BLOOD IN THE GLENS

BLOOD IN THE GLENS

TRUE CRIMES FROM THE SCOTTISH HIGHLANDS

JEAN McLENNAN

BLACK & WHITE PUBLISHING

First published 2009
by Black & White Publishing Ltd
29 Ocean Drive, Edinburgh EH6 6JL

3 5 7 9 10 8 6 4   10 11 12 13

ISBN: 978 1 84502 250 1

Typeset by Ellipsis Books Ltd, Glasgow
Printed and bound by MPG Books Ltd, Bodmin

CONTENTS

ACKNOWLEDGEMENTS

This book would not exist without HI-Arts and literary agent Jenny Brown, who encouraged me to pursue an idea. In a venture like this it is always hard to know how and where to start and for their help in finding my starting point I must thank my friend Ruth Wade and my daughter Jill.

So many people gave me of their time and shared their knowledge about the cases featured in *Blood in the Glens* and I am most grateful to them. Deserving of particular mention are David Barclay, Angus Chisholm, Alan Dawson, Cathy Gordon, Susan Gordon, George Gough, Peter Henderson, David Hingston, Jayne Marsden of the *Yorkshire Post* Library, Brian McGregor, Hugh and June McLeod, Peter MacPhee, Gordon MacRae Jnr, Ian Peacock, Katrina Reid, Linda Walker, Scottish Television's *Unsolved* production team and present and retired members of Northern Constabulary and others who preferred not to be mentioned specifically.

If I have forgotten anyone please accept my apologies.

I owe a huge debt of gratitude to another writer who helped me immeasurably in honing the manuscript, Eleanor Thomson and also to Andrew Burnet who did a sterling editing job. Thank you to the team at Black & White who have been easy taskmasters.

Thanks also go to Val McDermid who patiently tutored me at an Arvon Foundation course and whose advice to 'Let it all hang out,' has not been forgotten. She has very kindly produced the foreword.

This book is dedicated to all the victims.

FOREWORD

The Scottish Highlands is not a gentle landscape. Breathtaking, beautiful and unexpected it may be, but benevolent it isn't. Every year those mountains and lochs and coastal waterways beguile innocents to their death, their treacherous good looks a siren call to the senses, blinding us to their dangers.

But it's not just the landscape that kills. The Highlands resemble every other place colonised by human beings. They are also home to homicide, murders just as shocking as those that take place in any cityscape. These dramatic vistas have played host to crimes that resonate down the centuries.

People still travel halfway across the world to visit the site of the Glencoe Massacre of 1692, where accounts of the numbers dead vary according to the political perspective of the reporters. Whether the death of the MacDonald clan members at the hands of the Campbells was a shocking betrayal of traditional hospitality or an act of political expediency ordered by distant powerful masters also depends on point of view.

A mere sixty years later, land agent Colin Campbell of Glenure, known as the Red Fox, was assassinated by an unknown assailant as he collected rents in Appin. The events surrounding his death later inspired Robert Louis Stevenson to write one of the finest of all adventure novels, *Kidnapped*. The truth of what happened that day in Appin only became clear more than 200 years after the event, when members of the Stewart family finally revealed the story that had been handed down secretly from generation to generation.

The eleven cases that Jean McLennan anatomises here are all culled from the last six decades, but many of their elements are foreshadowed in these notorious earlier cases. Why were these victims chosen? Was the crime scene significant? Who benefited from the deaths? How did the killer escape? Was there more going on here than met the eye? Will we ever know the full story?

We are drawn ineluctably towards violent death, both in fiction and in fact. Stories of true crime fascinate us as much as the latest crime novel we curl up with in bed at night. There are many theories about the reasons murder exerts such a strong pull on our imagination and it's something I've thought about often over my years as a writer of crime fiction.

In part, I think it's like watching lightning striking someone else's house – there's a primitive feeling of relief: if it's happening over there, then it can't be happening to me. Reading about it is a talisman that protects us from the bad things out there.

In part, I think it's about comforting ourselves. Most true crime in books and on TV focuses on cases where there is a solution, so we can rest easy at night knowing that for every evil killer, there is a dedicated detective skilled enough to deliver justice on our behalf.

But mostly, I think it's part of our quest for understanding why human beings treat each other as they do. And by setting her accounts of these startling and terrible cases against the broader picture of homicide in Scotland and how we deal with offenders, Jean McLennan provides a valuable coda to this fascinating book. Criminal behaviour is invariably rooted in the society it afflicts, and *Blood in the Glens* provides us with a unique picture of the real Highlands. It's maybe not the one the tourist board would like everyone to see, but it's more informative than any guidebook.

Sit back with a glass of whisky and a plate of shortbread and take a walk on the unexpectedly wild side.

VAL McDERMID

INTRODUCTION

Some psychiatrists and psychologists say that we all have it in us to be killers, given the right (or should it be wrong) circumstances. So it isn't surprising that murderers look just like us – and in most respects they are like us. They don't have a label, and they don't have a physical characteristic that marks them out as different. They come in all shapes and sizes, all ages and genders. They have stepped over a line from which there is no going back, for either them or their victims. How and why they have done so, and the process of detecting their crime, of how justice is achieved for the victim and their loved ones, is what makes them fascinating.

The stories in this book have one thing in common – a killing that took place in the Highlands of Scotland, which for the present purpose includes Orkney. It is one of the safest places to live. There are only four or five murders each year, over approximately a third of Scotland's area, which compares with a national figure of around 130 murders per year. In the Highlands there are half as many murders per head of population as in the rest of Scotland, but the area has had its share of bizarre and unusual cases. Northern Constabulary, who police the area, are proud to boast a high detection rate. There are only three cases marked as homicides outstanding on detectives' books. As in any other force's patch, many killings don't challenge the detectives' forensic or investigative skills, but the solved cases featured in this book, with one exception, were puzzling and took police time, skill and patience to bring the killer to justice. The murderers in the unsolved cases may yet discover that they haven't committed the perfect crime.

The skills brought to bear by detectives are broadly the same across the developed world, but when an accused is indicted of murder in Scotland a distinctive legal system that pertains solely to Scotland comes into play. Understanding the basic principles of the system is the key to understanding what happens after the accused is arrested.

Prosecutions in Scotland are brought in name of the Crown, represented by the Lord Advocate whose department is called the Crown Office. Historically Scotland's criminal system was one of private prosecution but this resulted in powerful or wealthy criminals avoiding justice because weaker victims would lack either the means or the courage to prosecute, or were bought off with blood money. Private prosecutions are still competent but they are very unusual. An alleged killer, in the eyes of the law, is innocent until guilt is proved, and is likely to be remanded in custody pending the trial.

In Scotland there are time limits for bringing a case to trial. Lengthy remands, after which an innocent person is released on acquittal, don't happen in Scotland, unlike elsewhere. Until 2004 the Crown Office had only 110 days from the date an accused was taken into custody to start proceedings And this time limit – together with the one-year rule, of which more in a moment – was strictly observed. The Crown could ask a judge to grant an extension, but it would not be given unless there were circumstances beyond the prosecutor's control, such as the illness of the accused or an essential witness. If the trial didn't begin within the time limit the accused was liberated automatically, and, most importantly, he or she could not be tried for that murder or other crime in the future. The time limits were changed in 2004 as part of reforms recommended by Lord Bonomy. Currently, an accused can be remanded in custody for up to 140 days before a trial in the High Court begins and at the end of that period he/she must be admitted to bail. In spite of its obvious appeal in terms of human rights, other jurisdictions have resisted emulating Scotland by adopting this time limit, no doubt because it is quite a tall order to complete investigations and prepare for the trial of what may be a complex case in such a short time.

Even if an accused is not in custody (see for example Michael Ross in Chapter 4: 'A Position of Trust') the prosecutors have only one year from the date of the first appearance in court to begin the trial. Should they fail, the accused cannot be prosecuted in future for the murder described on the petition. The petition is a document setting out the charges according to what is known at the time. The indictment is the final version of the same document, which sets out the charge or charges on which the accused will be tried.

Lawyers use the Latin term *mens rea* to describe the mind of a killer guilty of murder. It marks the distinction which Scotland shares with many jurisdictions, between the killer who has it in mind to commit murder or whose actions are depraved enough that he is reckless of the consequences, and a lesser crime resulting in death – that of culpable homicide, as it is known in Scotland, or manslaughter elsewhere. In some rare circumstances, such as sometimes apply in a mercy killing, a conviction for culpable homicide need not lead to a custodial sentence. The distinction is an important one because a conviction for murder can bring only one sentence: life imprisonment. But life doesn't necessarily mean life behind bars: the Parole Board may decide to release a prisoner on licence. However any breach of the rules imposed on release on parole, or of the law by a parolee, results in an immediate return to prison.

In Scotland, crimes including murder, culpable homicide and others considered serious enough, are tried in the High Court. This can sit in any of Scotland's cities depending on volume of business, and not necessarily near where the alleged crime took place. A jury of fifteen men and women (not twelve as in England) hear the evidence, normally sitting with a single judge. The jury are masters of fact; it is solely for them to decide, on the basis of the evidence, whether a defendant – or panel, as the accused may otherwise be known – is guilty or innocent, or whether the case has been not proven. After a jury finds an accused guilty the judge, who has heard all the evidence, and who is then (and not before) apprised of information regarding previous convictions, hands down his sentence. Sometimes this seems unfair, but knowledge of an accused person's previous convictions might prejudice a jury against him and cause them to prejudge him.

Although life imprisonment is mandatory for murder, a judge must now make a recommendation as to the minimum period a killer will spend in prison before being considered for parole. On occasion a judge will say that life should mean life imprisonment. I am not aware of any case since Scotland adopted the Human Rights Act in 2001 in which a sentence of life meaning the whole of life has been handed down in a Scottish trial. Indeed, some killers who were sentenced years ago when the trial judge said life should mean life have benefited from this legislation. After a more recent hearing (a right bestowed by the Act), punishment tariff terms have been fixed that entitle them to be considered for possible release by the Parole Board. This can cause some concern. (See Chapter 2, 'Not Mad Enough').

The 'not proven' verdict is unique to Scotland and its application is often controversial. It leaves the family of a victim (or a victim in non-murder cases) without closure, and the accused with a stain on his or her name as innocence has not been accepted. It is a finding from which an accused person has no right of appeal and it applies when there is insufficient evidence to convict but there are doubts regarding innocence.

In Scotland, the double jeopardy rule precludes a retrial for the same offence, even if compelling new evidence is discovered. However, it can only be a matter of time before the Scottish Government brings Scotland in line with England and Wales, where the rule was banned by legislation in 2005.

Mention the Scottish Highlands to many who don't live there and a picture is instantly conjured up in their minds. It features mountains like sleeping giants, separated by deep clefts of picturesque glens; heart-achingly beautiful coastal scenery; a country still populated by kilt-wearing people. Highlanders in the 21st century mainly live in small communities where folk know most of their neighbours, so when violent death visits, it shocks more than in a large city where anonymity is more commonplace. Apart from the largely unchanged scenery, life has moved on and realities of modern life are reflected in the Highlands as much as anywhere else. Sadly, crime is part of that life, but fortunately there are few murders in the Highlands and the fascinating cases featured in this book have arisen over the last sixty years.

PART ONE
SCOTLAND THE GRAVE

1

THE BUTLER DID IT

There was something that worried Norman Wright about the two men who checked in to his North Berwick hotel on the snowy night of 15 January 1978. They were well dressed and on the face of it their story was credible: they had told him they were touring Scotland for the last time before one of them emigrated to Australia. But Wright suspected that they were con men who wouldn't pay their bill and, while they dined, he phoned the local police station and asked for a check on the number plates of their car. That phone call was the catalyst for a police investigation that stretched from London to the north of Scotland, involving six police forces and leading to the shocking discovery of five bodies. One of these was found in lonely, scenic Glen Affric in the Scottish Highlands.

The two guests at the quiet and select Blenheim House Hotel were Archibald Thomson Hall (who used the name Roy Hall) and Michael Anthony Kitto (who claimed to be John Blackman). As it transpired, both were ex-jailbirds. The weather had closed in and afraid of being involved in an accident or getting stuck, they had decided to make an unplanned stop for the night. Hall was a superstitious man. He had been troubled that the registration on their Ford Granada ended '999'. He had therefore asked Kitto to find another Granada, ascertain the name of the owner in case the pair were stopped, have plates made up to the other car's number and change the tax disc to fit. He had thought of everything but Kitto had neglected to carry out Hall's instructions. His lackadaisical attitude was to be the pair's downfall.

3

Kitto had picked a number at random and the one he had chosen fitted a Ford Escort. He hadn't even bothered to change the disc to coincide with the number plate, so a quick check made it clear to the police that there was something to investigate. Following Wright's call, two local constables came to the hotel. Little did the two uniformed officers realise that there was a body in the boot of the Granada and that they were picking up a couple of serial murderers who had left a trail of five bodies behind them. A consummate actor, Hall managed to appear unconcerned at the turn of events and even offered to buy the policemen a drink.

One of the officers drove the Granada and the other took Hall and Kitto to Berwick police station, where they had to wait for detectives to interview them. Hall asked to go to the toilet, where he flushed incriminating evidence from his pockets down the pan. His apprehension was growing while he waited. He was aware that it was only a matter of time before police found the body in the boot, and that what happened next was clearly going to lead back to prison and that for a very long time. He asked to go to the toilet again and this time made his escape through a small window.

He tracked down a local taxi driver who was the latest in a long line to be taken in by the con man. Hall's story of a sick wife in hospital evoked a sympathetic response in the driver who set out in deep snow to drive Hall to hospital in Edinburgh. While his driver struggled against hazardous road conditions, Hall was sitting back, his brain working double time as he tried to formulate a plan to complete his escape by getting hold of some money and leaving the country immediately.

At Haddington, flashing blue lights indicated a roadblock and the end of Hall's flight to freedom. He was taken from the taxi to the police station at Musselburgh where he was told what he already knew. The body of a young man had been found in the boot of his car. He told police nothing when they questioned him. Eventually he was put in a cell. He asked for a cup of water and proceeded to swallow some barbiturate capsules, which he had recovered from his rectum, the customary hiding place for drugs among prisoners. Hall already knew that prison for the rest of his life was inevitable and his preferred choice was death. But escape plan B didn't work either and he was discovered before the over-dose of barbiturates took full effect. He was taken to hospital in Edinburgh where staff pumped his stomach and saved his life.

Later, at Edinburgh police headquarters, Detective Inspector Tom McLean and Detective Chief Inspector McPherson questioned him. To begin with they got nothing from Hall but meanwhile Kitto was singing his heart out. According to Colin McEachran, the Crown Advocate Depute responsible for prosecuting the case in the High Court in Edinburgh, Kitto told police, 'I have an . . . incredible story. You might not believe it but there is another three bodies I want to tell you about.' Constable Webster, one of the two men called to Blenheim House Hotel, reckoned that Kitto might have had a lucky escape. He could well have been Hall's next victim.

Hall was recovering from his second suicide attempt in Edinburgh Royal Infirmary when police came to question him again, armed with the information they had obtained from Kitto. By that time they knew everything, with two exceptions – the exact location of three of the bodies, and details of the first murder. The first victim had been David Wright. Hall had carried out his murder alone before his killing spree with Kitto. Kitto couldn't remember exactly where bodies had been left. Hall, scornful of his accomplice's lack of intellect and anticipating enjoyment outside a cell or a court, agreed to help the police find them.

On 18 January 1978, a convoy of police vehicles, with Hall under vigilant guard, travelled to a lonely track leading to a game-keeper's house at Guisachan, in beautiful Glen Affric about thirty miles north of Inverness. The weather conditions were still wintry, but a constable eventually found an old man's skull in a rhodo-dendron bush and the remainder of the body strewn about where foxes and other scavenging animals had left it. This was the body of eighty-two-year-old Walter Travers Scott-Elliot.

By 19 January, antiques valued at £3,000 (worth about £13,000 today) had been recovered in Newcastle-under-Lyme, Staffordshire. Police were linking this to the disappearance of the Scott-Elliots and a burglary at their home. An antiques dealer had become suspicious of two men offering him a quantity of Minton pottery, Meissen china and silverware at well below its true value. He had taken note of their car registration number. Police investigated, and discovered that the number belonged to a car rented out in the name of Walter Scott-Elliot. The police visited the Scott-Elliots' flat in Chelsea and discovered that the place had been ransacked. There were also spatters of blood. Valuables were missing, including a collection of coins over 700 years old.

Two days later Hall led the police to David Wright's body at Kirkleton Estate, Dumfriesshire. The body of Mary Coggles, known as 'Belfast Mary', had been found on Christmas Day 1977 but remained unidentified until Kitto described how she had been killed and her body dumped at Middlebie near Lockerbie in Dumfriesshire. Finally, there was a two-day search in harsh winter weather at Ross Wood near the Comrie–Dalchonzie Road in Perthshire, using dogs trained to search in the Arab–Israeli war. The body of sixty-year-old Mrs Dorothy Scott-Elliot, wife of Walter Scott-Elliot, was found.

Hall and Kitto appeared at Edinburgh Sheriff Court on 28 January, both charged with the murder of Walter Scott-Elliot and theft of the coins from the Scott-Elliot house. Hall was also charged with the murder of David Wright. The two men were taken to prison on remand to await their trial. The police had all the bodies and the killers; they turned their efforts to gathering information and evidence for the trials. There were to be two. The first would be held in Scotland, in the High Court in Edinburgh, and would deal with the two murders committed north of the border. The other would take place in the Old Bailey, to hear evidence in the murders of Dorothy Scott- Elliot, Mary Coggles and Donald Hall, all committed in England. Despite confessions from the two accused, there was no certainty they would plead guilty to the murders and the investigation had to piece together what had happened to enable the Crown to establish 'beyond reasonable doubt' that both men were guilty of four murders and Hall of a fifth. And the police and Crown Office had good reason to wonder if a legal technicality might lead to the eventual release of the killers.

Headlines in the press reflected public revulsion at the murders, particularly those of the two elderly people, the former MP Walter Scott-Elliot and his wife. Some dubbed Hall 'The Monster Butler'. One paper, the *Daily Mail*, quickly joined up all the dots and, early in the investigation, on 19 January, even before all the bodies were found, printed an accurate account of the crimes. This was despite the police in Scotland keeping their cards close to their chest and releasing few details. During a press conference reporters had given the senior Scottish police officer a hard time because, they said, police in London were releasing more information. The police officer expressed some doubt that a fair trial could be had south of the border. Hall's lawyer, Mr Leonard Murray, agreed. He wrote to the Lord Advocate, Ronald Murray, QC, alleging that the coverage in the *Daily Mail*, much of which had been gleaned from police press conferences, was a contempt of court and would prevent his client from receiving a fair trial.

The Lord Advocate is responsible for the investigation of crime in Scotland, through the Crown Office, and for deciding whom to prosecute. Ronald Murray, QC did not agree to initiate proceedings so Hall's lawyers raised them on his behalf. A hearing in the contempt of court case took place on 3 March while Hall and Kitto were still awaiting trial for murder. Lord Emslie, who heard the contempt case, continued it for further consideration by a larger court of three judges. He said he was not happy that a decision in an earlier case was correct and it would have been binding on him unless more than one judge reviewed it.

At a pleading diet before the Sheriff Principal at Edinburgh Sheriff Court on 28 April, the accused were required to state whether they intended to plead innocence or guilt. (Pleading diets were hearings designed to oil the wheels of justice. They were abolished in 1980 but a similar procedure was introduced after Lord Bonomy's Report on procedure in the High Court in 2002. Interim hearings were then introduced to ensure that both Crown and Defence are ready to go to a trial, to prevent a trial being adjourned unnecessarily.) Kitto's advocate, Mr James McNeil, indicated that Kitto was reserving his plea until the contempt case was heard. The Crown Office must have been concerned.

In any event no final decision was made in the contempt case until after Hall and Kitto had been sentenced in Edinburgh High Court. At the trial which followed on 2 May, both men pled guilty.

Police records showed that both Hall and Kitto were thieves with extensive records, but neither had ever before been convicted of crimes of violence. Events that led to the trail of bodies were pieced together by police forces in London, Cumbria, Highland, Lothian, Dumfriesshire and Perthshire.

Hall had been a criminal all his adult life and he was 53 years old when he first killed. Why? He had previously been in situations where he could have killed, or at least been guilty of assault, if his first instinct had been aggressive. Instead, he had chosen to flee. So what had changed? To find the answer to that we need to examine his life up to the first killing, the time when he first stepped over the line.

Hall was born on 17 July 1924, the oldest of three children. He grew up in a terraced house owned by his parents in a poor, working-class area of Glasgow. His father worked in the sorting office of the Post Office. He was a former soldier and a lay preacher. Hall himself says that he did well enough at school but by the time he was in his teens he was already a small-time thief. He collected for the Red Cross using two tins, one for coin, which he handed in, and another for notes, which he kept. His career choice on leaving school was crime. His parents' marriage was not a happy one and eventually they separated.

Although Hall attended his father's funeral with leave from prison, he was much closer to his mother and his stepfather, John

Wooton. Wooton was another criminal whom Hall met in prison, and later introduced to his mother. His brother Donald, seventeen years his junior and the last of his victims, was almost certainly the product of a relationship his mother had had with a senior officer, while the family all lived at Catterick camp.

One of Hall's early victims was an older woman, Anne Phillips. She was a divorcee in her thirties with whom he had his first affair when he was just sixteen. Mrs Phillips was a newsagent with a shop near the Hall family home. She introduced him to fine dining and bought him his first dinner jacket, to his father's disgust. Hall found out where her shop takings were kept and dipped into them to fund his lifestyle, in spite of their relationship. He used her, as he was to use many others. He was still in his teens when he discovered his bisexuality. He embarked on a relationship with a lodger in his mother's house, the first of many homosexual affairs.

He assiduously cultivated manners and style to further his ambition to move among the wealthy. He hoped to pass himself off as one of them and Anne Phillips helped his early grooming for the role. Beguiled by Joan Fontaine's performances on screen, he started calling himself Roy Fontaine and trained himself to speak with a carefully modulated upper-class accent. He became a self-taught authority on jewellery and antiques. He was a very successful jewel thief and liked to think he resembled E. W. Hornung's fictitious 'gentleman thief', Raffles. Hornung's creation stole for 'excitement, romance and a decent living'. Hall's reasons mirrored these. He admitted that part of his reason for stealing was the adrenaline rush it gave him and that he felt a sexual frisson when he handled nice jewellery he had stolen. Crime and sex made Hall feel alive, but there was a huge difference between fiction and Hall's real life. Raffles was elusive, but Hall's criminal activities invariably caught up with him.

He spent most of his adult life in prison for robbery, theft and burglary. Interestingly, he was found insane and unfit to plead when, aged twenty, he appeared in Glasgow Sheriff Court in December 1944. He had been charged with four offences of theft by housebreaking. Instead of a prison sentence, he was detained during Her Majesty's Pleasure, a euphemism for being held in a mental institution. The course of his life thereafter demonstrates that any treatment given then was ineffective. Liberated, he simply picked up where he had left off.

Some of his exploits were very audacious and would not be out of place in a work of fiction. In one scam he used several times, he visited estate agents in Edinburgh or Glasgow pretending to be looking for a house for his family to live in when his father returned to Scotland after serving in the Diplomatic Corps in India. A convincing liar, he conned the house owners into divulging when they would be out and as he looked round he noted the valuables and worked out means of entry. Later, when no one would be at home, he returned. He either broke in or used a duplicate key – having taken the number from one he had handled during the 'viewing'. At that time he often made the forty-mile train journey from Glasgow, where he lived, to Edinburgh, 'just like any other commuter'.

During this period he managed to steal a very expensive ring and, having checked its value in Scotland, travelled to England to sell it. Hall immediately took to London, especially its Turkish baths, then a venue for homosexuals, and from then on he spent much time there.

Passing himself off as a well-to-do young man, he allegedly began a relationship with the bisexual comedian/musician Vic Oliver, who eventually became son-in-law to Winston Churchill. With Oliver, he attended parties held by the likes of Ivor Novello that were homosexual orgies. Among those he says he met at this time were Lord Louis Mountbatten, the playwright Terence Rattigan (with whom he claims to have later had an affair) and the writer Beverley Baxter. He was keeping himself on the proceeds of his crimes, which were then mostly opportunistic. For example, when he attended a party where the fellow guests were famous and wealthy people, including Elizabeth Taylor and Richard Burton, he tried bedroom doors, intending to pilfer jewellery if he could.

He managed to garner some capital from his thieving and decided to become a legitimate businessman. For a time he ran a second-hand shop with his mother. Unsurprisingly the business was not 100 per cent legitimate; they often dealt in stolen goods. During this time Hall befriended Esther Henry, who then owned Edinburgh's most prestigious antique shop. He cultivated his relationship with her and bided his time. Years later, she too became one of his victims.

Hall missed the buzz that he got from stealing and when the Second World War ended he gave up the shop. Between prison sentences, he learned how to be a valet and a butler. He honed his skills in service, working briefly at the four-star Glenburn Hotel in Rothesay to complete his metamorphosis into 'the perfect young gentleman'. He started working as a butler, creating false references and backing them up with phone calls from public phone boxes. While working for one couple, Mr and Mrs Warren-Connell, he took the opportunity of his employers' absence to accept an invitation. He attended a Royal Garden Party at the Palace of Holyroodhouse in Edinburgh, passing himself off as Mr Warren-Connell. He loved to rub shoulders with the titled and wealthy and he arrived in the Warren-Connell's Rolls Royce, which he had 'borrowed'. With his immaculate appearance, upper-class accent and careful manners, he looked the part.

Working as a butler, he sometimes stole from his employers while still in their employ, replacing valuable items with fakes. With his contacts from his spells in prison, he had no problem acquiring copies of all kinds of valuables. Sometimes he waited till he had moved on to another job and then either broke into the house where he himself had formerly worked or told an accomplice how to gain entry and what to take. Meanwhile, he made sure he had a sound alibi. More than once, police warned his employers of his propensities and he was dismissed before he could work out a plan that would impoverish them.

But he didn't draw the line at the crude approach of smash and grab, the forerunner of the modern ram raid. The usual team was

Hall and an accomplice with a getaway driver. One man would carefully smash the jeweller's window to expose the loot that Hall, with his eye for jewels, had already earmarked. Then Hall would reach in and grab the selected pieces. They were off and away with the alarm system shrieking, before there could be any response.

Hall was amoral, bisexual and promiscuous. He could charm the birds from the trees but he was disloyal to almost everyone. He had long-term relationships with two women and affairs with several other women as well as men.

Hall's life swung from one extreme to the other; the austere life of prison and the life of luxury in the homes of the wealthy during his spells of freedom. That wasn't the only contradiction in his life. He liked to rub shoulders with the wealthy and famous but he also had affairs with men and women who were at the opposite end of the social scale. Mary Coggles, an Irishwoman, was one of them. Mrs Coggles had worked as a prostitute in the seedy Kings Cross area of London. He met her in 1972, while he was on parole, and stayed in contact with her till her death.

Hall had a capacity to con people he met and an ability to think on his feet that got him out of many tight corners. He escaped from prison and the police on more than one occasion. He was clever but he was also cold and calculating and seldom empathised with anyone. However, he didn't commit any violent offences until he lost the man he described as the love of his life. The quality of his love for David Barnard, a fellow prisoner he met in Hull prison, was of a different order from anything he had felt before. Barnard was an armed robber who had shot a policeman in London and when they met in prison he was serving an eighteen-year sentence. The pair started a sexual relationship and were soon committed to each other, planning for the future when both were free. Hall was due to be released from prison first.

On his release on parole he worked at Whittingham Hospital for the insane for a time and formed a relationship with Ruth Holmes, a fashion designer, whom he married in spite of his commitment to David Barnard. He says he was prepared to leave his wife to live with Barnard but the marriage ended anyway when she was shocked to discover her husband's bisexuality. At around this time, he was also sleeping with his old friend Mary Coggles. She was now acting as go-between, visiting David Barnard in prison to carry messages back and forth. (Parolees were not allowed to consort with other criminals so Hall couldn't visit David himself.) For a short time, Hall managed to go straight, but then an old friend, a homosexual gigolo, contacted him. Hall learned he had stolen a briefcase from a high-ranking civil servant he had slept with, but that he couldn't open it. Its complex locks suggested the contents were important. Was Hall interested? All of his intentions to go straight evaporated.

Hall opened the case to find that it contained confidential documents that would have caused the government of the day great embarrassment. He decided to try to use them to bargain for David Barnard's release. His plan backfired, as many had before, and he found himself back in prison after telling a former fellow inmate from Hull prison what he was up to. His confidant was an informer and as well as giving Hall up to the police he told Hall's wife about his love for Barnard.

After a trial held in camera because of the nature of the papers in the briefcase, Hall was sentenced to two years' imprisonment. He was sent to Long Lartin prison in Worcestershire. Mary Coggles continued visiting David Barnard in Hull until Barnard's release. Then he started visiting Hall himself. Hall and Barnard continued making plans for a future together when Hall was free. However, just four short weeks after David Barnard was released from prison, having completed twelve years of his eighteen-year sentence, he crashed the car he was driving on the M6 and was killed. The love of Hall's life had been brought to an untimely end and that seemed to trigger the change in him that was to bring about the undue death of five other people. It seems that human life ceased to have any value for Hall from then on. He was cold and calculating before, but murderous after Barnard's death.

Even though Hall was committed to Barnard emotionally he

still had sexual needs. He met David Michael Wright, his first victim, when they were both serving sentences in Long Lartin prison in Worcestershire. A sexual relationship developed between them. Hall enjoyed Wright as a sexual partner but had no emotional involvement with him. This was a pattern throughout Hall's life in which he used people for his own ends without compassion. Wright was due to be released first and Hall told him about the home of a multimillionaire, Angelo Southall. He had cased the place while working there as a butler, but since this was by now known to be his modus operandi, Hall knew that he would be a prime suspect for the burglary. This way he would be in jail when the crime was committed and would have the best alibi ever. The pair agreed that Hall would get a percentage of the value of the robbery but Hall never saw it. This rankled with him.

Shortly after Hall completed his sentence, he saw an advert in *Country Life* magazine for a job as butler to Lady Margaret Hudson at Kirkleton, Dumfriesshire, a landed estate with a fine house in a nice situation. (The house now belongs to a successful businessman.) Lady Hudson was the seventy-four-year-old widow of Conservative MP Sir Austen Hudson, who had died in 1956. The couple had no children and few relatives. After her death there had to be a search for next of kin. Lady Hudson lived quietly with a companion and staff in a house full of antiques and valuables. Neighbours found the stout, elderly lady abrupt in manner but likeable. They thought she was quite lonely.

At the job interview, Lady Margaret wondered at Hall being interested in the job. He would be buried in the country, figuratively speaking. Hall assured her that he liked country living, all the while astutely assessing the value of the potential haul at Kirkleton and resolving that he would rob his future employer. He landed the job, and for a time he was happy just to stay there, enjoying the swimming pool, the beautiful gardens, shooting and socialising with the local gentry. He was seldom to be seen in the evenings without his formal suit and bow tie. Then David Wright managed to track him down and arrived at

Kirkleton intending to lie low for a time. The police were looking for him.

Wright had been involved in a mugging that had gone wrong and the victim had ended up dead. Hall looked forward to indulging his sexual desires with Wright, so it suited him to tell Lady Margaret that Wright was an old friend who had just come out of the army. She invited Wright to work on the estate in exchange for his keep. However, Wright was a thorn in Hall's flesh from the start. He pestered Hall constantly to rob Kirkleton with him, and was impatient to do the job. He threatened to tell Lady Margaret about Hall's past. Finally, Wright made two fatal mistakes. He stole a diamond ring belonging to Lady Hudson, which Hall later found in a rolled up sock in Wright's room. Then one night he drunkenly fired a rifle at Hall who was asleep in his bed, narrowly missing Hall's head, roaring that they were going to rob Kirkleton immediately. Lady Hudson and the household staff were away that weekend and Wright had taken the opportunity to raid her drinks cellar.

The following morning, Hall and John Wooton, his stepfather, had planned to go shooting rabbits and Hall invited the now penitent and sober Wright to join them, all the while cold-bloodedly planning his murder. As soon as Wright had fired his last cartridge Hall turned his gun on Wright, told him he was going to kill him and then shot him in the head. He shot him four times in all. Later, when police questioned him about the killing, he said calmly and dispassionately, 'I shot him again, then again, and then once more.'

After telling Wooton to leave immediately so as not to involve him further, Hall dragged the body into some bushes. He went back to the house to fetch a spade, but the ground was rock hard so he had to content himself with placing the body in a stream, having stripped it and removed all means of identification. He went back very early the next day and added camouflage to the body. A local farmer who met him out and about at 5am, was told, 'I'm just out for a quick walk.' Hall was looking rather less than his usual immaculate self. Ironically, he was always dressed to kill.

Within a fortnight of Wright's death, Hall's past caught up with him. An anonymous phone call to Lady Margaret warned her that if she had anyone using the name Fontaine in her employ she should be very wary, for he was a thief. Hall found himself out of a job but left with three months' salary thanks to his employer's generosity and affection for him. He had been an excellent butler and she was sorry to let him go – but then she had no inkling of his monstrous activities during his employment. After Hall and Kitto's trial in Edinburgh Lady Margaret expressed profound horror to her neighbours at the events on her property. Within six months she had sold off all but eighteen acres of the estate, retaining the house, and went off on a cruise to try to forget. During the cruise she fell on deck and broke a hip. She died within another six months. Perhaps she was Hall's sixth victim.

On leaving Kirkleton, Hall visited Cumbria. He liked the area and rented Middle Farm Cottage at Newton Arlosh. But the bright lights of London were irresistible. In the late autumn of 1977 he took a new job as a butler in Chelsea. His new employers were Eton-and-Oxford-educated Walter Scott-Elliot and his Anglo-Indian wife Dorothy who lived in a luxury flat in select Richmond Court, Sloane Street. Scott-Elliot was eighty-two years old and a former Labour MP. He had considerable wealth, much of it inherited. He had sold the family estate at Arkleton, near Langholm in the Scottish Borders and had been a director and sometime managing director of the Bombay Company, which became the Bombay Burma Trading Corporation. By 1977 he was frail, but having fought in the Coldstream Guards in the First World War he still had spirit, as Hall was to discover. Scott-Elliot had probably enjoyed exactly the background and start in life that Hall coveted. Dorothy, his second wife, was sixty. On taking up his job, Hall soon started steaming open their mail. He discovered that they held bank accounts across the world, and soon he was planning to empty them and retire. However, he couldn't resist the opportunity to burgle a neighbour's flat and he needed a younger, fitter accomplice to help him gain entry.

He was still seeing his friend Mary Coggles, by then aged fifty. One night, in the Lancelot Pub, Brompton Road, near Harrods, she introduced him to Michael Kitto. He seemed to fit the bill. Coincidentally, Mary Coggles had at one time been house-keeper/cleaner to the Scott-Elliots and was now a Post Office cleaner. Kitto was a petty thief from South London and was twenty-nine years old.

Hall and Kitto visited the house late one evening, at nearly midnight, when Hall thought it would be perfectly safe to give Kitto a guided tour. Mrs Scott-Elliot was supposed to be in a private nursing home and Mr Scott-Elliot was in bed asleep. He was taking prescribed sleeping pills. Kitto was ushered from room to room and shown the collections to which the Scott-Elliots had been devoting their time and resources. Hall told him he would be stealing it all in due course. They came to Dorothy Scott-Elliot's room and were about to open the door when the lady herself emerged and demanded of Hall what Kitto was doing in her house at that time of night.

There is doubt as to what exactly happened next. In early state-ments, Hall said he had overreacted, knocking her to the ground and smothering her with a pillow. He later claimed that Kitto sprang at her, covering her mouth and nose with his hand. Unexpectedly, he said, she had slumped to the floor. When they picked her up and laid her on the bed they were surprised to find that she was dead. However, her death certificate gives the cause of death as asphyxia but also 'blunt violence to head'. What is beyond all doubt is that both men were there and implicated in Mrs Scott-Elliot's death.

Now Hall and Kitto faced a dilemma. Mr Scott-Elliot was in bed in the flat doped on sleeping pills, but no matter how frail he was, he was soon going to be asking about the whereabouts of his wife.

It was already obvious to Hall that he had to share the same fate as his wife, but for the moment the plan was to travel north with her body, dispose of it and then decide exactly what to do with the old man. They kept him stupefied with sleeping pills in whisky, so he accepted what he was told: that his wife had gone ahead to visit friends in Scotland and they were travelling to meet up with her.

They needed cash and so before they set out Mary Coggles donned a grey wig to hide her brassy blonde hair and dressed up in Dorothy Scott-Elliot's clothes. With Hall accompanying her, she took cheques already made out to cash on which Hall had forged Dorothy Scott-Elliot's signature and they went from bank to bank. They made a series of withdrawals, none big enough to excite undue interest. John Wooton, Hall's stepfather, was summoned from Lytham to assist. Mrs Scott-Elliot's body, wrapped in a bedspread, was put in the boot of his car. Hall told his employers' banks and the caretaker at the flat that the Scott-Elliots had suddenly decided to go away to Italy for Christmas, so their friends and acquaintances were not suspicious of their disappearance. The party, which now comprised Hall, Kitto, Wooton, Mary Coggles disguised as Mrs Scott-Elliot and Scott-Elliot himself, set off with Dorothy Scott-Elliot's body in the boot.

After the party spent a night at Newton Arlosh, John Wooton left to go home to Lytham. Hall did not want him implicated any further. Hall then hired a car in Carlisle, in Scott-Elliot's name – the car the antiques dealer was later to describe. Hall and his two accomplices then drove the old man and his wife's body to a remote spot in Perthshire. Unobserved, Hall and Kitto dug a shallow grave beside a drystone wall at Ross Wood on the Comrie-to-Dalchonzie road and, after burying the body, covered the freshly turned soil with ferns and heather. It was December and the roads were snow-covered. Even when the police knew where to look, they found it difficult to discover the body.

The trio returned to Newton Arlosh with the old man and spent the night considering what to do with him. They still kept him doped with whisky and sleeping pills. They needed time to empty the bank accounts and clear the antiques and valuables from the flat in Chelsea. They formed a plan to take Scott-Elliot into the

Highlands and kill him there. Hall's confidence was such that they spent a night at the Bridge of Tilt Hotel at Blair Atholl on the way north, with Mary Coggles passing herself off as Dorothy Scott-Elliot. Scott-Elliot was fed in his room during the overnight stay and in the morning it was he who paid the bill.

They drove north, with the old man dozing in the back of the car, while they were looking for the ideal spot to carry out their evil plan, and on 14 December in beautiful Glen Affric, Scott-Elliot made the choice for them. He asked to get out of the car to urinate and walked towards the shelter of some nearby trees. At first, Kitto and Hall tried to strangle him with a scarf, but the old man put up a surprisingly strong fight. After a struggle, they finished the job by hitting him over the head with a spade until he was dead. His body was placed in a shallow grave and Hall, Kitto and Coggles returned to the cottage at Newton Arlosh.

Mary Coggles stayed at the cottage while Hall and Kitto returned to London and started clearing the Scott-Elliots' home of jewellery and antiques. Coggles was delighted with Dorothy Scott-Elliot's mink coat and jewellery. Hall was very concerned she would give them away, but she could resist neither the coat, nor boasting on the phone about her new-found wealth to friends in the Kings Cross area of London. Hall begged her to be less conspicuous, but she swaggered round the little village of Newton Arlosh wearing the mink. Her rough manner and appearance didn't fit the luxurious coat and Hall knew that she was drawing attention to herself, increasing the likelihood of arrest.

The rows between Hall and Coggles on this issue eventually erupted into violence. One night, Hall tried to burn the coat in the fireplace at the cottage. Mary Coggles started screaming and Hall turned on her with the poker. He struck her about the head. He then got a plastic bag and put it over her head. He and Kitto calmly sipped brandies while they watched her suffocate. Once again, Scotland was where the body was to be dumped. This time the chosen spot was near the village of Middlebie in Dumfriesshire, not far from Kirkleton, an area Hall knew well.

Hall and Kitto had a quiet family Christmas with Hall's mother and stepfather. John Wooton and his wife were living a respectable life in an area of Lytham where no one knew anything of their past. However, Archibald Hall's brother Donald had been released from prison in Cumbria and he headed straight for the Wooton household. From their first meeting in prison, when John Wooton had stopped a violent prisoner from beating up Archibald Hall, he had been a help and support to the man who became his stepson. Now Wooton was seeking his help. Don would soon mess up the ordinary lifestyle into which he and his wife had settled. John didn't have to ask twice. Hall's first thought this time was of murder – the 'easy solution' to every problem.

Kitto and Hall took Don back with them to the cottage at Newton Arlosh. Hall had always hated his brother. The two could not have been more different, apart from the fact they were both criminals. Archibald Hall was meticulous about his person. His bearing was of someone of substance; he even dyed his hair. Donald Hall was scruffy, unshaven and slovenly with dirt under his fingernails. He had a drink problem. He had worked as a labourer, a baker and a street-sweeper when not in prison. His first offence was for indecent assault when he was just sixteen and, unlike his brother, he had been found guilty of assault several times. Donald was, however, and always had been, a petty thief. He recognised his brother was in a different league and hoped they could work together. This was the last thing Archibald Hall wanted.

The first night back at the cottage, on 14 January, Kitto and Hall took their chance. Donald was demonstrating how to tie someone up using only six inches of string, with himself as guinea pig. While he was trussed up with his thumbs and toes tied together, Hall held a pad of chloroform over his mouth and nose. Then, to make sure he was dead, Hall and Kitto filled a bath and held him under the water for about five minutes. This time, they decided, the disposal of the body was going to take a bit more thought. Mary Coggles' body had been found on Christmas Day, but identification had proved difficult for the police and there had been nothing to link her to Hall and Kitto. Donald Hall had a criminal record and identifying his body would be easy for the police. And of course he was Hall's brother.

Once again, Scotland was the place selected to dump the corpse and Hall and Kitto drove north. As they reached North Berwick they made the fateful decision to spend a night at the Blenheim Arms.

At the trial in Edinburgh High Court a psychiatrist said Hall was suffering from a personality disorder which might be termed psychopathic. Another psychiatrist said he lacked a sense of shame and concern for his victims. He was however judged sane and fit to plead. Kitto's counsel said Kitto was completely under the control of Hall. Both men were sentenced to the mandatory sentence – life imprisonment. The High Court judge, Lord Wylie, recommended that Hall should serve at least fifteen years, after which he might be eligible for parole. Of course Lord Wylie was aware that there were other cases pending which could influence the amount of time the men would spend in jail.

Of the killing of Walter Scott-Elliot, Kitto was reported to have said, 'We turned the old man over onto his back. Roy [Hall] kicked him on the neck. I tried to strangle him with my bare hands. Roy put his foot on the neck. The old man was still and we walked away from him. We heard him moaning. Roy said, "I know what will do it." We went to the car and got a spade. Roy passed it over the fence to me. He said, "Hit him with that." This I did and the old man stopped moaning.'

On 25 May 1978, Hall and Kitto were remanded in custody at Horseferry Magistrates' Court in London, charged with the remaining three murders and with conspiracy to rob the Scott-Elliots. The case was bizarre enough, but another fact makes it even more so. In an unconnected crime, Alan Gough, a furniture-remover and an intended witness at the trial in London, was murdered in August 1978.

At the subsequent trial in England, both men pled guilty to the murders of Mary Coggles and Donald Hall and the manslaughter of Dorothy Scott-Elliot. On 1 November, the Recorder for London, Judge James Miskin, QC, handed down sentences for the murders of Mary Coggles and Donald Hall. Hall received a further life sentence and Miskin recommended he be detained for the rest of his natural life. He said that Hall was the leader, who heavily influenced Kitto, and this was reflected in the sentencing of the pair. Kitto was jailed for life, with the recommendation that he serve fifteen years for his part in the killings. Charges relating to the killing of Mrs Scott-Elliot and conspiracy (Hall) and trespass and theft (Kitto) remained on file, meaning that proceedings relating to these crimes could be raised in future. They never have been.

In March 1978, a memorial service was held for the Scott-Elliots in the crypt chapel of the Palace of Westminster. It must have been a time of great sadness for their family and friends. At the time of his death, Wright was still married to his second wife and his parents were still alive. Nothing is known of Mary Coggles' family, though she is believed to have had five children. Donald Hall, a divorcee, was disliked by most of his relatives, so it seems unlikely that his killing provoked much mourning.

In *The Perfect Gentleman*, the first edition of his autobiography, Hall wrote: 'There is a side of me when aroused, that is cold and completely heartless.' His dealings with people throughout his life demonstrated that heartlessness, but it was only after Barnard's death that he stepped over the line.

In prison – from which he had no prospect of ever being released – Hall expressed revulsion at the activities of paedophiles following the death of Sarah Payne. He believed that hanging should be brought back for perpetrators of crimes against children – though he admitted that this might seem strange coming from him. He had said that part of the justification for killing his brother was he thought Donald had been interfering with children. Donald Hall's criminal record doesn't bear that out. The only sexual offence of which he was ever convicted was indecent assault and it was when he was little more than a child himself.

Until close to his death, Hall campaigned unsuccessfully to be transferred to a prison in Scotland. He died of natural causes on 16 September 2002, having been transferred shortly before his death to hospital in Portsmouth. He had served twenty-four years of his final sentence. His autobiography was reissued with some amendments in 2004 as *To Kill and Kill Again*. Hall's final words in the second edition are: 'To any criminal, to anyone who thinks they might have the capacity for murder, to anyone similar to myself, I would urge you not to do it. Think again. In the final analysis my life is an impoverished nightmare. Let me be a lesson to you.'

Kitto has been released from prison on licence and is believed to be living in London.

2

NOT MAD ENOUGH

Most visitors travelling into the Highlands by car or bus either arrive or leave on the A9 road. It is a route that features in both this story and also that of the disappearance of Renee MacRae and her son, Andrew told in Chapter 9. This road wends its way from Falkirk in the centre of Scotland to Scrabster, the small but busy port close to Thurso on the north coast. As far north as Perth the road is now dual carriageway for much of its length, but further north the route is a conventional two-way road for the most part. The A9 travels through several different scenic zones, from the wide flat plain around Stirling, to the pretty rolling green hills and plentiful trees of Perthshire and on to the bleaker but majestic Highland landscape of heather-covered mountains, plantations of spruce and pine and sparkling blue lochs.

Challenging mountains in the Cairngorm range draw climbers from all over the world and although they are not the highest in Europe, it is an unwise person who assumes that they are safe or easy to climb. Every year, these peaks claim lives of the unwary, the ill-equipped or the simply unlucky. Circled by mountains forty miles or so south of Inverness lies the resort of Aviemore. In the 1960s it was popular with winter sports enthusiasts and walkers, but now the resort is busy all year round with a variety of activities on offer.

This story began to unfold on the afternoon of 15 March 1962, near Newtonmore, just a little south of this winter sports playground. Retired police sergeant Alex Matheson, in his new role as water bailiff, was going about his business of policing the fishing on the banks of the River Truim, a narrow tributary of the River Spey. He came upon what must have been the last thing he expected. He first noticed a bloodstained road map fluttering about on an embankment between the river and the A9, where his car was parked. When he had a closer look he saw a man's foot protruding from below a pile of twigs and soil in a shallow grave. The man had been shot in the head.

By dusk that day, Detective Inspector Roderick Fraser, chief of Inverness-shire CID, was at the scene with a team of detectives. By torchlight they examined the location to find they had been left nothing to help in their identification of the deceased. They discounted the likelihood of his being a tramp as he was too well dressed. Fraser noticed that the right shoe was worn in a circle on the sole, as it would have been on a man who was a driver. Perhaps, they concluded, the killer was now driving the dead man's car. The only other initial clue came to light when they examined the items back at police headquarters, then located in Inverness Castle. An address in Leeds was faintly pencilled on the back of the map Alex Matheson had found. However, when Leeds police contacted the people at that address they said they knew nothing that could help the inquiry. They had no idea how their address came to be on the map and had no knowledge of anyone fitting the description of the dead man.

It seemed probable that this case was going to involve forces over a large area of the country. DI Fraser and his team figured out that either the killer or his victim was probably from the Leeds area and it was likely this inquiry was going to stretch their resources. In 1962, the Inverness-shire police, forerunners of Northern Constabulary, had had few murders on their patch. They were ill equipped both in numbers and expertise to deal with a major inquiry of the kind they were facing. Early on in the inquiry, two of Scotland's top murder detectives travelled north to help their colleagues. They came from Glasgow, then as now Scotland's murder capital, where they would have gained more than adequate experience. They were Chief Detective Inspector James McLaren and Detective Sergeant Hugh Sloan. Their boss, Detective Superintendent Robert Kerr, head of Glasgow CID, also made the trip to meet DI Fraser. The Glasgow police were very helpful in co-ordinating the inquiry but they were back south when the case was finally cracked.

Although he was outranked, Fraser led the police team. He set about identifying the dead man and seeking out clues that would help them locate and apprehend the killer. One problem, which took some time to resolve, was pinning down the date of the killing. The body had been well preserved in wintry conditions, but pathology and forensic science were not so well developed in the 1960s as they are now. The first step was to conduct a thorough search of the area. A mobile incident caravan was set up in the lay-by near where the body was found. Police searched the verges of the A9 and eventually the army was called in to help. Tracker dogs were deployed. Plaster casts were made of marks on the ground near where the body had been found.

The difficult task of identifying the victim was carried out at the same time, a job made more difficult because everything that might have helped had been removed from the body. Using a photo of the dead man, police carried out door-to-door inquiries at every house in the area and visited businesses he might have used, including places he might have stayed. The area was full of skiers and walkers and even in those days there were many places to check and people to interview.

Everyone who was known to have been in the area at what police believed to have been the relevant time was interviewed by police forces over the whole of Scotland. The first breakthrough came on 21 March. Mr and Mrs Wild of Lowell Street, Leeds contacted Leeds police. It was their address that had been written on the map. When they were initially contacted by police, they had no idea of any connection with the dead man, but now they thought they might know who he was. George Green was their daughter Sheila's boyfriend of about sixteen months. He had left for a holiday in Scotland on 7 March and had not returned when expected a week later, nor had he been in contact. Sheila hadn't accompanied him on his trip. Their shared interests were tennis and car rallies; Miss Wild owned a vintage Riley. But she wasn't keen on skiing and had opted to stay at home. Sheila Wild had also discovered George hadn't been in touch with his boss and this was out of character.

Meanwhile, Mrs Marion Green, George Green's mother, had contacted police in Leeds to report her son missing. Mrs Green had been worried, but she hadn't reported her son missing at first, supposing that, as a thirty-year-old man, he could look after himself. When the police in Leeds connected her report with the news from Inverness-shire, they arrived on her doorstep with shattering news.

George lived with his mother in a two-bedroomed house in Woodlea Street, Leeds. A keen skier, he had timed his holiday to allow his married sister from Hampshire to stay at their mother's house for a visit. His plan was to spend his week's holiday on the slopes around Aviemore. When his sister left, he was expected back home to resume his job as an engineer with the Yorkshire Electricity Board.

Green's mother, accompanied by his aunt and uncle, travelled north by train to Inverness for the harrowing experience of identifying her son, praying on the way that she would find the body wasn't his. Sadly her worst fears were realised and later that day she appealed to the public for anyone who knew anything about the killing to come forward. She said that her son had never been in any kind of trouble and she couldn't understand why anyone would want to kill him. With incredible prescience she said, 'The terrifying thing is, it could happen again unless the killer is caught.'

The remoteness and isolation of the Highlands, even adjacent to its busiest trunk road, meant that there were no eyewitnesses who could help. The killer had struck and disappeared. Mrs Green said George had been driving his Ford Anglia and gave them a detailed description of the vehicle, which by now police were sure the killer had stolen. DI Fraser was heartened by the information. He reckoned the killer had made a big mistake and that the car would lead them to him. He was to be proved right, but not immediately.

Through the media, a nationwide appeal was made to members of the public for sightings of Green's car, a black Ford Anglia with its distinctive number plate YUM 772. No money had been left on the dead man. This was well before the days of ATMs, so Green would have been carrying his holiday cash. Robbery was an obvious possible motive for the killing. Green's friends, interviewed shortly after his death, described him as a kind and popular man, 'the sort of man who would give a lift in his car to a stranger'. His mother confirmed he was in the habit of picking up hitchhikers. Another friend told how Green was always trying to improve himself, taking a course every year and applying himself wholeheartedly to studying the chosen subject.

Green had previously visited Scotland with his younger brother (who at the time of the shooting was a student at London University) where they had enjoyed walking and hostelling. It was in Scotland that Green had first tried skiing and he had taken it up again on a Scandinavian holiday in 1961.

From information given by Mrs Green, it appeared unlikely that her son had ever got to his destination on the ski slopes. He had told her he would be in touch to tell her which hotel he was in but she received neither a phone call nor a postcard.

Mrs Green said she couldn't get the James Hanratty case out of her head. Hanratty had confronted a couple who were strangers to him and forced them to drive him to a place, which in a strange twist of fate was called Deadman's Hill, situated near Luton on the A6. There, in what became known as the 'A6 murder', he shot physicist Michael Gregsten twice in the head. He then raped Gregsten's companion Valerie Storie before shooting her five times in the chest. Gregsten died but Miss Storie survived to pick out her attacker at an identity parade. Hanratty was hanged in April 1962, one of the last people to be executed in the UK before the abolition of capital punishment.

We can only imagine the nightmare that must have played in

Mrs Green's mind as she remembered the lurid and prolific media coverage of Hanratty's trial (which concluded just months before her son was killed) and related it to what had happened to George. The parallels between the two cases were striking – and they must have seemed especially so to the dead man's mother. Hanratty's sentence was carried out while the search for George Green's killer was still underway.

Hanratty's mother claimed that George Green's murder was proof of her son's innocence, saying that the real culprit must still be at large. The resemblance between the two incidents was enough to give the Scottish detectives pause for thought, but a check of the circumstances convinced them that the two killings were unrelated.

Hanratty maintained his innocence to the end of his life, and wrote to his brother from prison saying he was not to blame for the shooting. As a result, his family took up his case, working to prove his innocence. They finally succeeding in having the matter considered by the Appeal Court as recently as 2002. In the run-up to the appeal hearing, Hanratty's body was exhumed. The DNA evidence was duly analysed, and tied him to the rape of Valerie Storie with odds of 2.5 million to one. This was enough to convince the Court of Appeal that Hanratty's conviction should be upheld.

A week after the discovery of George Green's body, the Chief Constable of Inverness-shire, James McIntyre, made an appeal to the public. He admitted that detectives were 'up against it' and went on to say, 'We must find the murdered man's car. It is the duty of every man, woman and child in Britain to help us track down this killer.'

Territorial Army troops were called in to help in a search of the area between Newtonmore and Dalwhinnie and mine detectors were used in the search for the gun. The inquiry team were still trying to piece together Green's movements after leaving home. There had been no reported sightings of him and the police concluded that he might have been killed as early as the day he set out on his holiday and at a location several miles south from the one where he was found.

There had been a major army exercise underway around the time of the murder. One of the officers who had been involved and was now helping police with the search said he recognised the car number plate. As he and his men were on manoeuvres they had set up a roadblock near Dulnain Bridge. The car had been stopped and the soldiers had had a conversation with the driver. He had been chatty, whereas his passenger had been slumped against the passenger's side door, apparently asleep. The driver had passed off the appearance of his companion, explaining that he was sleeping off an overindulgence of alcohol. As the car drove off it had slid in snow and stuck: the soldiers had got behind it and given it a push. The roadblock had been set up on 7 March, the day Green left home. Police now believed that Green had been killed on the first day of his holiday.

Police disclosed that they were almost certain the killer had used a .22 bullet but they couldn't say whether the weapon had been a gun or a rifle. A bullet had been recovered and sent to Glasgow for what was then described as scientific examination.

The post-mortem carried out by pathologist Dr Richmond revealed that Green must have eaten a meal shortly before his death and detectives checked every hotel and restaurant in the area. They struck gold quickly. Two waitresses in a restaurant in Newtonmore remembered a man fitting Green's description. Statements were taken from them, but a vast amount of information was being collated and it was some time before their significance was realised.

Then officers searching the edges of the A9 eight miles south of where the body had been discovered found bloodstained clothing and a holdall in a stream nearby. It matched the description of the dead man's luggage given to police by his mother. This supplied police with the clue that the killer was travelling south after dumping the body. They didn't believe that Green had died at the location where the luggage was found. They reckoned the killer thought that he had put sufficient distance between the body and the property so that the two would not be connected if they were found. DI Fraser concluded it must have been dark when the killer tried to bury the body or he would have noticed that he had left the map and part of the body was exposed. The killer was obviously trying to cover his tracks.

Police frustration mounted as the only clue that would help them find the killer, the location of the black Ford Anglia, eluded them. A month after the killing, the car had still not been found and still no one had come forward to report having seen Green as he made his way north – except for the sighting in the restaurant. All that the police had were questions. They knew that Green was friendly and kind-hearted and they conjectured that he might have picked up a hitchhiker and told him about his planned holiday. The passenger would know then he was carrying a lot of cash. Cops wondered if Green had planned to drive the 320 miles plus from his home in one go, sleeping in his car when he became tired. Did his killer come upon him then? Detectives were fairly sure that Green had been killed on either 7 or 8 March. After the first flurry of discoveries, the trail seemed to be going cold but the investigation carried on apace.

Police records were checked and the whereabouts of anyone with a record for violence involving firearms was followed up. A search was also conducted for escapees from borstal, prison and mental institutions as the jigsaw was being put together. This was in the days before offender profiling became a science. Common sense and experience suggested that the killer could be mentally unstable and might have a record. Police were still appealing for the public to help find the car with registration YUM 772. There was always the fear that false number plates might have been put on it, particularly in view of the distinctive number, which would be likely to stick in the minds of the public.

As the search for George Green's killer went on, police believed that he was still using Green's car and sightings of it came from as far afield as England, Wales and Aberdeen. Every one of them was checked, along with gullies and disused quarries where the car might have been dumped. A signalman from the Welsh village of Llandrillo reported that he had seen a car similar to the missing vehicle on the borders of Merionethshire and Denbighshire.

A woman who lived near the Erskine Hospital at Bishopton, Renfrewshire said that she had seen the car close to her home. It had been travelling very fast in the direction of Greenock. She told police that her eight-year-old daughter, Marion, was a collector of car numbers. On seeing this car, she had said, 'Yum, yum. ' At the time the woman had thought nothing of it, but when her husband told her about the car police were trying to find she remembered. Marion was in the habit of memorising number plates and writing them down later in a book. Her mother asked her about the number, which she gave without hesitation as 'YUM 772'.

An English holidaymaker told police at Fort William he had seen the car near Invergarry on the A82 about two weeks after George Green's body was found. The report said there were two people in the car. DI Fraser was amazed at the gall of the killer, returning to the area so soon after the murder. He must have driven past the incident caravan.

DI Fraser and his team reviewed all the statements taken and at last attention focused on those of the two waitresses who had served Green's last meal. They said he had been the only customer in the café at the time and they had sat and chatted to him while he ate. He had recounted to them how he had picked up a hitch-hiker somewhere around Pitlochry or Blair Atholl and that the man was a 'head case'. Green told the waitresses that his passenger had been wearing a clerical collar, and seemed to be a religious crank. He had been in a mental institution and had also served time in prison for activities he said were prompted by messages from God. Green said that although his passenger had made him feel uncomfortable he hadn't felt threatened, as the man was smaller than himself. He said he had felt confident that if the man became violent he would be able to defend himself.

Green explained that when the conversation between him and his diminutive passenger changed to the subject of Green's plans to marry, the man became very agitated and shouted that Green would be sinning. Green decided he had had enough and pulled over at a lay-by about two miles south of Newtonmore, where he asked the man to leave the car. As he ate his meal, his erstwhile passenger walked past the café and Green pointed him out to the waitresses. They described him as a small man huddled in bulky winter clothing.

The major breakthrough came out of the blue on Saturday, 5 May. Detectives in Manchester received a phone call which led to them detaining a Scot and taking a Ford Anglia car to their headquarters. It was thanks to the vigilance of nineteen-year-old Mark Davenport. Mark, the son of a garage proprietor, had lived and breathed cars since he was able to toddle, and knew the make, model and year of production of any car on the road. He had spotted a 1957 Ford Anglia, sprayed grey and red (obviously by an amateur). It was bearing a number plate that was too new for the model of car. He remembered the notice on the wall of his Dad's garage about the car police were anxious to find and put two and two together. Davenport was driving through rush-hour traffic but he managed to attract the attention of a uniformed policeman and urged him to jump in. Davenport explained as he drove that he thought the car was the one connected to the murder in Scotland. They followed the car, which was driven to a lock-up in Daisy Bank Road, and they watched the driver enter a house on Hathersage Road. Within ten minutes he was in custody.

This was the break police had long been waiting for. Mrs Green went to see the car at a police garage in Manchester and confirmed that it was definitely her son's car. 'It has been re-sprayed and the number plates changed but I have no doubt about it. I have ridden in it many times and I know little points about it,' she said. She had earlier told police that the car had two broken wing mirrors, a special fixture had been made and added below the boot to carry the spare wheel, the rear bumper had been bent into the rear offside fender and the car had a GB plate on the rear. These features were included in the notice Mark Davenport had remembered. Examination of the engine number established beyond doubt that this was Green's car. As detectives from the Highlands made their way south, a Manchester police spokesman confirmed to the press, 'This is the car we have been looking for.'

Before interviewing the suspect, DI Fraser examined the car. He found documents in the vehicle that didn't fit with Green's murder. They did however relate to a Swiss man recently reported missing by Interpol. His suspect was now in the frame for two murders. Fraser went to the house in Hathersage Road where the suspect had lodgings. Nearly everything in the man's room had belonged to either Green or the missing Swiss man, Hansreudi Gimmi, a twenty-four-year-old textile designer who had been living in Edinburgh and working in Dunfermline. Mrs Marion Green's prediction that there would be another killing had been proved accurate. A friend of the accused, Arthur Shaw, was also interviewed. By now Fraser had enough evidence to convict his man of at least one of the murders. He was ready to interview his suspect, Iain Simpson, a twenty-six-year-old Scot.

When he was charged with the murder of George Green and theft of his car and property, Simpson at first said he had found the car in Manchester. He went on to say that when he was in Dumfries Infirmary the previous July he had told a doctor that he was going to kill someone. Then his mood appeared to change and he made a candid confession in the course of which he seemed to be quite proud of what he had done. He said he had fallen out with Green and after he had been put out of the car he had decided Green was a menace and that he would shoot him. Green relented as he passed and stopped again to offer him a lift. Simpson took his chance, getting the gun out as he walked round the back of the car. He said Green had leant across and opened the passenger door and he had shot him then. He had pushed his victim over to the passenger seat and taken the wheel, driving north for a while. At first he had intended to take Green to hospital, but he later realised his victim was dead. Then, having, as he put it, 'cleared his mind', he turned back towards the south. He claimed his shooting of Green was, 'A mission of God'.

When Fraser asked about the property of Hans Gimmi found in his room, Simpson confessed, in a completely emotionless voice, to shooting Gimmi and offered to show police where he was buried. The following day, 6 May 1962, the accused was transported by police from Manchester, where he had been charged with the theft of the car, to Inverness. On the way north, Simpson led police into Twiglees Forest in Dumfriesshire where, about fifty yards off a Forestry Commission track, he pointed out the grave of Hansreudi Gimmi. The body might never have been found had Simpson not confessed and led police to it.

Simpson was hustled into and out of the court in Inverness with a coat over his head. At a brief hearing in private in the Sheriff's chambers he was remanded in custody and taken to Porterfield Prison, Inverness.

His brother Donald, then only eighteen years of age, visited him while he was in Porterfield Prison. He was weeping when he came out, shocked by his visit. Donald Simpson said, 'His eyes were vacant and he kept staring into space. The only thing he was sincere about was his climbing equipment. I asked him what had made him do what he had done. He just shook his head and said, "I did it – but what does it matter anyway . . ."'

Donald Simpson then said, 'It's a terrible thing to say – but when I left I was frightened of my own brother.'

Police found the original number plates of George Green's car in Ladybower Reservoir, Buxton, Derbyshire. Simpson had covered a lot of ground in the car, much of it before the number plate was changed. He boasted that he had been to London as well as back to the Highlands. Few people had remembered seeing George Green, but there had been many sightings of Simpson. Numerous people remembered odd conversations they had with him. He was so distinctive. More than forty years later, he is still remembered in Inverinate, Ross-shire for his weird appearance, described as 'gnomic', and his unusual choice of headgear, a balaclava-type hat with sides that rolled up.

Fraser's team discovered that before flagging down Green, Simpson had hitchhiked from Perth to Tomatin, fourteen miles south of Inverness, and back again. The drivers who carried him had lucky escapes. They had simply not triggered his killer instinct. The two drivers reported that Simpson, only 5ft 3in tall, tried to speak with a cultured accent. Then Green had picked him up between Perth and Pitlochry.

Simpson admitted that he stopped at a lay-by three miles south of Newtonmore and stripped George Green of all identification, then dragged his victim down a steep bank and covered him with twigs and soil. In the dark he wasn't aware that he hadn't made a very good job of hiding the body. He made a better job of disguising Green's car by painting it grey and red and putting on a false number plate, DJA 20. If it hadn't been for the sharp-eyed mechanic Mark Davenport, Simpson might have taken more victims before he was caught.

Less than a month after he had killed Green, Simpson felt compelled to kill again. He headed back into the Highlands to Loch Duich, on the north-west coast. Picturesque Eilean Donan castle, built on a promontory into the loch, is much visited in this area, where every corner turned produces a more breathtaking view than the last. The original castle was built in the fourteenth century to defend the territory of the Lord of the Isles at a time when the main highway was the sea. It will have been the scene of much brutality in the past. It is a short distance from Inverinate. In April 1962, that was where Simpson met up with Hansreude Gimmi, a twenty-four-year-old from Zurich who was holidaying in the area. In fluent German, Simpson introduced himself as a professor. He often claimed to be an academic. He offered Gimmi a lift. Simpson would have killed Gimmi almost immediately but Gimmi disclosed that he was due to return to his lodgings in Edinburgh to pick up his belongings and more cash. Simpson must have been running out of money at the time.

Simpson had been stationed in Germany during National Service. Having an interest in antiques, he had built up contacts in the trade there. He had enough knowledge to know what would sell in Germany and he travelled the UK, visiting shops and pricing items. When he found something of interest he said he couldn't afford it but asked for permission to photograph it; a request that would seldom be turned down. Then he produced a catalogue using the photographs and sent it to his contacts in Germany. When he had an order he would buy the item and sell it immediately, making a quick profit.

The two men spent a night at the youth hostel at Ratagan, eight miles from Eilean Donan, and on 7 April they set out for Edinburgh. Gimmi slept in his flat in Gilmore Place, Polwarth, while Simpson spent the night at a youth hostel and rejoined Gimmi for what was to be his last journey in this world.

As they drove, Simpson casually suggested a picnic in lonely Twiglees Forest in Dumfriesshire and before Gimmi got out of the car Simpson executed him, shooting him in the head as he had done with Green. Gimmi had been expected in Zurich for his sister's wedding on 14 April but hadn't turned up. His family had reported him missing.

Simpson was a consummate liar. He had courted a young woman Estelle Kierans, a hospital worker in Warrington, who was devastated to find out his true nature. She had loved and trusted him. She had even accepted his proposal of marriage. However, he had created a fantasy life for himself, which he 'sold' to her. He told her he was a student from Glasgow studying in Manchester, and managed to give Estelle the impression that his family were well off. He even travelled with her in Green's car, such was his confidence. At the same time he was wooing another woman called Dorothy who lived in Cheshire.

In the period around the killings he befriended a van driver, Arthur Shaw, who trusted him. He knew that the car Simpson was driving had originally been black and had the number plate the police were looking for. He also knew that Simpson had dumped a gun in the Mersey. In spite of this, when Simpson told Shaw that he hadn't killed Green he believed him.

Shaw believed that he had cheated death. He was sure Simpson planned to kill him when the pair of them were on holiday in the stolen car at Ben Liathach in Wester Ross. As they climbed a steep ice slope, with Simpson climbing ahead, the two men were tied together. Simpson started jerking the rope fiercely. Shaw just had time to untie the rope before it yanked him off his feet. It seemed to Shaw that Simpson's life was all holidays.

Simpson had been one of a family of ten who grew up in Coatbridge. He was a problem teenager with a record for petty crime and spent time in an Approved School before joining the army to do his National Service. He served mostly in Germany, where he acquired fluent German. He was demobbed in 1959.

Frequently in trouble, he was the black sheep of the family and had no contact with them for three years before the killings. He had worked at several fairly menial jobs, latterly as a grocery assistant and, of course, was dealing in antiques as a sideline. He rarely seemed to be short of cash. Like Archibald Hall, he had aspirations to move in higher circles than his modest upbringing allowed. At different times, he passed himself off as the son of a famous Glasgow brain specialist, a distant relative of the Royal Family and a lecturer at Manchester University.

After a prison sentence for theft from a church, Simpson headed for the Highlands, where he burgled churches and isolated houses. In one of the latter he found the pistol and ammunition he had used to carry out the shootings of Green and Gimmi.

At his trial in the High Court, Simpson was found insane and unfit to plead. Had he been found guilty of the murders, which were then capital crimes, there would have been only one sentence – capital punishment. He would have been hanged.

Two consultant psychiatrists gave evidence of his insanity. Dr Martin Matthew Whittet, consultant psychiatrist to the North Regional Hospitals, examined Simpson while he was on remand in Craig Dunain Hospital, Inverness. The psychiatrist told the court he had investigated Simpson's background. He had been in trouble as a small boy, as young as eight, when he set fire to a haystack. Thereafter he had been in and out of trouble of all sorts. At one stage he had started a church of his own and had been involved in the acquisition of communion vessels and plates from other churches. Then he had started his own church in Barlanark, Glasgow, and built up a congregation of around 200. Soon a real church was founded nearby. His flock began to question his credentials and to wonder about what was happening to the plate collections. When they challenged him, Simpson disappeared. In May 1960, he had tried to hang himself. Afterwards he was admitted to Crichton Mental Hospital as a voluntary patient. After a period in Barlinnie Prison, Glasgow, he was diagnosed as of unsound mind and admitted to Hartwood Hospital in July 1960. He stayed till 1961, when he absconded.

Lord Kilbrandon asked whether it was the case that in June 1960 he was certified by a consultant psychiatrist as a person of unsound mind and a danger to the lieges and whether it was on that certificate that he went to Hartwood. Whittet said it was. Whittet told Lord Kilbrandon that when he examined Simpson, at times during the conversation Simpson seemed to be far away. He screwed up his brows and rolled his eyes from time to time and then broke into laughter unrelated to what was being said.

Dr Whittet said he knew that Simpson was charged with the capital murder of two people. In his opinion, Simpson felt that he had achieved something by their killing. He felt he was doing this to impress on people that the world had a wrong standard of belief and that his victims were not really killed but what he described as 'changed'. His own beliefs were what motivated him to kill. Whittet was sure that Simpson would kill again given the chance.

Mr J. A. Dick, Simpson's defending counsel, asked Whittet, 'Does it come to this, that because of certain discussions he had with Mr Green and Mr Gimmi, he considered that they did not size up to his standards of moral values and therefore he should kill them?'

Whittet answered, 'Yes.'

The second psychiatrist to give evidence to the court was Dr

Ronald Cadell. He said there was an abnormal religious motivation in Simpson's mind. He told the court that Simpson had posed as a minister of religion for nine months at one stage and that he had occasionally passed himself off as a doctor. In Dr Cadell's opinion, women were never really in any danger from Simpson. Simpson believed that he had been put on Earth to protect women. His violent responses were triggered by remarks which were derogatory to the gender, or which didn't coincide with his religious views. 'He was quite sure he would be caught eventually but he wanted to continue to carry on what he felt was good work.'

Sentencing Simpson to be detained without limit of time at the State Mental Institution at Carstairs, Lord Kilbrandon said, 'The outstanding feature of this case is that the accused had in 1960 been certified as a public danger and confined as such. He escaped from this confinement. He was not discharged as cured but was just subjected to the old routine of a short prison sentence. I am not blaming anyone for this – it is the system. If this is the system and if this gives rise to serious public uneasiness, I cannot say that I am in the least bit surprised. I do not suggest there is any individual to blame. But I hope this case will never be forgotten by those responsible for this country's mental administration.

It is not known whether the prison authorities had Simpson assessed before his release but it certainly seems unlikely. The Mental Health Act of 1983, which is currently in force, contains a similar provision to that when Simpson managed to abscond. However, the period of freedom without recapture which is deemed to prove sanity is now six months.

During his trial, Simpson was shackled to cop John Cameron (later to be Detective Superintendent and head of CID in Northern Constabulary). As Cameron carried out his duties, Simpson threatened him that if he was ever freed he would kill him.

Police reckoned that there were other unsolved murders in the UK that could be laid at Simpson's door and that he might have carried out similar crimes while he was in Germany. Since there was no evidence, he was tried only for the deaths of Green and Gimmi.

The trial and incarceration of Simpson do not bring this story to an end. At Carstairs State Mental Hospital, he had the misfortune to get in the way of a couple of other inmates who were bent on escape and didn't care who they killed. They were Robert Mone and Thomas McCulloch. Simpson could have stepped back and let them get on with it, but instead he showed a humanity that suggests he might have been on the road to sanity. It cost him his life.

He was certainly a model prisoner at Carstairs. He adapted to life in the institution quickly and responded to the treatment given him. He studied and achieved a Batchelor of Arts degree, which was presented at a ceremony in Edinburgh; and subsequently achieved an honours degree in science and social studies.

Mone had grown up in Dundee, where he had attended St John's Roman Catholic School for a time before being expelled. From there he was sent to Approved School and when he was old enough he joined the army. On 1 November 1967, Mone – by now a private in the Gordon Highlanders – went AWOL from the army in Germany, bought a gun in London and returned to his old school in Dundee, looking for revenge.

He entered a classroom, where a class was in progress, and barricaded the door of the room. He terrorised a young, pregnant teacher and eleven pupils, sexually abusing some of the girls and raping one of them, while the school's principal ushered the remaining pupils to safety.

Police tried to talk to Mone and persuade him to give himself up. They managed to track down a former girlfriend of his, Marion Young. At her own insistence, she entered the classroom and tried to calm him. Mone shot and killed the teacher. He was captured in the aftermath and later was found to be insane and unfit to plead. He was sent to Carstairs. Both the teacher, Nanette Hanson (posthumously) and Marion Young were awarded the Albert Medal for their courage.

Thomas McCulloch was from Clydebank, near Glasgow. In 1969, he was in a hotel in Renfrewshire when he fell into an argument with staff over a minor matter – a sandwich that was not to his liking. He left, and later returned with four guns. He was overpowered as he tried to murder a chef and the manageress, but not before he had shot the chef in the face and the manageress in the shoulder as well as firing at police. He was diagnosed as a psychopath and was detained without limit of time in Carstairs.

Mone and McCulloch became close friends at Carstairs, holding hands in the chapel, decorating their rooms in a similar way and wearing identical clothing. They began to plot their escape together.

On 30 November 1976, Mone and McCulloch's plans reached fruition. Using materials they had garnered, some from the props of a planned Christmas show, McCulloch proved himself to be very able at creating weapons including a garrotte, a wooden sword and an axe. The pair had also managed to make fake nurses' uniforms and a rope ladder.

Mone and McCulloch attacked a male nurse in the hospital's social club and Iain Simpson went to his aid. Mone and McCulloch threw paint stripper in their faces. Mone had planned to disable the nurse in this way long enough to get the keys off his belt. When that didn't work, Mone and McCulloch hacked the two men to death, continuing their assault long after the men were disabled and dead or dying. In a sickening parting shot, McCulloch sliced off both of Simpson's ears. Then Mone and McCulloch scaled the perimeter fence. The plan was to hijack a car. Mone lay down on the road, pretending that he was hurt and the pair waited for a motorist. A passing driver stopped, but had a lucky escape as a police car pulled over too.

Police Constables George Taylor and John Gillies were the next victims, hacked with cleavers and axes. Gillies survived, but Taylor was stabbed to death and Mone and McCulloch took the police car. The roads were icy and they crashed, disabling the police car. McCulloch posed as a cop with Mone as his prisoner, and in this guise, they stopped a van with a driver and passenger. As soon as William Lennon and John McAlroy got out they were set upon, hacked and stabbed and thrown in the back of their own van.

McCulloch thought he saw a roadblock up ahead and drove off the road, wrecking the van.

Mone and McCulloch next went to a farmhouse, where they terrorised the Craig family and stole their car. Eventually they were stopped on the A74, just north of Carlisle. Their eventual capture was almost an echo of the final standoff in *Butch Cassidy and the Sundance Kid*, thankfully without guns. Mone and McCulloch fought on, but the police were brave and six hours after their escape, they were back in custody.

At their respective trials in 1976, both were jailed for life. McCulloch was sent to Peterhead, a prison for Category A prisoners, unpopular with most prisoners because of its remoteness, which makes visiting difficult. Mone was sent to Perth Prison, where he too was categorised A, the most dangerous type of prisoner.

Today's Human Rights legislation allows life prisoners the right to have the punishment element of their sentence fixed. This is the period that must be served behind bars before consideration for parole. McCulloch's was fixed at thirty years. He was eligible for parole in 2006. By 2005, he was attending a programme which seems to have been intended to prepare him for release. He was also studying for a law degree and had become a trained counsellor to help other inmates with their personal problems. All these initiatives would potentially influence the Parole Board favourably. Has he been rehabilitated? By January 2009 McCulloch was in Noranside Open Prison near Forfar with predictions that the next move would be to a hostel in Dundee.

Mone had also been sentenced to life and, as with McCulloch, the trial judge, Lord Dunpark, had said that life should mean life. Lord Dunpark stated that this recommendation had nothing to do with punishment for murder but had been made because Mone was likely to kill again, given the opportunity. However, in 2002, Mone had the punishment element of his sentence set at twenty-five years. Lord Carloway, who presided over the hearing, commented that release would be a matter for the judgement of the Parole Board, who have the responsibility to have regard to public safety. The current rules do not allow the judge to take public safety into account in sentencing or fixing the punishment element.

The police are very concerned that those convicted of killing a policeman may be liberated – and rightly so. Mone too has attended a course, in his case at Shotts Prison, which authorities say is designed to help rehabilitation. It consists of lectures, discussions and interviews with psychiatrists. The authorities say this was normal and part of the management of long sentences, but it seems very likely it is also a route towards release. Mone was also allowed out of jail for a day in July 2007, when he was spotted window-shopping in Crieff, Perthshire.

But then there was a further indication, if one was needed, that Mone is still dangerous. He was involved in a brawl at Shotts Prison in 2008 and as a result was sent once again back to a maximum-security prison, the one at Peterhead, all hope of an early release dashed. Many breathed a sigh of relief at the news, not least the women who were victims of his depravity in Dundee forty years ago.

The links to violent crime that ripple out from Iain Simpson's story don't stop there. Robert Mone's father, Christopher (known as 'Sony'), was a notorious Dundee hardman, drunk and thief. He was convicted of killing three women at New Year in 1979 and was later knifed to death in Craiginches Prison, four years into his sentence. He was unashamed of his son's crimes and boasted of them. With a father like that, even without his own mental illness, Mone was always going to have a poor start in life.

Neither McCulloch nor Mone is what society today would call an 'old' man. They are in their late fifties and still capable of violent criminal acts. You will recollect that Simpson was in the prison system and was released into the community instead of back into a secure institution. His freedom cost two lives. Only the future will tell what the price of liberating McCulloch and Mone may be, if and when they are released.

3

THE CASANOVA KILLER

When a milkman sees the bottle he had laid on the doorstep of an elderly man still sitting there two days later there he wonders. A milkman would know if his customer was the kind to go on holiday and forget to cancel his milk. John Shuttleworth, Jack to all who knew him, wasn't like that and anyway he had just come back from a holiday. The milkman mentioned his concern to Jack's next-door neighbour in Molleton Terrace, Back Gate, Ingleton, Yorkshire. The neighbour, Stephen Morphet, said he hadn't seen Jack for a couple of days. Worried about the old man, the two men tried his front door. They found it open and called out but received no reply. Neither felt comfortable about searching through the house just then. Though his neighbours were fond of him, Jack was a private man and they were respectful of his privacy. Still puzzled and concerned, they went about their business.

Ingleton is a village in the scenic Yorkshire Dales near Settle, an area popular with tourists, a community where people keep an eye on their neighbours. A community much like many of those in the Highlands of Scotland, where events connected with Ingleton on this day, 5 August 1989, were also to be played out over the next few weeks.

Later that day, Mr Morphet heard Jack's phone ringing continuously and went into the house to answer it. Jack's daughter in Morecambe had been trying to contact her father. At her behest the neighbour searched the whole house and found no sign of the old man. She asked him to look in the shed in the back garden that her father used as a workshop. Taking another neighbour with him, he did so. They noticed that the shed door was fastened on the outside by a piece of metal pressed through a hasp. Inside they found Jack dead. The scene was a horrific and bloody one. Their neighbour had been brutally murdered.

Police were called and Detective Superintendent Ian Peacock of North Yorkshire Police was appointed senior investigating officer. It was late and dark by the time he arrived at Ingleton. He appraised the scene. Early advice from a pathologist was that the victim had been dead for a couple of days, so he arranged for the scene to be sealed to await daylight. He began to pull together the team necessary to investigate a violent murder. The personnel included a forensic pathologist, a forensic scientist, scene-of-crime examiners, a task force, additional detective resources to those available locally and an incident room manager. In addition, he arranged to gather all CCTV information from local sources that might be helpful. In the following days, experts gathered evidence, which they expected would prove crucial in the event of a trial.

The tiny stone-built shed was spattered with blood and the state of the dead man's body left no doubt that he had been subjected to a violent attack with several blows to his face and head. A piece of wood left in the shed had been used as a weapon and the team was excited to see that a fingerprint had been left in blood on the wood. It was to be of no help; the fingerprint belonged to the deceased. Jack's clothing had been searched and his wallet and cash were missing from the pocket of his trousers.

The victim was eighty-eight years old. He had been a prizefighter in his youth and was fit and active for his age. Jack had worked till he was seventy driving the school bus. He had lived in Ingleton for the last twenty-five years, on his own for the last two after his wife died. Violent crime was practically unknown in this part of the Dales and the area was rocked by Jack's murder. Elderly people particularly were afraid for their safety. The village police station was tiny and for the inquiry it was connected up to the incident room twenty-five miles away in Skipton by fax and telephone.

Stephen Morphet had last seen Jack on Thursday, 3 August, when the old man had been working on his car at the front of his house trying to repair faulty indicators. Morphet had tried to help with the repair without success. There were clues that pointed to someone having been in Jack's house; there were two cups in the sink. The bonnet of Jack's car was still slightly raised and the bonnet lock cable was in the vice in the shed where Jack was found. Jack's front door had been left open and the back door closed. Jack followed a particular routine regarding his doors. He left his front door open only when he was working at the front of the house. The back door, which was accessible from either end of the row of cottages, was then locked. He had the opposite practice when he was working in the shed with the back door unlocked and the front door locked. It seemed likely someone had been helping Jack repair his car, had been in the house and then taken round to the shed.

Most victims are known to their killer, but inquiries suggested to the police that this wasn't the case. It seemed possible, or even likely, that the old man's killer wasn't local or known locally. Ingleton is close to a busy route from the industrial towns of Yorkshire to the west-coast resorts of Blackpool and Morecambe and, particularly in summer, this takes a lot of strangers close to the village. Could the killer have been someone passing through?

The media pack is always pressing for information when a murder has taken place. Police are keen to allay local fears of a violent person operating in the area who might kill again – and also to galvanise the public into providing information. Accordingly, the usual pattern of press conferences, sometimes held on a daily basis in the early stages of a murder inquiry, is a system that suits both.

At the first press conference, while a door-to-door inquiry in Ingleton was under way, Peacock made his first appeal to the public, asking them to help police by reporting anyone seen with bloodstained clothing. He also asked whether anyone had found the dead man's wallet and driving licence, or had seen the dead man after 4pm on Thursday, 3 August. That was when Jack had last been seen alive, alone and in the village shop.

Mr Shuttleworth's two sons, Rodney and Garth, attended a press conference and added their appeals to those of the police. Rodney, who lived in Devon, revealed that his father had just returned from spending a holiday at his home only four days before he was found dead. His father had driven himself to and from Devon. In spite of his age, Mr Shuttleworth had been fit and robust. Just before he left, Rodney had looked in his father's wallet to see how much cash his father had. He was in the habit of removing some of the money and putting it in his father's bank account for security. There had been £540, which he left there.

Both sons made an emotional appeal for help in catching the 'animal' who had brutally killed their father, saying that anyone with information should come forward and that it could be their father next.

The Shuttleworths told the press that their father always carried a substantial sum of cash with him – often in the region of £1,000. They had tried to dissuade him from this but he had remained adamant. He had always been interested in cars and as well as buying and selling vehicles he often bought items at auctions and car boot sales which he repaired and then sold on. Jack argued that he needed to have the ready money in case he saw a bargain. They thought that, in the past, their father had been careful about disclosing how much cash he had on him, but they felt that he might have become more careless. He always told them that he would put up a fight if anyone tried to take his money. Horrifyingly, he had told them that anyone trying to take his money would have to kill him first.

It appeared that was exactly what had happened. There were no defensive injuries on the dead man so it was likely his assailant had taken him by surprise. Peacock confirmed via the media that the likely motive for the killing was robbery. Jack Shuttleworth had been harassed for the last eighteen months of his life by someone knocking on his door in the middle of the night. He had told his sons and daughter about this irritation. Peacock didn't think that the person responsible for this had anything to do with the killing. He had a pretty good idea who it was and what it was about. Newspapers speculated that Jack might have asked a stranger who had befriended him to stay with him overnight and help him catch this nocturnal pest, but Peacock was certain that this very private man would never have invited a stranger to stay.

The post-mortem carried out by Home Office pathologist Michael Green confirmed that the dead man had been struck four times on the head with a blunt instrument – the piece of wood which was found at the scene; he had also been punched on the face at least twice. In a move designed to shock and hopefully gain sympathy for the victim and his family, Peacock released some information to the media. He revealed that in the pathologist's opinion Mr Shuttleworth had not died immediately. The assault had happened on the Thursday evening and death had occurred in the early hours of Friday. The killer had locked Jack in his shed so that even if he had been able to seek help he was prevented from doing so.

Soon after the press conference there was a breakthrough. Several locals reported that they had seen Jack Shuttleworth outside his home with a man they did not know at about 2.30pm on the last day he was seen alive, Thursday, 3 August. They reported that the boot and bonnet of Mr Shuttleworth's red, T-registered Vauxhall Viva were open and the stranger seemed to be helping Jack work on his car. Police now had a description of a man. He was 5ft 8in tall, with black hair and a swarthy complexion.

On the Saturday a week after the discovery of the victim, police carried out a stop-and-check of all vehicles going through the village in the hope that this would jog someone's memory and elicit more information about the stranger. This produced another three or four people who had seen Jack with the stranger, but there was no new information that could help identify him.

It was likely that everyone living locally would have seen a newspaper or a TV newscast reporting the crime and relaying the police and family appeals. However, the police team also arranged for posters to be hung in various places all over Ingleton where the residents would be sure to see them. These posters asked anyone who had seen Jack after 4pm on 3 August, or had information about any wallet that had been found, to contact them at the local police station or the incident room. This paid off. A guesthouse owner in Ingleton, about two minutes' walk from Jack Shuttleworth's house contacted the detectives. She had found an old empty wallet behind a wardrobe when cleaning a bedroom. The room had been occupied by a man who had stayed on 2 August and had paid for two nights but had suddenly left on the evening of 3 August, having stayed only one night. The description given by the guesthouse owner and her family was very similar to one given by people who had seen the man with Jack at his car that day. Rodney Shuttleworth identified the wallet as belonging to his father.

The guesthouse owner and her family told police that the man, who used the name David, had said that he was waiting for his car to be repaired in a nearby town, that he was a mining engineer and that his wife had left him. As well as the wallet, he had left a painting in the guesthouse, which police soon found had been stolen a few days before. Many of these elements were to be part of a pattern, with a deadly outcome for at least one other victim.

Peacock's team discovered colleagues had a report of two paintings stolen from a guesthouse at Osmotherley, near Northallerton, North Yorkshire, about thirty miles from Ingleton. They were by local artists, twin sisters Elizabeth Mary Alderson and Dorothy Margaret Alderson, who had became well known because, unusually, they had collaborated on some of their works. One of the paintings was *The Wheel Shed*, and the other, the one recovered from the guesthouse at Ingleton, was of the 1936 Derby winner, Mahmoud. Using the name David Rogers, the man had stayed overnight at Osmortherley on 31 July. He had also stolen a camera, which was later found in a car belonging to a French couple he befriended in the Highlands of Scotland. He left the guesthouse at Osmotherley without paying his bill. His description fitted the stranger seen with Jack Shuttleworth. Police now had a name for their suspect, but a check of criminal records revealed no match with the name.

The pattern of obtaining accommodation without paying led police to Carlton Miniott near Thirsk, about sixty miles east of Ingleton where a man, again fitting the description of the suspect, had been using the name David Kerr. His landlady, Mrs Doreen Corner, described him as a charmer, a laugh a minute, who was in the lounge shortly after arrival chatting to two elderly guests. He even showed fellow guests the two stolen paintings. She said she would never have suspected him of doing anything illegal. After trying to cadge a lift with two elderly guests who were not going his way, he left in the morning without paying his bill. He left behind clothes, toiletries, a key and a bottle of gin. Perhaps he intended the landlady to think he was going to return, buying some time to put a distance between him and the site of his fraud. He told Mrs Corner that he was heading for Scotland and so he was, but first he went to Ingleton.

Fingerprints from the English guesthouses were lifted and sent to Yorkshire Police Fingerprint Bureau, but the suspect could not be identified from them. He now had two known aliases. What was his real name?

Regular press conferences were held and new information was dripped to the media to keep the case in the public eye as police hoped that someone would come forward with new information. It was from their own colleagues that help came. On 16 August, a national circular was sent out by the Yorkshire team with all the information collated about the crime and the suspect thus far. It was circulated to all police forces up and down the UK. It produced virtually instant results. Officers in both Strathclyde and Lancashire responded the following day.

The force in Lancashire did not have a particular interest in the case but, to his credit, an officer there spotted that the suspect described by the Yorkshire force had an uncanny resemblance to someone being sought by colleagues north of the border, in Strathclyde. Strathclyde's police bulletin said they were seeking a man implicated in a theft of jewellery on Mull. He was using the name David Kerr. It was too big a coincidence to ignore.

Officers from the inquiry team in Yorkshire immediately set off for Mull, one of the islands off Scotland's west coast. They discovered that in mid-July the man using the name David Kerr had been on the island. In a hotel bar there one evening, he was introduced to a local woman, Anne Wood, a divorcee who worked as a shop assistant. He spent the evening in her company, charming her with tales of his life as a wealthy man in New Zealand. He spoke of horses, boats and cars that he owned. When he proposed to Mrs Wood that evening she laughed at him.

However, Mrs Wood was enchanted by the prospect of a life very different from the one that she was living. She reasoned that although she was not in love with Kerr she was fond of him and concluded that that would be enough. The following day she accepted his proposal. Over the next few days the couple got to know each other better. Mrs Wood's daughter Laura took an instant dislike to Kerr. This may have simply been her teenage antipathy to the prospect of moving to the other side of the world, but Laura was instinctively correct. For Kerr was not what he had told Mrs Wood, as she was soon to discover.

A few days after their first meeting, Kerr took the ferry from Mull to Oban on the mainland, where he said he had some business to transact. He was accompanied by Mrs Wood, her daughter, her sister and the sister's children. On the ferry, Kerr gave Mrs Wood an engagement ring.

When they disembarked at Oban, Kerr said he had to make a phone call and he left, having arranged to meet up later. They never saw him again. One disappointment followed another for Mrs Wood. Within a few days she discovered that the ring Kerr had given her had been stolen. It was among a haul of jewellery valued at £35,000 he had taken from her friend Mrs Eileen Stanmore, owner of the Glen Maree guesthouse at Salem, Mull, where Kerr had been staying during their brief courtship. It was Mrs Stanmore who had introduced Kerr to Mrs Wood.

The Yorkshire police team discovered that during his short time on Mull, Kerr had been photographed with a group of Mrs Wood's family and friends. They now had a photograph of the wanted man. It raised a dilemma. It was tempting to show the photograph to potential witnesses in Jack Shuttleworth's murder case; particularly the landlady in Ingleton, but it might prejudice identification at a trial. They kept it in reserve for the moment.

The very next day, Constable Paul Eddington, based at Bettyhill in the far north of Scotland, was reading the Yorkshire police bulletin. He realised the description of the man being sought by police in Yorkshire closely resembled a man being sought in the Highlands, who had been travelling around using bed and breakfast establishments and leaving without settling his bill. Eddington phoned Detective Superintendent Ian Peacock in the incident room in Skipton. Praiseworthy though his observation skills were, he bypassed his superior officers and hence wrong-footed his own force in what was to follow. Head of CID in Northern Constabulary at the time was able Sandy McGillivray, who had come to the north force from Derbyshire Police. He had an explosive personality, earning him the nickname 'Semtex'. Eddington was probably hauled over the coals for his failure to follow protocol.

By now the pattern of Kerr's behaviour was recognisable. He operated north and south of the border as a charmer who would con any vulnerable woman: he told stories of being wealthy; he stayed in small hotels and guesthouses and invariably left without paying. The officers who were in Mull travelled north to Bettyhill and Tongue without delay. These were the last places Kerr was known to have been.

Yorkshire detectives arrived in the north and quickly discovered that Kerr had been a frequent customer at the bars in Tongue. On interviewing the staff they discovered that he had given two rings to a barmaid. Anticipating that the items had been stolen, they retained them. Peacock contacted DS McGillivray and apprised him of his team's presence and activities in the north of Scotland.

Following the trail of unpaid bills, Yorkshire Police were by now hard on Kerr's heels and they arrived at Smoo Cave Hotel just one day after he had left. It was the closest police were to get to capturing him for some time. His behaviour at the hotel was, by any reckoning, bizarre. He had arrived and checked in with a French couple. The hotel proprietor, Mr Lew Montgomery, said that Kerr talked non-stop and told everyone who would listen that he made his living by buying and selling boats all over the world. The Smoo Cave Hotel had been on the market and although Kerr was told that it had been sold he was adamant that he wanted to buy the hotel. He insisted in handing over a cheque for £40,000 as a deposit, saying his agent, a Mrs McOnie, would pay the rest. The cheque was drawn on Mrs McOnie's bank account.

Kerr told the hotelier he had met the French couple when his boat broke down. Mr Montgomery thought that Kerr's companions understood little of what was being said and would not have been in a position to confirm or deny any of the story he was giving. This was as well for Kerr, as he had told them something quite different. When the French couple were found and interviewed in the north of England, they said he had told them he was a boat importer and was on his way to pick up a new boat to deliver it to its owner. At the Smoo Cave Hotel, the three stayed in a lodge attached to the hotel. They departed in the morning without paying, having run up a big bill. They left behind a rucksack later identified as belonging to Mrs Margaret McOnie.

The senior cops from both sides of the Border were concerned that when Kerr became seriously strapped for cash he might kill again. On 22 August, Ian Peacock held a press conference in Scotland and issued a copy of the Mull photograph to the media. This step had been agreed with McGillivray and approved by the Crown Office, which would have been concerned if release of a photograph could prejudice a future fair trial in Scotland.

Peacock did not mention a murder inquiry but said, 'There is no doubt that this is the same man we want to eliminate from our inquiries. We wish to trace him urgently and speak to him. He is clearly a ladies' man who preys on single women. He wears smart clothes and likes to give the impression he is very wealthy.'

Peacock asked for help to trace the man and also to find out his real identity. It was the start of a series of press conferences that were carefully considered in their wording, designed to 'steer' Kerr back into England. This was an attempt to avoid the difficulties that would have followed an arrest in Scotland for the murder of Jack Shuttleworth committed in England. The rules for detaining and interviewing a suspect were then, and remain different in Scotland and England.

Later that day, Mrs Margaret McOnie was reported missing by her family. When anyone is reported missing, police have to make a decision based on the information available whether there is a risk to the health and safety of that individual. Most adults who go missing return safely within a few days. Some are deliberately turning their backs on their existing lives and making a fresh start. In the latter case, police adopt a hands-off policy, respecting the rights of the individual. But there are sometimes compelling reasons for immediately opening an inquiry on the assumption that a serious crime may have been committed. This was such a case. Detective Superintendent McGillivray recognised that Mrs McOnie was almost certainly another victim of Jack Shuttleworth's killer and that the inquiry would soon be classified a murder.

In 1989, Margaret McOnie was a respectable fifty-five-year-old widow. Her late husband Alec, who had died in 1984, had been a security guard. She now lived with her only child, an adult daughter Sandra, in Sinclair Street, Milngavie, Glasgow. She was working as companion/housekeeper to an elderly, wheelchair-bound gent who lived in a retirement flat.

Margaret had decided to do something different for her summer holiday in 1989. She would, for the first time, have a walking holiday in the Scottish Highlands. She planned to go with a friend but between their talking about the holiday and setting off they fell out and she decided to make the trip alone. She bought a ruck-sack and walking shoes and joined the Youth Hostelling Association. On 6 August she set off for a fortnight's break. She had no firm plans for her route but had arranged to meet up with a friend in Oban on 16 August.

Her plan was to head north up the west coast towards Cape Wrath. Margaret was already familiar with the Trossachs, the area lying to the north of Glasgow, which was within reach of her home on day trips. The scenery of the west coast mainland and the Western Isles is idyllic and largely uncultivated. The coastline, longer than that of France, is populated by seabirds including gulls and puffins and home to seal colonies. It is sometimes rocky and often girdled by unspoilt golden sandy beaches where there is seldom human company. It is as different from Blackpool's crowded beach as it possible to be and is a paradise to tourists looking for a peaceful break away from the hustle and bustle of the city. The roads are mostly single-track and they are generally quiet, even at the height of the summer season. There are not enough superlatives in the English language to describe the beauty of the scenery.

This area offers visitors a variety of experiences, including woodland walks, sea and loch fishing and challenging mountains to be conquered, such as Ben Loyal at 2,506 feet. Highlanders in this area mainly live in tiny villages, among them Bettyhill where the late John Lennon holidayed with his family as a boy.

This part of Scotland is homeland of the Mackay clan, a surname that still dominates the local telephone directory. The area was badly affected by the scourge of the Clearances, a time in the nineteenth century when landlords brutally evicted their tenant crofters to make way for more lucrative sheep. This terrible episode from local history is still talked of with passion as if it was yesterday. Today, crofters have rights of security and purchase and a better relationship with estate owners, though there are still problems with absentee landowners in some places.

The north-west Highlands is the biggest police beat in Scotland, extending to 900 square miles policed by a single officer; an indication of the volume of crime. Policing in this region is by consent – there is no gun or knife crime and little drug crime and the vast majority of people are law-abiding and ready to help the local cop. This, then, was the area to which Margaret McOnie headed, unaware that it was to be where she would breathe her last.

Margaret had set off, her steps light with excitement at her courage in taking this journey alone, and with a great sense of freedom. She had no car; she would be using public transport including the network of post buses that connect the more remote communities in the north. She arranged to phone her daughter regularly and to send postcards. Sandra received one postcard and so did another family member. Then, on 11 August, Sandra received a phone call from her mother in which Margaret told her of having met a wonderful man on Skye. His name was David Kerr, she said, and he had swept her off her feet. She was madly in love with him. He was a wealthy mining engineer and had a boat at Mallaig. He had proposed to her and she said that she was thinking of accepting his proposal. She told Sandra that she was travelling on with him and that they intended heading for Orkney. It was a call that caused Sandra some concern at the time and it was the last time she spoke to her mother. It was only after the conversation had ended that Sandra realised that her mother hadn't said where she was calling from, although a postcard from Orkney did arrive days later.

Margaret McOnie was due to return home to Glasgow on 19 August and when she didn't appear, Sandra and Mrs McOnie's two sisters, with whom she was also very close, began to be worried. They contacted the friend she had been due to meet in Oban to hear that she hadn't turned up. The family thought about it over the weekend and when there was no further contact from Mrs McOnie on 22 August they reported her missing.

A massive search for the missing woman began. As with all such searches in the vast area of the Highlands, much of it unpopulated, the problem is where to start. They started where Mrs

McOnie had last been seen. An incident room was set up in Tongue village hall with computer connections to Northern Constabulary HQ in Inverness and thirty cops were drafted in to begin house-to-house inquiries.

The house-to-house soon revealed that on 13 August Mrs McOnie had checked in to Castle View Guesthouse, Loyal Terrace, Tongue. Tongue lies at the junction of the two main roads in the area – the one northwards from Lairg, in central Sutherland, and the road along the north coast towards John O'Groats in Caithness. It's a quiet village on the north coast, which has just a couple of shops, a filling station and two hotels.

Mrs McOnie had arrived at the guesthouse with a man fitting the description of Jack Shuttleworth's killer and using the name David Kerr. The pair had checked in together. They told the proprietors they were on a walking holiday. On 16 August, they had gone out in the morning and when Kerr returned later that day he was alone. That evening he went for a drink in the Ben Loyal Hotel. He told fellow customers that Mrs McOnie had met up with friends while they were out and had chosen to go off with them. The owner of the guesthouse heard this story too and thought it very odd. On the morning of 17 August, Kerr had checked out and, uncharacteristically, paid the bill. Police from both sides of the Border knew the chances of finding Mrs McOnie alive were remote. The jewellery the Yorkshire team had recovered in Tongue was taken to Mrs McOnie's family in Glasgow. They identified it as hers.

McGillivray made an appeal to Kerr through the media, asking him to come forward to assist in tracing Mrs McOnie. He said the couple might have gone their separate ways but that police were now sharing the family's concern for Mrs McOnie's safety and needed his help.

The local community responded wholeheartedly to the task of searching for Mrs McOnie. A search party was formed of about eighty people, including police, locals, Assynt and Dundonnell mountain rescue team, equipped with search and rescue dogs and an RAF helicopter. They focused first on the village of Tongue and then fanned out around Tongue and towards the village of Durness, about thirty miles to the west. The terrain around the village was made up primarily of boggy peatland and difficult to search, so the focus was on the areas close to roads, tracks and paths. Logic suggested that if Mrs McOnie was walking voluntarily she would have encountered the same problem. And if she was dead, her killer would have had similar difficulties trying to carry away and dispose of a body. She was unlikely to be found in the middle of a peat bog.

Kerr's movements between his departure from Tongue and his appearance at Smoo Cave Hotel were tracked. Kerr had travelled south on the post bus from Tongue to Lairg and then, strangely, he had come north again immediately, to Bettyhill, another small Highland village on the north coast, thirteen miles east of Tongue. There he hired a caravan for two nights – the 17 and 18 August – and on 19 August he turned up at the Smoo Cave Hotel. When he left Smoo Cave, he was still travelling with the middle-aged French couple. There was now concern for their welfare. He was seen again with the French holidaymakers in Inverness on 21 August and at that time they were reportedly safe and well.

Inquiries on both sides of the Border had by now discovered several aliases Kerr had been using and also the extent of the fantastic stories he made up about himself. Kerr was showing himself to be a Walter Mitty. The fictitious creation of James Thurber, Mitty was an accountant with an overbearing wife. He pretended to be a pilot, a courageous soldier and a surgeon to escape the reality of his dull existence. Kerr's stories were every bit as imaginative and improbable, but the extent of his fantasies could only be guessed at until his real identity was known – and, of course, Kerr proved not to be his real name.

The wanted man could be almost anywhere so Peacock decided to tap into the great British public as a resource. He asked the media in England to make an appeal, but not to print the photograph of

Kerr which had already been publicised in Scotland. By now the police were as certain as they could be without a second body that they were looking for a double murderer. Peacock was still fearful that showing the photograph could prejudice the trial identification of Kerr as the stranger seen in Ingleton with Jack Shuttleworth. The English press responded to his request but the photograph was aired once, on the evening news on ITN. By seven o'clock that evening, police had shown the photo to one of the potential witnesses who had seen Jack with the stranger and who fortunately had not seen the news on TV. She unequivocally identified Kerr. The Yorkshire cops had the confirmation they needed that placed the suspect in Ingleton with his victim there. If it came to a court challenge of that identification, then the police had done all they could.

That evening, 24 August, Mrs McOnie's body was found in the north of Scotland, a praiseworthy result given the size of the area that had been searched. She was buried in a shallow grave beside a single-track road leading to Melness, across the Kyle of Tongue (an inlet) from Tongue. Her daughter and sisters were asked to travel north for the unenviable task of identifying her body. In spite of the widespread coverage given to the description of the wanted man by then, no one had come forward to offer help in identifying him. A warrant was issued for Kerr's arrest in Scotland, naming him as Gary David Kerr and stating that he was wanted for the murder of Margaret McOnie. From then on, the Crown Office would not approve public appeals by the police in Scotland, on the grounds that they could be prejudicial to a fair trial. Therefore, most of the subsequent publicity emanated from Skipton, though it was fully reported in Scotland.

Liaison between the two police forces made it clear that the English force was better placed to deal with Kerr after his arrest. Northern Constabulary was not then equipped to carry out taped interviews whereas their Yorkshire colleagues were. In Scotland there is always the issue of fairness, taking into account particular vulnerabilities of the interviewee. Fairness is not easily demonstrated in a written transcript where the tone of a question can transform an interview into an interrogation. (The current gold standard is for interviews in serious crimes to be recorded on video. Northern Constabulary don't yet have facilities for videoing interviews although at the beginning of 2009 preparatory work had begun.

The day after Mrs McOnie's body was found, there was a discussion between Ian Peacock, Yorkshire Assistant Chief Constable Peter Sharpe and the Crown Prosecution Service in England. The possible prejudice of identification evidence at a trial was weighed against the risk to the public of the suspect remaining at large, and it was decided that he must be found as soon as possible. A photo of Kerr was released to the press, who were informed that the man was now a suspect in two murders. The press release warned the public that both victims had been robbed and that the man could kill again. Sharpe emphasised that Kerr was dangerous and should not be approached. Motorists were warned against picking up hitchhikers.

Kerr's swarthy face looked out from the front page of many of the country's newspapers. Airports and ports were warned to look out for him in case he tried to flee the country. Shocked by the revelation that he was wanted now in connection with two murders a relative of the killer came forward and identified him as Brian Newcombe, a fifty-one-year-old mechanic from the Nottingham area.

Now the fantastic tales he told could be compared to the reality of his life. Newcombe was born on 9 September 1937 in Mansfield, Nottingham. He had a thirty-year history of petty crime, with convictions for burglary, theft and deception. His criminal activities ranged from Southend-on-Sea in the south-east of England to Newcastle upon Tyne in the north-east, but nothing in his past record indicated he had a capacity for serious violent crime until his actions in 1989.

He had been married twice. His second marriage, which was to Penelope Jane Hamlett, was on 11 February 1984, and although he was an unemployed mechanic he had described himself as a Development Engineer on the marriage certificate. She too must have been taken in by him but loved him enough to stick around even when she discovered his deceit. The marriage was fiery and at the height of a row Newcombe would walk out and be gone for several days.

Newcombe's younger sister Anne had Down's Syndrome. She and his eighty-one-year-old, widowed mother lived in a terraced house in the mining village of Huthwaite, near Mansfield. His father had been a mining engineer, an occupation Newcombe sometimes claimed for himself. In 1989, Newcombe and his wife Penny were living round the corner from his mother and sister in a flat in Springwell Street, Huthwaite.

Earlier in 1989, Newcombe had wanted to start his own business as a gardener using the trading name Downham Landscapes. He had lost his driving licence for a time and as a result would have found it difficult, if not impossible, to get work as a mechanic. His elderly mother gave him £1,000 to help to get his gardening business off the ground and a neighbour allowed him to use her telephone until he got a phone installed in his flat. His business had not taken off. The neighbour reported he had only received one or two calls.

Newcombe was described by villagers who had known him throughout his life as a Billy Liar-style loner. To some he claimed he had been a Formula One racing mechanic for Ferrari and said he had lived in Italy. He told others he had been a personal assistant to Lotus chief, Colin Chapman, and had driven his racing cars. He even claimed to have a villa in France. Locals knew everything he said had to be taken with a pinch of salt. One neighbour described him as a Romeo and a conman. His cars were flash and spotless. He spun yarns about his work but no one believed it or took much notice.

By the time Newcombe was identified as the suspect, his wife Penny had been living with friends for several weeks and he hadn't been seen in Huthwaite for about six weeks. He had left, as usual, after an argument, but this time he had been gone for longer than usual. Penny thought he had gone for good, that he had walked out on her for another woman. He was always 'chatting up' other women. She had moved in with her mother-in-law for a few days and then had gone back to Harrogate, her home town.

The English murder team discovered Nottingham police had been looking for Newcombe in connection with a reported theft of £11,000 from Mrs Gwen Leason of Tibshelf, near Alfreton, Derbyshire. She seems likely to have been another of his conquests, who was charmed by him and later became a victim of his pilfering, but she never spoke publicly about their relationship. It may have been the knowledge that he was wanted for this offence that set him off on his murderous trip.

When police visited Newcombe's home in Huthwaite, there was a small, black car parked outside with French registration plates. Their first thought was that Newcombe had killed the French couple and had returned home using their car. Their second thought was that all three – Newcombe and the couple – were in the house. But in fact, in a weird twist of fate, a French couple, totally unrelated to the investigation, had rented the flat for six months after Penny Newcombe had vacated it.

Ian Peacock made a personal plea to Newcombe though the media. 'Give yourself up now. Ring me personally. You have my word you will be treated fairly,' he said. 'I urge him not to engage in any acts of violence. His best chance is to give himself up right away. He has my personal word of receiving fair treatment. Speak to me – ring me immediately.' Peacock also tried to ensure that the media mentioned that ports and airports were being watched. He had recent experience of two murder cases where the wanted men managed to flee to France, adding complications and delay in returning them to England.

Sightings of Newcombe began to flow in. In Scotland, the sudden death of a pub landlady looked suspicious, but on investigation it turned out the woman had accidentally fallen down the stairs and there was nothing to link her death with Newcombe. Once it was established that Newcombe had returned to England, Peacock tried to stress that the English/Scottish border was being watched to keep his quarry in England.

The French holidaymakers were found safe and well in West Yorkshire, where they were interviewed. The camera, which Kerr had stolen from a guesthouse in Yorkshire, was found in their car. When police had the film developed, there was a photograph of Kerr in a church on Skye. It was presumed to have been taken by Margaret McOnie. Evidence was stacking up.

Information about Newcombe was still being gathered. He had been using several names including David Kerr, Phil Kerr and Gary Kerr. He wooed older single women who were vulnerable to his charming manner, frequently spinning them a yarn. He had proposed marriage to several women on short acquaintance, including a tourist he met in Fort William. The wanted man had by this time been dubbed 'the Casanova con man' by some of the media. He boasted, to anyone who would listen, of owning a £65,000 yacht berthed in the Western Isles and of driving expensive BMW and Mercedes cars. Sometimes he claimed to be a mining engineer whose car had broken down and was being repaired locally. On other occasions he said he was a doctor or a bomb-disposal expert. In spite of his north-of-England accent, he passed himself off as coming from New Zealand.

The post-mortem report on Mrs McOnie's remains showed that she had been attacked from behind with a rock. She hadn't carried much cash, though she had a chequebook, which Newcombe had stolen. Police thought that this time the motive was unlikely to be robbery; it was more likely that Mrs McOnie had challenged him about something he had said. Mrs McOnie's property, apart from her jewellery, held little interest for her killer. He mostly gave it away to other women. He left some of her clothing in the guesthouse in Tongue, some on the post bus to Lairg and some at Smoo Cave Hotel.

Newcombe was sighted in Heath near Chesterfield. Then on

24 August he was seen in Morecambe, where he paid for accommodation with a cheque from Mrs McOnie's chequebook and stole a chequebook from a business called Utilidata Ltd. He then went on to Melrose Guesthouse, Church Street, Ambleside in the Lake District. His landlady there, Helen Ireland was quoted in the *Yorkshire Post* as saying, 'He turned up at the door on foot and asked to stay four nights but we could only put him up for two. We hadn't seen any pictures of him and we had no idea who he was. He was no different to any other guest, nothing out of the ordinary at all and there didn't appear to be anything wrong with him. He wasn't dishevelled, he looked tidy and responsible. He was very pleasant and quite natural but he didn't have much to say for himself. He said he was working as an engineer and had come up to sort out a problem at a site. He seemed quite plausible because we get a lot of workmen here and when he didn't appear for breakfast on Friday I thought he had gone off early to sort out the problem. But when he didn't turn up on Saturday we alerted the police.' Newcombe left the clothes he was wearing when he arrived in the single room he had occupied.

On 26 August, Newcombe was in Bolton, where he stole a Colt Galant with the registration number SOS 370X. In one of their many press conferences, police asked the media to alert the public that Newcombe might be travelling with a woman who would have no idea of the police hunt and to keep this in mind. The police were right. Newcombe was cunning enough to realise that he might draw more attention travelling alone and when he was caught, he had done his best to create an illusion that he was one of a group of colleagues.

A great deal of police attention was focused on Newcombe's home ground in the Nottingham area. It is very common for criminals to return to their home area even when to do so is to risk capture. Detectives also believed that Newcombe was cool and blatant enough to mingle with holiday crowds anywhere. Through the media there were appeals to anyone who might have transported him by public transport, taxi drivers and private individuals who might have given him a lift. There was concern that he could strike again and in particular lonely, middle-aged women were told they should beware, as they would be at the greatest risk. Police would not even discount the possibility that he might return to another guesthouse in the Lake District. He had stayed close to Tongue for several days after killing Margaret McOnie. More of his aliases were discovered – among them Phillipe Kerr, Dr Stephen Barbour and Richard Greaves.

From Bolton, Newcombe travelled through Derbyshire using Utilidata cheques to pay for fuel and food. As days passed, at one of the daily press conferences Ian Peacock commented to the media that Newcombe must be getting desperate, as his resources would be nearing exhaustion. The next report bore that out. Newcombe filled up the car at a petrol station near Ashbourne and then called at a bakery near Chesterfield where he purchased nine bread rolls and some chocolate with an Utilidata cheque. He told the shop assistant that he was starving, that he had just come off work on an oilrig. She described him as unshaven and very dark and dirty looking. He was probably sleeping in the car by this time. In an interview later he admitted stealing a purse in the bakery.

On 29 August, police released details of the stolen car Newcombe was using, stressing that fifty million pairs of eyes belonging to members of the public could help find it. That night at 3am, police swooped on the Derbyshire house of Mrs Leason, the woman who had reported him to Nottingham police for the theft of £11,000. They believed Newcombe might be sheltering there, but were disappointed. Mrs Leason later admitted she was relieved when he was arrested. She had by then realised that she could have lost something much more valuable and irreplaceable than her money.

On the night of 30 August, Inspector Andrew Roy noticed a car in the car park of the Parkhurst Guesthouse, Mansfield, just three miles from Newcombe's home. Guesthouses were high on the list of places Newcombe might appear and the proximity of this one to his home meant it merited special attention. Roy knew the car fitted the make, age and colour of the car the wanted man had been using. On checking with the police national computer he confirmed that the number plate didn't match the type of car to which it was attached. He realised the implications and called for back-up.

Newcombe had checked in to the guesthouse at about nine in the evening with two other men. He signed the guesthouse register with yet another alias – T. Reynolds of Preston. The three men gave the name of their supposed employer – Utilidata – and booked in together. The manageress of the guesthouse, Mrs Maria Incerti, gave them the first-floor family room. Mrs Incerti didn't tie Newcombe in with the manhunt even though police had visited her earlier in the day. His ruse of arriving with two other men had successfully misled her even though cops had shown her Newcombe's photograph. Nevertheless she had become suspicious. When she had told Newcombe where to park the car, he had refused, which she had thought odd. Later, the cheque he tendered to pay for the accommodation was for £40 and not £37, the cost of the room. He said his boss had already made it out.

Mrs Incerti was managing the guesthouse temporarily while the owner was on holiday. She felt uncomfortable and phoned the owner's daughter-in-law who said she would send her husband round. Before he arrived, however, police were on the phone asking her to leave the front door unlocked because they would be coming in to arrest someone and they didn't want to have to ring the bell.

When eight policemen entered his bedroom, Newcombe submitted to arrest without a struggle. His two companions were also arrested. One of them was later released without charge; the other was found to have an outstanding warrant for firearms charges and was handed over to South Yorkshire police. Newcombe had picked up the two men in a pub and spun them a yarn of being able to offer them work on an oil rig. They had been travelling with him for two days, between Northumbria and Somerset.

They had neither knowledge of, nor involvement with, either of the murders.

Newcombe was interviewed at Skipton, by two experienced Yorkshire detectives who had been preparing for this since the moment the identity of the wanted man was known. He declined to have a solicitor present. He showed no remorse for his actions. He freely and frankly admitted the killing of Jack Shuttleworth, saying that he had met Jack in the street and helped him repair his car. They had removed the bonnet lock mechanism to adjust it, he said. While they were in the shed, he claimed, Jack had become argumentative and hit out at him. He had struck back. When Jack was on the floor, he had seen the wallet sticking out of his pocket and decided to help himself.

He also admitted murdering Margaret McOnie. He claimed that when they were out walking on 16 August she had told him that she knew who he was; that he was wanted for the murder at Ingleton. He also claimed that he had pleaded with her not to tell the police. Then, as she was sitting with her feet in a brook, he had struck her on the head with a stone and continued striking her till she was dead. This story was demonstrably false. There was no national publicity about the killing in Ingleton until 24 August, by which time Margaret McOnie was dead. Therefore she could not have known he was a murder suspect. He offered no other explanation as to why he killed Mrs McOnie.

Even though he made his confession to police there could be no certainty as to which way he would plead when his case reached the court. Detective Superintendent Ian Peacock prepared for a trial of the case in England. He knew that he had many pieces of compelling evidence. Among them was Jack Shuttleworth's wallet, left in the Ingleton guesthouse. He wasn't just relying on Rodney Shuttleworth's identification either. The dead man had repaired the wallet using thread he had also used for shoe repairs and some of this had been left in the shed where he died. Forensic science proved that the thread was exactly the same. The crime scene had been meticulously sealed off and carefully searched – and this had paid off.

Mrs Penny Newcombe was interviewed by the police and said that she had been suspicious that her husband had relationships with other women. She routinely searched his pockets when he returned after his periodic absences. On one occasion she had found a return ticket to Blackpool and a wallet she didn't recognise as belonging to her husband. She was able to give this to the police. The dates on the ticket placed Newcombe in Blackpool on the day of the violent death of another elderly man whose wallet and cash had been stolen. Unfortunately the deceased's family were unable to identify the wallet. This information confirmed what the English inquiry team had already suspected. A search of crime pattern analysis using information from Jack Shuttleworth's killing had already picked this out as a possible match. There was never sufficient evidence to pin this case definitely on Newcombe but we can draw our own conclusions.

Newcombe was expected to face two trials, one in Scotland and one in England. As his files on the accused's activities were completed, Ian Peacock took copies of everything to Sandy McGillivray in Scotland, in the expectation that it would help to prepare for the trial to come north of the Border. In view of the chronology of events, the English trial was to take place first.

Newcombe appeared in court in Skipton, charged with the murder of Jack Shuttleworth. While he was in police custody he was constantly monitored because he was a suicide risk. After appearing in court he was remanded to Armley Prison, Leeds. He was put in the hospital wing for three weeks for mental and physical assessment. Then he was put into a cell on D wing. He was a category-A prisoner, considered extremely dangerous and so subject to the greatest security. He was in a cell on his own and checked on frequently.

In spite of this, on 13 November 1989, a prison officer found him hanging from the bars of his cell window. He had managed to plan his own death and carry it out with meticulous detail. He had torn strips from three bed sheets and had used lengths of thread from at least two prison-issue blankets to wind round the rope made with the strips to strengthen them. He had managed to stuff a piece of material from a prison T-shirt into his mouth and partly block the peephole in his cell door with a crumpled piece of paper.

Shortly before Newcombe's death, in a report produced for the Howard League for Penal Reform, Armley Prison was described as the most overcrowded in Britain. Three warders were suspended after inmates made allegations of brutality. Newcombe's death was the sixth suicide among remand prisoners in the jail in just over a year. However, Newcombe left three suicide notes in which it was quite clear that prison conditions had nothing to do with his death. There was one note for his mother, one for his wife and a third for his solicitor.

Following any death in custody in England there must be an inquest and in December 1989 an inquest was duly launched into the death of Brian Newcombe. At the opening of the inquest, his wife Penny Newcombe made a statement. She said that when she had visited her husband in Skipton Police Station he had admitted to committing the two murders in Ingleton and Tongue. Police there had been concerned that he was a suicide risk and that the risk would be heightened if he knew his wife was thinking about divorce. He didn't know that she had left the marital home and she agreed with the police she wouldn't tell him.

Penny Newcombe said that Newcombe had told her he would starve himself to death. She didn't believe he would have had the strength of character to see that through. When she visited him in Armley Prison five days before his death, he had been quite upbeat about the future. He had accepted that he would be in prison for a long time – about thirty years, he thought – and he was thinking about doing an Open University course. The coroner said that although Newcombe was found hanging at three minutes past midnight on 13 November, the three letters he had left were dated 10 November.

The letter to his solicitor read: 'I take this decision to end my life with a clear and well-balanced mind – in fact, it has never been more clear.' Of the prison authorities he wrote, 'They have treated me with consideration and kindness. They are blameless.' He added that his action was to spare his wife and family more distress and humiliation. 'It is simply a matter that if I am found guilty of a charge I didn't in my wildest nightmare intend to commit, then I could not even cope with the knowledge of such guilt.'

Brian Newcombe's funeral was held in the village cemetery at Huthwaite on 24 November 1989. The service was held ninety minutes earlier than originally planned, at the suggestion of Rev. Alan Roberts, the minister of the local Methodist church, who was conducting the service. There had been opposition from local people who had forebears already interred in the cemetery. They did not want someone who had committed such cold-blooded and heinous crimes to be laid to rest beside their loved ones. Rev. Roberts had earlier appealed for calm, saying he respected the view of those opposing the burial but also had to respect the feelings of the Newcombe family. Only family members were told of the change of time to avoid disruption from objectors and only nine people including his mother, his wife and nephews and nieces attended.

Detective Superintendent Peacock described Newcombe as 'a glib, smooth-talking con man with a fast tongue. Not for one moment did Newcombe ever express any remorse. In twelve hours of interviewing he never said he was sorry. They were matter-of-fact conversations in which he admitted killing two people.' Peacock said he was not surprised that Newcombe had taken his own life. While Newcombe was in police custody he had done everything to prevent it and when the man was sent to Armley he had again done all he could. 'I felt considerable sympathy for the families of both victims,' he said, 'as they would not then see justice done.'

The inquest into the death of Jack Shuttleworth came after that of Newcombe. There it was revealed that Newcombe had struck the old man four times on the back of the head inflicting a fractured skull during the old man's brave struggle. He had not died immediately.

At the inquest, Peacock said that he was completely satisfied that Newcombe was solely responsible for Jack's death. Jack's son Rodney felt justice had been cheated by Newcombe's suicide. He said that the letters left by Newcombe showed no remorse for the families of his victims. He expressed a hope that there would be justice in the next world. Mrs McOnie's family remain silent but if they expressed a view it is reasonable to think they would concur.

Because of his suicide, the extent of Newcombe's crimes will never be known and nor will the reason why he suddenly embarked on a course of violent, murderous behaviour. There are several parallels between him and Archibald Hall (See Chapter 1, 'The Butler Did It'). Neither was happy with the hand that life had dealt him and both men lacked scruples that might have prevented them from dispatching anyone who stood in their way.

PART TWO
HOME-GROWN KILLERS

4

A POSITION OF TRUST

In a scene that would not have been out of place in a thriller, the door of the Mumutaz restaurant suddenly opened and a man entered, his face masked by a black balaclava. Those who glanced at him thought at first it was a joke and the gun in his hand was a water pistol. The gunman strode past a waitress and diners up to the manager, Shamsuddin Mahmood, who was serving local businessman Donald Glue and his family. He calmly lifted a gun to Mahmood's face and shot him once at close range. The killer then turned and fled. It was early in the evening of 2 June 1994, in Kirkwall, the capital of the Orkney Islands. This was the beginning of a case that took fourteen years to come to trial.

The murder of Shamol, as the well-liked Bangladeshi was known, was the first in Orkney since 1969 (also the year when Orkney's Longhope lifeboat went down with a loss of all hands). In that case, the body of Andrew Kennedy, an elderly disabled man, had been found. He had been shot dead at his home on the island of Burray at teatime on Friday, 14 March 1969. Showing great efficiency and expedition, the police had an accused in custody by 3am the following day. Evidence pointed at Alexander Walter Bruce, an eighteen-year-old neighbour of the deceased who had been using the shotgun that killed the old man earlier that day. He had had both the means and the opportunity to carry out the murder.

Bruce was in bed asleep when cops came to arrest him. He was taken to Kirkwall, where he was questioned without either legal representation or the presence of his parents. In 1969 the age of majority was twenty-one so he was still legally a minor. The accused was flown to Aberdeen to await trial on the same day as his arrest and on the same plane as the body of Andrew Kennedy, which was being carried to a post-mortem examination. No time had been wasted and local police were probably patting themselves on their backs.

However, three months later, when Bruce was tried for the lesser charge of culpable homicide in the High Court in Aberdeen, the judge was highly critical of the procedure the police had adopted. Then, as now, the treatment of suspects must be fair and as a result the accused walked free.

The murder of the Bangladeshi waiter was not so easily solved. This time, police were meticulous in following procedure and biding their time, even though their interest focused on one person early in the inquiry. Under the law of Scotland, unlike in England and elsewhere, there is only one chance to try a suspect, because an acquitted accused cannot be retried for the same crime. In a recent notorious case in England, Sion Jenkins was convicted of killing his foster daughter Billie-Jo Jenkins, appealed and was retried twice and finally acquitted. He was tried for the same murder three times. That could not happen in Scotland, at present.

Following Shamol's shooting, the populace of these normally peaceable islands was stunned. They were afraid that an armed killer was on the loose. For the first time ever, many people started to lock their doors. Many thought that the killer wouldn't be an Orcadian; they felt they knew their neighbours too well to think that any of them was capable of a cold-blooded killing.

Kirkwall, where the shooting of Shamol took place, and Stromness are the two main towns on mainland Orkney, the largest of the group of seventy islands. Each of the towns has a distinctively different character. Stromness is compact with narrow cobbled streets and old grey buildings huddled into the lower slopes of a steep hill around its harbour. Kirkwall is hilly too but the buildings are generally more spread-out and most of the streets are wider. The two towns are home for most Orcadians. The Orkney

Islands lie just a short distance over the treacherous Pentland Firth from the north of mainland Scotland. Ferry and air services make them easily accessible.

Mainland Orkney is linked to two islands to the south, Burray and South Ronaldsay, by a series of defensive causeways called the Churchill Barriers. These were constructed in the Second World War to prevent German vessels reaching the vast sheltered area of water encircled by some of the islands, known as Scapa Flow. Previously, blockships had been strategically positioned between the islands to prevent entry to the natural harbour. These proved to be inadequate in the first weeks of the Second World War, when a German submarine managed to get into Scapa Flow and sink a Royal Naval battleship, the *Royal Oak*, with the loss of 833 lives. Previously, during the First World War, the German fleet had been scuttled in Scapa Flow. Nowadays, the Barriers are essential to the infrastructure of the islands, with roadways running along them facilitating travel between the three islands they link.

Orcadians have their own particular festivals and events. One of the most distinctive, unique to Orkney, is the Christmas Day and New Year's Day street game known as The Ba'. Two competitions – one for the men and one for youths – are held on each of the two days. Up to 200 men and boys compete with each other in a game of street football. Two teams respectively called 'the uppies' and 'the doonies' aim to get the ba' to one of the 'goals'. There are many scrums and in the general mêlée most of the players will have little idea where the ba' is at any given time. Throughout the town centre, shop windows are boarded up in the expectation of a contest lasting five hours and sometimes longer. The Mumutaz's windows will have been among them.

Kirkwall was bathed in early-evening sunshine when the shooting of Shamol shattered its peace. The Mumutaz, in Bridge Street, is still an Indian restaurant today but under new ownership and a new name. Bridge Street is a narrow street, part of Kirkwall's main shopping area, which carries one-way traffic westwards from the harbour area towards the massive sandstone structure of St Magnus Cathedral, towering over the town centre. The cathedral is the most significant landmark in Kirkwall. The double rope once used by Orkney's hangman, unused of course since the abolition of capital punishment, is stored in the cathedral within a few minutes' walk of the Mumutaz.

Bridge Street bustles with traffic and pedestrians during the day, but by early evening, once the shops have shut, it is quiet apart from a few pedestrians and cars. A network of lanes radiates out from it to the east and west, a feature that helped Mahmood's attacker to escape.

At the time of the shooting, the restaurant was busy with fourteen customers, including children, at its tables. Waitress Marion Flaws and Shamol were attending them while proprietor Moina Miah and his brother were upstairs in the kitchen. Miss Flaws, who was close to the door when the killer entered, didn't think he was there as a joke. She thought he intended to rob the restaurant. She ran outside to summon assistance but there was no time. As she hesitated at the end of the lane adjacent to the restaurant she heard the fatal shot and a few seconds later she watched as Shamol's assailant left the restaurant and fled down a lane at the other side of the Mumutaz, heading westwards away from the scene.

Two of the diners, Donald Glue and his half brother, David Lowry, who had been dining with their families, gave chase but soon thought better of it. The possibility of becoming the gunman's next victims dawned on them when the killer stopped and looked back. They returned to the restaurant where police had been called and others had done all they could to make the victim comfortable. A local doctor came quickly but nothing could be done for Shamol and he was pronounced dead shortly afterwards in the town's Balfour Hospital.

The islands' police complement was only thirty-six officers, spread across three shifts, and the most senior detective was a sergeant. They were sufficient to police the islands in normal times, but were not equipped to deal with such a serious crime. A contingent of officers from the Inverness headquarters of Northern Constabulary were shipped across from Scrabster to Stromness on the evening of the incident in an unscheduled run of the ferry. Detective Superintendent George Gough had been appointed to lead the inquiry and he quickly discovered that a motive for the killing was elusive. It was to remain so for a long time. Police acted quickly to seal off the islands. The killer had to be contained and caught.

Forensic experts examined the restaurant and removed a bullet and casing. These were the only pieces of tangible evidence left at the scene, apart from the body. The diners were interviewed, but their recollections of this horrifying incident proved inconsistent. Some had been sprayed with brain matter and blood as the bullet passed through Shamol's head. Their shock, coupled with the assailant's disguise and the unexpectedness of the incident, prevented them from providing police with a description accurate enough to inform an e-fit sketch of the killer.

Psychiatrists say that witnesses would have preconceived perceptions of the type of person who would commit a murder and that too could have coloured the diners' descriptions. Those preconceptions would also extend, in a community like Kirkwall, to disbelief that a local could be the killer. This was not a view that Gough shared. His gut instinct said from the first that the gunman was an Orcadian. The killer's confidence spoke to him of local knowledge and familiarity with the locus. There was one thing on which the witnesses were agreed – this was a cool, proficient killer who calmly and purposefully walked in, held the gun in both hands with arms extended, fired, turned and left.

The restaurant remained closed for days, even after scene-of-crime examiners had finished their job. The view through the windows resembled the *Mary Celeste*. Tables were still set, left as they had been when the shot was fired, a poignant reminder to Orcadians, had they needed it, of the rare violence that had visited their community.

The small team that had landed on Orkney on the day of the shooting was inadequate to carry out the initial, manpower-intensive part of the inquiry, but there were logistical problems. The tourist season was in full swing and there was a shortage of accommodation. About twenty Northern Constabulary officers from other areas were shipped in – this was as many as could be accommodated. There was plenty to do. For three days, everyone leaving the islands by ferry or plane was subject to a stop-check and hundreds of statements were taken. People who had left the islands before the stop-check was implemented were traced and questioned about what they might have seen. The day after the shooting, house-to-house inquiries started in Kirkwall. Local shop-keepers and businesses were asked to produce their CCTV tapes.

The motive is often the key to finding a killer and so the inquiry team looked at the victim's background, hoping to find the answer there. Most killers know their victims or have had some contact with them. Twenty-six-year-old Shamol was popular on the islands. People described him as likeable and friendly. He seemed to have no enemies. He was the youngest of a family of seven and an economics graduate whose family had aspirations for him that he should become a lawyer like one of his brothers. He had a girl-friend in Bangladesh who was studying to become a doctor and he was expected to marry her. The dead man had his own ideas that didn't match up with those of his family and, for the moment at least, he was happy working in restaurants.

Shamol had worked as a waiter in the Mumutaz restaurant for a time during 1993. He had only returned to work there as manager in April 1994. Between his spells in Kirkwall, he had worked in London and Southampton. Police forces in those areas helped their Highland colleagues and looked for clues in their respective areas that might point to a motive for the killing. They found nothing.

Predictably, the killing was on everyone's lips in Orkney. Local speculation raged over potential motives. Had Shamol had a liaison with a local girl that caused friction; had he been in debt to loan sharks; had he been the victim of a contract killing; had he been involved with drugs; was the motive racial? Mr Miah, Shamol's employer, believed the latter. He was so concerned he took his wife and children to live in what he described as a safe house and asked the head teachers at schools attended by his children to keep them in at lunchtime. In 1994, Orkney and the far north of mainland Scotland had a tiny immigrant community. In recent years, this has been swollen by immigrants from new EC countries. For the most part, immigrant workers were then, as now, well integrated into the local population.

Local firearms expert, Constable Eddie Ross, examined the bullet and casing and identified them as 9mm and of a type manufactured in the Kirkie arsenal in India. This information was potentially useful, but didn't move the investigation forward because the bullets were commercially available in the UK. Ross took all legally registered firearms held on Orkney away for ballistic examination. He test-fired them to see if they were capable of firing the murder bullet. A normal part of Eddie Ross's duties included destroying any illegally-held firearms on the islands. He would usually dump these out at sea, a fact that was to become potentially significant later.

As well as the house-to-house inquiries and the check on everyone leaving the islands, the team of detectives invited people to come forward with information and they did. On day two of the inquiry, Lynn Railston, then a teenager, and her mother came forward to report an incident that occurred on 19 May, less than three weeks before the murder. From their house, which overlooked Papdale Woods, they had watched a young man wearing a black balaclava and clothing that was similar to the killer's. For over an hour he had skulked in the woods, going from tree to tree as if he was stalking either human or animal prey. While they watched, the man removed his balaclava and dark jacket exposing a distinctive top, put the items he had removed in a rucksack and left the woods. Neither Lynn nor her mother recognised the man. They had been worried by the incident at the time but since no one was harmed they hadn't reported it. Now they did. Gough's team noted the information and its possible significance, but at this early stage of the inquiry they were keeping open minds.

Another local woman reported that she had received a chilling phone call in the days just before the murder. Her telephone number was similar to that of the restaurant.

'This is it. Your life is at an end,' the caller had threatened. There was a report of a cartridge casing found in a Kirkwall taxi three days after the killing. The police seemed to have plenty of clues but they had no suspect and still no known motive.

The local media were used as a conduit for requests, focused on particular help the police needed. Early appeals for information sought witnesses who had seen a man, probably no longer wearing a balaclava, in the vicinity of Junction Road, one of the main roads into the town, or in Bridge Street during the period from 6.45 to 7.20 on the evening of 2 June. The man could have been anything between sixteen and sixty and between 5ft 6ins and 6ft 2ins tall. The diners in the Mumutaz had given such widely varying descriptions.

Everyone who had been in the area at the time was asked to come forward to say what they had seen, to account for their movements and to check the activities of others. Three Asian door-to-door salesmen on South Ronaldsay found themselves treated as prime suspects for a time. After they were eliminated from the inquiry they immediately left the islands, clearly panicked by events. A local man whose past record suggested he might be the killer was taken in for questioning but he was soon eliminated from the inquiry.

Shamol's body was flown to Aberdeen and on 4 June a post-mortem was carried out. This is necessary in all cases of violent death, even when there is no doubt as to the cause.

The house-to-house in Kirkwall continued for over a fortnight. Every householder was interviewed. Then all males living in Kirkwall between the ages of sixteen and fifty were questioned. All the information was inputted into the Home Office Large Major Inquiry System (HOLMES). For the first time in Northern Constabulary's patch, information was being processed remotely while work was being carried out in Orkney, with administrative back-up provided by a support team in Inverness. This case was Northern Constabulary's biggest HOLMES inquiry at the time.

Information kept flowing in. There were sightings of a male fitting the description of the killer in the vicinity of the public toilets at Kiln Corner, a short distance from the restaurant. Immigration officials, looking for illegal immigrants, had been at the Mumutaz in March and there had been a more recent investigation by the same organisation at a restaurant owned by Mr Miah's brother in Stornoway on the Hebridean island of Lewis. A balaclava was found in a bag in the toilets of the popular and busy Ferry Inn in Stromness.

Two Austrian holidaymakers came forward. They had met Shamol the previous year and when they revisited the Mumutaz a couple of days before the shooting he had chatted with them. They had witnessed an altercation between the dead man and two other men. Shamol had refused them entry to the restaurant and one of them had threatened to shoot him. The Austrians said Shamol had seemed upset by the incident. Intensive inquiries followed in an attempt to identify and locate these men.

Ten days after the killing, Mr Miah reopened his restaurant in response to what he described as overwhelming support from islanders. He was still concerned for the safety of his family and staff and thought it was going to be very difficult to recruit another waiter while they could be at risk of another attack. The Bangladeshi newspaper in London that he normally used for recruiting staff had fully reported the murder.

Investigations continued into Shamol's lifestyle for pointers to the motive for his murder. He had made a £100 bet on the result of the World Cup and this fuelled speculation that he might have been in debt as a result of gambling.

The net widened. Police started to examine similarities in the killing of thirty-year-old Asian waiter Abdul Maneer, who had been stabbed and disembowelled two years earlier in Helensburgh, on the west coast of Scotland. His killer had not been found despite an intensive investigation and an appeal through the BBC's *Crimewatch* programme.

Three weeks after the shooting, police were no closer to finding out who had made the threatening phone call, or to discovering the identity of the two men who had been involved in the heated argument with Shamol shortly before the killing. There had however been two sightings of the suspected killer. One of these was on the road from Orphir at about 6pm. This route passed through the community of St Ola, which later proved to be very significant.

Using the local press and television, Detective Superintendent George Gough made what he described as unprecedented disclosures to the public in response to local concern. Islanders were naturally anxious to know if the armed killer was still in their midst. In the face of his own belief, he wasn't able to offer reassurance, but the presence of so many policemen on the islands must have afforded locals some comfort. Gough reiterated his appeal for help in identifying the men seen arguing with Shamol two days before he was murdered. Now he also asked for help in identifying the man who had behaved so strangely in Papdale Woods.

Racial incidents on the Orkney Islands were rare, but within three weeks of the shooting, two young men appeared in court, charged with threatening to shoot a female Asian taxi driver. Ian Eunson and Steven James Foubister, from the Deerness area of mainland Orkney, had approached her taxi, one of them muttering about a balaclava while the other exposed himself. In the climate of fear after the killings, particularly in the tiny Asian community on Orkney, their behaviour was extraordinary. In court, the pair admitted that their behaviour was due to the driver's colour. When they appeared for sentencing on 5 July, they were sentenced to 200 hours of community service and instructed to pay £400 compensation to their victim.

At the end of June, British National Party literature was found in telephone boxes in both Kirkwall and Stromness. Mr Miah told the local paper that one of his young sons had been threatened on the way home from school. Racism was emerging as the most likely motive.

Police completed the house-to-house and followed up various lines of inquiry, but there was no breakthrough. Members of gun clubs on the island were interviewed and asked to complete a questionnaire. This required them to declare what firearms they owned and what experience they had of shooting. In mid-July, inquiries had been extended to other restaurants in the Highlands and Islands. Interpol was involved in a detailed investigation into Shamol's past. Police from Scotland's mainland continued to have a presence on the islands; eight officers were still there working exclusively on the investigation. George Gough was called away to an inquiry in Dundee and Detective Inspector Angus Chisholm, who had up till then been responsible for managing the HOLMES aspect of the case, took over as senior investigating officer on the ground. He followed up every possible lead reviewing statements and information in the system.

On the morning of 12 August, almost six weeks into the investigation, Detective Inspector Chisholm and his colleague Detective Sergeant Alan MacKenzie arrived at Kirkwall police station to start work at 8am. They met Constable Eddie Ross at the door of the police station. Ross had just completed a night shift. To the amazement of the two detectives, he told them that he had a box of 9mm bullets from the Kirkie arsenal – bullets of the same type as the one used in the shooting. Almost every adult on Orkney will have known from early in the investigation that the detectives were looking for anyone who had this particular type of bullet. It was incredible that this police officer, the local expert and the cop who had been test-firing legitimately held firearms on the islands should suddenly come forward with this revelation.

Chisholm sent Ross home with a driver immediately to bring the box of bullets to the station. On his return, Chisholm asked Ross where he had got the bullets. Ross said he couldn't remember. Chisholm, suspecting Ross was prevaricating but not yet understanding why, told him that wasn't good enough and he should go home and think about it. He arranged to speak to Ross at the same time the following day. In retrospect, Gough believes that Ross thought that the inquiry team were getting close to discovering he had the bullets because of the intensive and extensive nature of the inquiry. Uniformed officers – even Ross, who had been involved in the firearms aspect of the investigation – would be carrying out their normal duties and would have little knowledge of the progress of the murder inquiry. Until Ross admitted it, detectives had no idea he had bullets of this type.

When Eddie Ross was next questioned about the bullets he said he had remembered who had given them to him, but needed to speak to that person before disclosing the name. Even when pressured, Ross was simply not willing to give Chisholm the name. The Detective Inspector told Ross to go and get the person and bring them in to the station for interview. Ross left and returned some time later saying he couldn't find the person. He was still refusing to give up the name. This set warning bells ringing. Chisholm expressly told Ross not to speak to the person who gave him the bullets. He contacted George Gough, told him of the development and asked him to come back to Orkney to resume his former role leading the inquiry.

The following day, Eddie Ross again spoke to the detectives as he was going off night shift and they were coming in to begin work. He said that the person who had given him the bullets was called Jim. Despite his senior officer's direct order that he should not speak to this person, he had seen Jim at 6.30am and arranged for him to come to the police station to see DI Chisholm that afternoon. It was arranged that Eddie Ross should come back to the police station at 2pm. Chisholm and Gough, who had by then returned, questioned him and he said he had received one full box, still sealed, of 9mm bullets and some .22 bullets from Jim Spence, a street cleaner and former marine. Ross said he had previously forgotten that he had some of these bullets.

When Spence came in later he was interviewed under caution and made a statement. He was confused about what he had handed over to Ross. He said he had found the bullets while a serving marine with 45 Commando near Arbroath in circumstances that might have delayed his discharge, which was imminent, so he had secreted them into his own property and taken them home.

He had handed them to Ross as someone well known locally to have an interest in firearms and because he was a policeman. The detectives digested the implications of this development.

Ross was easily eliminated as a suspect. He had been at home when the killing took place and had responded to a phone call asking him to come in. He couldn't have got home to St Ola from Kirkwall in the time between the shooting and the telephone call. The inquiry team were puzzled. They didn't believe that Ross would have forgotten he had that type of bullet. On the other hand, there seemed no reason for him to delay revealing he had them; or to have been less than forthcoming about where he got them. The detectives couldn't see how this fitted into their investigation.

Shamol's body was released for burial in Dacca in mid-August. Gough told the local press that the persons who made the threatening phone call had been traced. It had been a hoax. Two children had made the call and their parents had been so horrified that police had to ask them not to overreact. In Scotland, when children are involved in an offence the matter is reported to the Children's Panel rather than the Procurator Fiscal. Police decided no report to the Children's Panel would be made in this case.

By the end of August the inquiry was scaled down. Officers from the mainland were redeployed and DI Angus Chisholm, who was again in charge of the inquiry, reassured Orcadians that he would be very much in touch if there was any new evidence. Then, on 9 September, came a breakthrough. Lynn Railston contacted the local Detective Sergeant, David Mateer. She was the lass who had watched with her mother while the balaclava-wearing man behaved strangely in Papdale Woods. She told Mateer she had seen the same man at lunchtime in a shop in Kirkwall town centre.

The following day, DS Mateer and Lynn Railston took up a position in the window of a café across the road from the shop at lunchtime and watched to see if the young man came back. He did. Miss Railston pointed him out to DS Mateer. CCTV images of the man were taken to the police station and he was identified as fifteen-year-old Michael Ross, elder son of Constable Eddie Ross. There was now a possible explanation for Eddie Ross's tardiness in admitting he had some bullets of the type used in the murder.

Until this point, the inquiry had been stagnating. It had already been arranged that the case would feature on the BBC's *Crimewatch* programme and the inquiry team were committed to seeing that through. There were now two lines of inquiry pointing in the same direction, but there was no certainty that Michael Ross was the killer. Even if he was, *Crimewatch* might produce new key evidence. The cops needed to keep an open and objective approach. By now detectives involved in the inquiry must have been wondering if Eddie Ross had been hiding, destroying or corrupting evidence. Involvement in making the programme, which included a re-enactment, absorbed detectives' time and it was later in September before they could follow up on the recent discovery placing Michael Ross in Papdale Woods.

On 24 September, Michael Ross attended the police station in Kirkwall accompanied by his father. He was formally interviewed on tape and denied he was the male in Papdale Woods seen by the Railstons. He couldn't provide an alibi for the incident at Papdale Woods but said that at the time of the murder he was in Papdale East housing estate and that he had met and talked to two of his contemporaries, Ingrid Watson and Hayden Hourston. He said he had been cycling home past Bignold Park when he head the sirens of the emergency services heading for the murder scene.

Police checked Michael Ross's alibi. Ingrid Watson said she knew Michael well and was adamant that she had not seen him on the evening of 2 June. Hayden Hourston didn't think he had seen him either.

Crimewatch featured the killing on 6 October 1994. On the programme, Gough appealed for information about the male who was observed behaving suspiciously in Papdale Woods in May, the two people seen arguing with the victim on the day before the shooting, a man seen at the side of the restaurant at 5.10 on the evening of the shooting and a man seen in Junction Road shortly after the killing. In a media interview after the programme, police said there had been a good response but there was little possibility of an early arrest.

On 2 December, detectives decided to interview Michael Ross for a second time. Eddie Ross collected his son from school and brought him to the police station. By agreement, Michael was interviewed initially without his father and without a tape recorder. He immediately changed his story and admitted that he was the person in Papdale Woods. The interview was suspended and resumed fifteen minutes later, on tape and with Eddie Ross present. Michael Ross repeated that he was the individual behaving strangely in Papdale Woods. He explained that he had been waiting for Jamie Wetherill, one of his contemporaries. The woods are adjacent to Kirkwall Grammar School, where both boys were pupils. Ross said he had heard that Jamie had beaten up one of his ex-girlfriends, Nicola Wyllie, and he was bent on teaching him a lesson. He said he hadn't planned to do any serious harm to Wetherill, just give him a fright. Nicola Wyllie was later interviewed and confirmed that there had been an incident involving Jamie Wetherill and that Ross would have known about it.

If Ross was completely innocent and this was the explanation for his behaviour in Papdale Woods, why had he not come forward sooner? Why had he not admitted it was him the first time he was questioned? What else was he hiding?

Later that day, Michael Ross was interviewed separately about the murder. He stuck to his original story and gave the same alibi as when detectives had first questioned him. Again the inquiry team interviewed Ingrid Watson and Hayden Hourston, who confirmed what they had said previously. They had not seen Michael on the evening of the shooting.

Police worked on the obvious possibility that Michael had used a gun and bullets from his father's collection. Eddie and both his sons were members of a local gun club, the Orkney Full Bore

Association, where they practised shooting. The boys were also members of the local cadet force where again they used firearms. Michael Ross was certainly more than capable of firing a gun.

DI Chisholm decided to interview Jim Spence again. This time he admitted that he had given Eddie Ross a box and a half of the 9mm bullets. He now said that Ross had spoken to him three times, pressing him to say that he had only handed over one sealed box of the 9mm bullets.

Michael Ross's girlfriend was interviewed. She told detectives about an incident in the months after the shooting. She and Michael had been walking along Scapa Beach one evening. He told her he had taken the key of his father's gun cabinet and removed one of the guns. He said he had it in his pocket. Obviously access to his father's weapons was not a problem to Michael.

It was time to search the Ross home. On 6 December, Eddie Ross and his son were both taken into the police station for interview while the search was ongoing. Michael was held and questioned for the full permitted six hours and during that time, he stuck to his story about having met Ingrid and Hayden. During this and all interviews, Michael Ross showed himself to be a confident young man, mature beyond his years.

The searchers noted that Michael had a decommissioned machine gun hanging on the wall in his bedroom. Eddie's extensive collection of firearms and ammunition was examined. There was no sign of the murder weapon. The search produced some material that suggested that Michael Ross was racist. It was potential evidence.

Records of Eddie Ross's legitimately held firearms were checked. Jim Spence had told the cops that he gave Eddie the bullets because he was a policeman and his interest in guns was well known. Detectives now wondered if Eddie Ross might have acquired the murder weapon in a similar fashion.

Little of this was disclosed to the public as it unfolded although Orkney, having such a tight-knit community, got part of the story right. Rumours of the search of the Ross home buzzed round the islands. There was even speculation that the garden had been dug up.

Six months after Shamol was killed, George Gough made a further appeal to the public in Orkney:

> This gun did not just appear one day. Someone must have had it before then ... I return to the belief that the solution lies in Orkney and perhaps even in Kirkwall. Obviously, it is more likely the weapon used to commit the murder was not legally accounted for by the person responsible and, in connection with this line of inquiry I request that the people of Orkney seriously consider the following questions:
>
> Have you, or do you know anyone who had, over the past four of five years, a 9mm handgun which they eventually decided to dispose of?
>
> If so, did you destroy it, throw it away, or give it to someone?
>
> I would be very interested to know of any disposal of a 9mm handgun in the recent past, particularly if you gave it to someone, even someone you consider a reliable and responsible person.

A considerable amount of important evidence was in the system. It had been gathered from diners and staff in the Mumutaz, from people out and about in Kirkwall and elsewhere – particularly on the road between the Ross family home at St Ola and Kirkwall, and at the public toilets at Kiln Corner in Kirkwall, another key location. Michael Ross's friends and his fellow cadets were interviewed.

In January 1995, police staged an identity parade in Kirkwall. Michael Ross was in the line-up but none of the witnesses could identify him. By March 1995, Eddie Ross was suspended from duty, charged with various firearms offences which had come to light.

Between January and August, detectives checked every statement and piece of information, ensuring that every possible line of inquiry had been followed up. Forensic experts from Glasgow, double-checking Eddie Ross's part in the investigation, test-fired firearms on the islands. Early in the investigation, a local uniformed officer had been instructed to interview all Orkney gun club members and complete a questionnaire with them. It was a fact-finding exercise about their experience of firearms and the source of the guns they used. This had been his only role in the investigation. In August 1995 he heard a rumour that the detectives considered Michael Ross their prime suspect and he admitted to Chisholm that he hadn't actually seen the Ross boys but had given their questionnaires to Eddie Ross for completion.

Michael Ross left school aged sixteen in the summer of 1995 and signed up to join the Black Watch. In August 1995, DI Chisholm completed a crime report libelling a charge of murder against Michael Ross and sent it to the Crown Office. In his view, there was enough evidence to warrant a prosecution. The lawyers in Edinburgh did not agree and the case against Michael Ross was shelved for the meantime to the frustration of the detectives who had been involved.

In May 1997, Eddie Ross was tried at the High Court sitting in Inverness. The charges on the indictment specified his failure to disclose to his superiors that he had some of the 9mm bullets until considerably after the shooting and his possession of an unlicensed handgun. It said the motive for his actions was to prevent suspicion falling on himself, his family or friends, that men in Kirkwall had helped him in the cover-up and that he had asked Spence to lie about the quantity of ammunition he had been given.

In the course of Eddie Ross's trial his advocate, Herbert Kerrigan QC, asked DI Chisholm to name the prime suspect in the murder. It was an unusual question, but so were the circumstances. Chisholm's initial response was that this was a question he should not answer. There was a short adjournment and a legal debate before the judge with the jury removed from the courtroom. After this Chisholm was directed to reply. He named Ross's son as the prime suspect in the killing. He confirmed that Michael Ross had been identified as the person who had behaved oddly in Papdale Woods shortly before the murder and that on that occasion he had been wearing the same clothing as the killer and fitted the description of the killer. He also told Mr Kerrigan that Michael Ross's alibi for the time of the shooting had been 'confirmed as being incorrect'.

DI Chisholm confirmed that early in the murder investigation Eddie Ross had told his colleagues that the bullet was one made at Kirkie in India and that although it was made to be fired in a machine gun it could have been fired by a handgun. He also said that Eddie Ross had been responsible for test-firing all 9mm guns held legitimately on the islands and that none of them could have fired the weapon used in the killing.

In the witness box, Detective George Gough explained that when Michael was questioned about his bizarre behaviour in Papdale Woods he said he had been lying in wait for someone who had hit a girl at the school. He also said that when the investigation linked the Papdale Woods incident to the shooting, all households in Orkney were asked to give any information about it. Neither Michael nor Eddie Ross had come forward.

The extent of the dilemma that had been facing Eddie Ross was clear. As a father, his first instinct would have been to protect his young son, then fifteen years old. Once he had embarked upon that course, he would probably feel committed to continue, even if he thought better of it later. Within a couple of weeks of the killing – and perhaps as soon as he recognised the type of bullet – he was already trying to muddy the waters. As a firearms expert, he would have known as soon as he saw the casing left at the scene that he had bullets of that type in his own arsenal. The serial number would have identified it to him as belonging to the same batch. He must have been concerned that the man who gave him the bullets would talk to police and he would not be able to ensure his long-term silence.

Eddie Ross can have had no other motive for keeping quiet about the bullets aside from defending his son. We can only wonder whether he tackled Michael about his suspicions. As a cop, his instincts must have been to question his son and it is difficult to believe he didn't. Whether Michael told him the truth is another matter for conjecture. Although he didn't have to enter the witness-box at his own trial, as is the right of every accused, Eddie Ross chose to give evidence. He told the jury he had no reason to suspect his son was implicated in the murder. He also said that his guns and ammunition were kept at his home in specially secured locked boxes and that the keys were hidden in his house in places known only to himself and his wife. On being questioned further, he admitted that either of his sons could, if they had searched carefully, have found the keys and gained access.

Ross had the job of disposing of illegally held guns and after disabling them would dump them at sea. Did he get rid of a gun used by his son this way, or did Michael Ross hide the gun himself? An island with vast areas of open countryside surrounded by sea would offer many places where a gun could be hidden and never found.

James (Jim) Spence, the former marine who had given Eddie Ross the bullets, told the court that Ross had asked him to lie about how many bullets he had handed over. About ten years before the shooting, he said, he had handed the cop a full, sealed box and an open box containing about ten to twelve rounds of the 9mm bullets. Spence admitted he had said nothing about the open box when he was first questioned by police, though he had later revealed the truth.

Robert Hall, a local firearms dealer and hairdresser, told the court that a dying friend had given him four guns to dispose of safely. They were unregistered and hence illegal. He had sold one to an Aberdeen dealer but had given the other three to Ross and to Angus Mackay, another policeman, who had now left the force. He said that none of the guns passed to Ross or Mackay were 9mm and so would not have been capable of firing the fatal shot.

Angus Mackay also gave evidence. He said that after the murder, Ross had told him to get rid of the gun Hall had given him. The police were interested, Ross had explained, and they knew there had been a 9mm gun among those Hall had received from his friend. Perhaps George Gough was right. Eddie Ross may have admitted to having some of the 9mm bullets because he thought the murder team were close to finding out.

On 29 May 1997, Eddie Ross was found guilty of deliberately hindering the investigation and attempting to defeat the ends of justice. An exemplary police record did not sway Lord MacLean from imposing a custodial sentence. Nor did a record of service in the army, during which time he did three or four tours in Northern Ireland. Nor did Eddie Ross's service to the Orkney community. He was sentenced to four years in prison. In imposing the sentence, Lord MacLean commented, 'To attempt to defeat the ends of justice as a police officer, by frustrating a murder investigation, strikes at the very heart of the criminal justice system. You knew where your duty lay and you wilfully failed to carry out that duty.'

Three years on from the killing of Shamsuddin Mahmood, police had stated publicly that they had a prime suspect but there was still adjudged insufficient evidence to bring Michael Ross to trial. In 1969, during the last murder trial in Orkney, police blunders had resulted in an acquittal. This time the inquiry had been competently and thoroughly carried out, but the Crown Office had to be sure that the prosecution would have every chance of success. In Scotland there is only one bite at the cherry. This case had many twists and turns yet to come.

After Eddie Ross's trial, George Gough appealed for anyone who had surrendered weapons to Ross, either in Orkney or during his previous police posting in Kingussie, to come forward. The search was still on for the missing 9mm gun. It has never been found.

In the period after Eddie Ross's trial supporters of the family pronounced themselves shocked and disbelieving of the outcome of the trial. A petition and approach to the local MP, Jim Wallace, were considered, though Wallace would have had no means to overturn the verdict. The only way to do that would have been by an appeal, which could be lodged against conviction, sentence or both. For an appeal against conviction there would need to be a technical legal reason, such as the judge's direction to the jury being flawed, or new evidence demonstrating that the verdict was unsafe. An appeal against sentence would be competent if the punishment was disproportionate to the crime and out of line with the sentence in similar cases. In the event no appeal was lodged.

Allegations from friends and supporters of the Ross family were published in the local press. They said that police had not pursued every lead. Gough responded to these allegations, assuring the public that all the evidence had been examined. It had not been possible to make public the results of follow-up on their information, he said, due to the volume of information received.

Shortly after Eddie Ross's trial, the *Sunday Times* printed an article saying racial prejudice was a problem on the islands and that a wall of silence had surrounded the incident. Gough was quick to rebut that allegation, saying that people on the islands could not have been more helpful.

Eddie Ross had something to say about it too. On 19 June 1997 the Orkney press printed a letter he had written from prison. He insisted that no firearm he had owned had been used in a crime and that neither he nor any member of his family had ever been a member of the British National Front or the British National Party.

He served two years of his four-year sentence, getting full remission possible for good behaviour. A person used to army life usually adapts to a prison regime quite easily, but Ross will have come up against inmates who would have a go at him for being a cop. He will have served hard time. On release, he returned to Kirkwall, where he took up work as an undertaker.

In 2001, Orkney was rocked by another killing in Kirkwall, but this time there was no puzzle for detectives. Local man Paul Bullen beat and kicked his victim, Tommy Miller, to death. Both men had been drinking all day, Miller having four times the alcohol limit for driving in his blood. Bullen pled guilty to the offence at the earliest opportunity and was sentenced to life with a nine-year punishment tariff (the minimum sentence to be served in prison before parole could be considered). Detection and conviction caused the police and Crown Office little difficulty. As in the vast majority of murder cases, the killer was quickly detected and caught. It seemed that Orkney was catching up with the rest of Scotland, a fact that will be regretted by its predominantly peaceable population.

In September 2006, twelve years after Shamsuddin Mahmood was shot, a letter was handed in to the police station. It read:

> This is a true letter. I promise that I saw the person who killed the Indian waiter. I saw his face in full and the handgun. It was in the toilets at Kiln Corner. I have lived long enough with the guilt of not coming forward. The person was about 15+ years approx – white, and had a balaclava on head but still not turned down, colour was either dark blue or black dark clothing. He came out of cubicle but went back in quick when he saw me. I looked over and saw his face in full. The handgun was of natural polished metal or silver and was like a big Beretta. This may sound stupid but the way he held the handgun looked like he had handled a firearm before. I just don't ken what to do!

It was signed 'Worried sick witness!'

Police traced the writer. He was Orcadian William Grant. He was interviewed at length many times and consistently identified Michael Ross as the man he had seen with a gun inside the toilets at Kiln Corner, Kirkwall on the evening of the shooting. Grant revealed that on the night of the shooting he had been drinking heavily. This was not an unusual event for him, and it was clear he would not be a good witness. A clever defence advocate would be able to tie him in knots. Nonetheless, having taken several statements from Grant, police were prompted to review the case and a new report was submitted to the Crown Office. This time it was adjudged there was enough evidence to arrest Michael Ross and try him for the murder of Shamsuddin Mahmood.

Life is stranger than fiction and two very odd coincidences occurred during my research of this case. The first was the timing of my visit to Orkney. I arrived in Kirkwall in May 2007, almost thirteen years after the killing. And as it turned out, I set foot on the islands on exactly the day that Michael Ross appeared on petition in Inverness Sheriff Court. This date was known in advance only to the prosecuting authorities. Ross was by now a sergeant in the Black Watch, and this was the first step towards his trial.

The second coincidence was that on the day Shamol was murdered, back in June 1994, a court report had appeared in the weekly *Orcadian* newspaper. It detailed the case of a man accused of owning a dog of the prohibited pit bull type. This was a relatively petty crime, but the man's name, Ronald Peter Tobin, eerily foreshadowed a much more recent case. In May 2007, Peter Tobin had just been convicted of the murder of Polish student Angelika Kluk in Glasgow. In 2008, following a trial in Dundee, he was also convicted of the murder of 15-year-old Vicky Hamilton in 1991. The following year, he stood trial for a third murder, that of fifteen-year-old Dinah McNicoll in 1991. On 7 July 2009, his trial was halted due to his ill health.

It was to be almost another year, just within the legal time limit for bringing the prosecution, before Michael Ross's trial began. Preliminary hearings were held, designed to ensure that both prosecution and defence were ready and the date for the trial was fixed. Ross, by now twenty-nine years old, was to be represented at his trial by Donald Findlay QC, one of Scotland's best known and perhaps most notorious defence attorneys. In 1999 Findlay was in hot water himself for injudiciously singing anti-Catholic songs at a party for Rangers Football Club, of which he was then vice-chairman. Now, as well as making what must be assumed to be a decent living at the bar, he offers his services as an after-dinner speaker.

The trial began in Court Room 3 at Glasgow High Court on Monday, 12 May 2008 before Lord Hardie and a jury of ten women and five men. Brian McConnachie QC was the Advocate Depute prosecuting the case. The charges on which Ross was tried were that he:

Between 3 May and 24 May 1994, inclusive, the exact date unknown, at Bridge Street, Kirkwall, outside the Mumutaz Indian Tandoori Restaurant, along with others unknown, committed a breach of the peace by uttering racist abuse, threats of violence, shouted, swore and acted in a disorderly manner;

On 19 May 1994, at Papdale Woods, Kirkwall, face masked and head covered, committed a breach of the peace by loitering and crouching behind a wall and trees;

On 2 June 1994, at the Mumutaz Indian Tandoori Restaurant, 7 Bridge Street, with face masked and head covered, shot Shamsuddin Mahmood in the head and murdered him;

On 2 June 1994, at the Kiln Corner toilets, Junction Road, and elsewhere in Kirkwall, having committed the crime in Charge 3 and being conscious of his guilt, changed his clothing and footwear worn while committing the crime and disposed of the weapon. This he did to defeat the ends of justice and avoid detection, arrest and prosecution.

Breach of the peace is defined as behaviour which might cause fear or alarm to the lieges (meaning any other person). It is one of the commonest crimes prosecuted in the lower courts in Scotland as it covers a multitude of activities which do not fit the definition of other specific criminal acts. Its flexibility allows the justice system in Scotland to respond to crimes such as stalking before any specific Act of Parliament is enacted.

Members of the public and press crowded into the courtroom every day of the trial. Ross, who was living in army quarters in Inverness with his wife and children, was not remanded in custody and with a fixed gaze he ran the gamut of photographers as he walked into court each day. During the trial he sat impassive in the dock behind a glass screen listening to the evidence, flanked by a security officer from the firm Reliance.

At the beginning of the trial, Donald Findlay told the court that Ross was lodging a special defence of alibi and that he had been elsewhere in Orkney at the time of the murder. There are several special defences, such as incrimination and self-defence, which must be 'lodged' before a trial gets under way, thus giving the prosecution notice of the defence case. The prosecution run their evidence first and need to know what the accused will say in his defence to have the opportunity to rebut it. By the time the defence are leading their witnesses it is too late for the prosecution to lead new witnesses to challenge the defence.

The dead man's brother, Shaffudin, came from Bangladesh to tell the court of Shamol's background, of the family's hopes and ambitions for him. He said he knew of no reason why anyone would have wanted to kill his brother.

Shamol's colleagues in the restaurant spoke of him as an amiable man. One young workmate said he had been treated by Shamol as a younger brother. The jury was told Shamol was not rude to customers but when necessary dealt with them firmly. Then diners who had been in the restaurant on the evening of the shooting gave evidence of what they had seen.

Several of Michael Ross's contemporaries, many of them fellow cadets, were called to give evidence by the prosecution and they told of Ross's abilities as a cadet, particularly his shooting skill. One of the former cadets told the court that Ross's nickname among cadets was 'Arnie', a reference to his resemblance to Arnold Schwartzenegger. More than one of the cadets said the accused was among a group of youths in the unit at the time who expressed racist views. On at least one occasion Ross had said, 'Blacks should be shot.'

Ross's former girlfriend told of the walk along Scapa Beach when Michael had said he had a gun in his pocket. There was evidence of the incident at Papdale Woods and of sightings of a male wearing distinctive clothing and carrying a rucksack walking on the road from Kirkwall towards St Ola, where the Ross family lived, early on the evening of the shooting. One of the men who saw him there said he saw the same person at about 7.45 that evening back in Kirkwall. He recognised him as the same man because he was carrying the rucksack and wearing a jacket, even though it was a warm evening.

Hayden Hourston was called as a witness to tell the court that he had not seen Michael Ross on the evening of the murder. The court could not hear evidence from the other person Ross claimed to have seen that evening. At the time of the trial, Ingrid Watson would have been in her late twenties, but she had died tragically in a road accident.

John Rendall described how he had been using the urinal in the public toilet at Kiln Corner on the evening of the shooting. He said he had heard a lot of activity in one of the cubicles and had hung about to try to see who it was. The noises had made him curious. As he walked away outside he was too late in turning round to see the person's face.

William Grant, the new witness who had come forward years after the shooting, told the jury that he was standing at the urinals in the Kiln Corner toilets that evening when a young man came out of a cubicle holding a gun. On seeing him, the young man swore and went back into the cubicle. Grant described how they stood for a moment looking at each other full in the face. He said he had been scared to come forward but by 2006 he could no longer live with the guilt. The Procurator Fiscal will have precognosed Grant (taken a statement from him in advance of the trial). As he will have anticipated, it took only a few moments for Findlay's cross-examination to tie Grant in knots. He admitted to telling lies for no particular purpose and by the time Findlay had finished with him he had contradicted most of his previous evidence. His credibility as a witness had been pretty well destroyed. McConnachie used his re-examination to ask Grant to identify the person he saw with the gun. Grant reiterated that it was Michael Ross. He pointed to Ross in the dock. What the jury made of Grant's evidence can only be guessed at.

Members of the Ross family had been cited as prosecution witnesses. This gave them no option but to turn up and give evidence or be found guilty of contempt of court. Colin, Michael's younger brother, spoke of a close relationship between Michael and his father. Michael's mother was questioned about the items found at her home that suggested that Michael was a racist. She dismissed Nazi-type drawings and lettering in a book of Michael's found at the Ross home, saying it was 'just boys' stuff'.

When Eddie Ross got into the witness box, he claimed that his own conviction was a miscarriage of justice. He still insisted that Spence had only given him one box of the type of ammunition used in the shooting and alleged that Spence was a drunk who did not know what he was saying. He had to admit, when asked by McConnachie, that Spence could have no motive for lying about the bullets. Eddie Ross was asked once again whether he thought his son had anything to do with the shooting and again he denied it.

Having proved that Michael Ross had motive, means and opportunity to commit the murder and – if Grant was believed – had been identified as the killer, the prosecution case rested. Findlay led his witnesses in the defence case. The defence depended largely on the evidence of Fijian soldiers who had served in Iraq under Michael Ross's leadership. The two Fijians spoke of Ross's heroism (he had been decorated for his service in Iraq), the support he had given them and how he had shown no sign in his dealings with them of any racial hostility. No alibi evidence was given, despite the notice of the special defence at the beginning of the trial.

The prosecution and defence summed up their respective cases and Lord Hardie gave the jury his direction. In every case, the jury are told that to deliver a verdict of guilty they must be certain beyond a reasonable doubt. A criminal prosecution requires this high standard of proof. In a civil case, the standard is a balance of probability. On Thursday, 16 June the jury retired to consider their verdict.

No one else can ever know what goes on when a jury retires. The jury's anonymity is protected and it is extremely rare for a juror to make any public comment about a trial. It is certain that the personalities within a jury must have an influence on the decision. One strong character could sway the opinion of others. One thing is certain, the jury in Michael Ross's case must have considered the actions of Eddie Ross, for which it is hard to find any tenable explanation apart from the defence of his son.

Although the exact history of juries in Scotland is unclear, they are believed they have been part of the Scottish criminal courts system since the fifteenth century. In England, juries are used to make decisions in some complex civil cases, but that is being reap-praised because in complex commercial cases the average juror would have difficulty understanding the evidence. Given that judges are accustomed to assessing evidence objectively, one must wonder whether the jury system has had its day. Maverick judges are fortunately rare. If there was a right of appeal for a retrial by both the Crown and the defence, coupled with double indemnity, that could be a sufficient safeguard to help ensure justice was served. I know of at least one senior cop who wishes it was so. In 2008, the Scottish Government consulted on the form of, rules pertaining to, and even the necessity for juries in Scotland. Change may be in the air but probably not so radical as to abolish the jury system.

The jury were unable to come to a decision on the Thursday afternoon when they retired, but by lunchtime the following day their foreman told Lord Hardie that they had reached a verdict. They found Michael Ross guilty by a majority of murdering Shamsuddin Mahmood. Lord Hardie addressed Ross, telling him he would be seeking social inquiry reports before sentencing. He went on to tell him he would be remanded in custody till July, when he would return to be sentenced. At this point, Ross looked up for the first time since the trial began. To gasps from court officials and the public, Ross swept the security man aside and vaulted over court furniture. His advocate, Donald Findlay, called out, 'No, Michael, no.'

Ross managed to reach a door and leave the courtroom. In the corridor outside, a short distance from a fire exit, his route to freedom, a court official brought him down with a rugby tackle and held him down till a policeman handcuffed him.

In the period before Michael Ross's sentence was imposed, Eddie Ross said that he believed the evidence against himself and his son had been concocted by the police. He said that there would be an appeal against Michael's conviction. To bring such an appeal there would have had to be specific grounds such as new evidence, or legal points such as the judge having misdirected the jury. It would in any case be entirely appropriate that Michael Ross's defence team consider whether such grounds existed, just as his father's defence team will have done years before.

In the aftermath of the trial, rumours abounded in Orkney of other men who fitted the description of the killer and were in Kirkwall on the evening of the shooting. There was also talk of information given to the police which seemed to have been disregarded. But most people seem to have accepted that justice had been done and to have appreciated that at last Shamsuddin's family had closure.

The last place police expected to find a killer was among the family of one of their own, and it is rare for a criminal to try to escape the dock, but these were not the only unusual features of this case. In the days immediately after the trial ended, police discovered that Ross had hired a car at Glasgow airport, filled it with weaponry including a submachine gun and grenades, and parked it in a Tesco car park at Springburn, about two miles from the High Court. Who knows what he had in mind if he had reached it when he made his bid for freedom, or if he had not been remanded in custody while awaiting sentence. He certainly had experience of living rough, even before his army service. He would spend weekends on Orkney away from home, trapping rabbits and living on what he could catch but he wouldn't have needed the weapons found in the car to trap rabbits. And where did he get such weapons?

His attempt to flee and the possible outcome if he had succeeded raised a debate about whether Ross should have been remanded in custody for the duration of the trial. His actions won't have enhanced his chances of leniency when it came to fixing the punishment tariff, the minimum time he would spend behind bars. Sentencing was delayed until October 2008 because Lord Hardie became ill. Then, the judge handed down the mandatory life sentence with a punishment tariff of twenty-five years for the murder and an additional five-year sentence for his attempt to escape and the cache of weapons in the hire car. Lord Hardie told Ross that it was a 'vicious, evil and unprovoked murder.' He added: 'Your actions in murdering him were an act of cowardice and, despite what was said about your army career, it is clear from your actions after conviction that you are still a coward.'

One month later, in November 2008, an anonymous businessman advertised in the *Orcadian* newspaper, asking for information that would lead to the capture of the real killer and the acquittal of Ross. He offered a reward of £100,000. Amanda Swanney, an Orkney woman now living in Aberdeen, who was thirteen at the time of the murder, came forward to claim that she had been with Michael Ross that evening and could provide him with an alibi. She said she was not interested in the reward. If she was correct, her statement could have saved Michael Ross from prison. But if it was true why has Ross never mentioned it and why has she taken so many years to come forward? She must have seen the huge amount of publicity given to the murder inquiry, the arrest, the trial and the events since. Miss Swanney has been very careful to say, 'If I am right in the way I remember it . . .'

After sentencing in October 2008, Michael Ross's legal team lodged a notice of intention to appeal against sentence and against conviction and followed that up with detailed grounds of appeal. Those grounds, together with a report from the trial judge, Lord Hardie, will be judicially considered to see if they have merit. Assuming they do, a date, will be fixed for a hearing before three judges, probably in 2010.

One has to wonder whether there will there be further developments in this story and also to hope that Shamol's family will finally be able to have closure. They have waited long enough.

5

UNDUE INFLUENCE

This is the story of the life and death of Inverness's own Maria Caldwell, Jasmine Beckwith, or Victoria Climbié. Sadly the list grows on, with the recent additions of Baby P and Brandon Muir. The story is worth telling because there is just a chance that someone reading this might be in a position in future to ensure that his or her city, town or village is not the one where no one spoke up and another child died.

The Keg Public Bar on Baron Taylors Street, Inverness was busy on Hogmanay 2002. It's a traditional, city-centre pub, frequented mostly by men, and one of the customers that evening was regular Hugh McGrogan. He had enjoyed a few drinks by the time he was joined by Christopher Gaytor. The men knew each other quite well in spite of a difference in their ages; McGrogan was a generation older. McGrogan's partner's daughter Tracy Reid was in a relationship with Christopher's brother Lee.

The men chatted for a time and the conversation turned to Danielle, Tracy's five-year-old daughter. McGrogan said that it was a while since his partner, Danielle's granny, had seen her. His tongue loosened by alcohol, Gaytor dropped a bombshell. He told McGrogan that Danielle Reid had been 'done in'. Shocked, McGrogan pressed him for more information, to be told that either Lee had killed her or she had fallen down the stairs.

McGrogan wasted no time and telephoned the police. Despite his obvious drunkenness, the duty officer at the police station took the call seriously. A uniformed sergeant was detailed to meet

McGrogan in the city centre and heard the inebriated man's story. McGrogan repeated what Gaytor had said, explained that Danielle hadn't been seen by any of Tracy Reid's relatives for three months, and said he was fearful for the bairn's safety. Taking McGrogan with him, the cop went immediately to the address given for Tracy Reid.

She was living at 66 Argyle Street, in the Crown district of Inverness. Although the prison is nearby, Crown is a desirable area, close to the city centre with many large private houses set in sizeable well-tended gardens. The house at 66 Argyle Street stands out from others in the street. Well maintained dormer bungalows and semis fronted by tiny gardens line the street, while number 66 is a two-storey house positioned end-on with a gable wall facing the street. The police sergeant arrived in the early hours of 1 January 2003 with McGrogan in tow. When McGrogan went to enter the house, Tracy Reid became belligerent. The cop asked McGrogan to wait outside and she became more co-operative. She told the officer that her daughter was staying over with a friend but she couldn't provide the address. The sergeant was not satisfied with Tracy's story and told her that officers would contact her again in the morning. When he returned to the police station he discussed the case with an on-call social worker.

About 8am the following day, 1 January, Tracy Reid arrived at Burnett Road police station to make a complaint against McGrogan. While she was being interviewed about this, she was also asked about Danielle's whereabouts and this time she said the child was with her partner, Lee Gaytor, in Bishop Auckland, County Durham, but she said she didn't have the address where they were staying. She said that her contact was by mobile phone and she provided what she said was the number. The police tried to contact Lee Gaytor immediately and rang several times thereafter but received no answer. Tracy Reid explained away what she had said the previous evening about Danielle staying with a friend, claiming she hadn't wanted McGrogan to know anything about Danielle.

Convinced that Tracy was not being honest with him, the

interviewing officer was concerned that Danielle was lying in the house at Argyle Street. Accompanied by another officer, he took Tracy home, ostensibly to get a photograph of Danielle, a normal procedure in a missing person inquiry. Tracy claimed to have lost her key when they arrived at the house. The cop thought Tracy was stalling, and his anxiety for the child increased. He offered to open the house forcibly. Tracy agreed and they waited for a ram to be brought from Burnett Road police station.

The two cops took a look round the house while Tracy produced the photograph of her bonnie wee blonde daughter. There was no sign of Danielle and there was no children's clothing evident in any of the rooms. In the course of that day the officers made several unsuccessful attempts to contact Lee Gaytor at the phone number Tracy had given.

In the early afternoon Tracy again went to Burnett Road police station to make a formal complaint against Hugh McGrogan, saying that he had been banging on her door for about ten minutes and she wanted him warned to stay away. She was asked if she had spoken to Lee Gaytor that morning. She said that she had and confirmed that she had used the number she had given the officers earlier. The number was tried again and again it just rang out. Tracy couldn't explain why she didn't ask Gaytor for the address where he and Danielle were staying. Police challenged her about her story, telling her they would not give up till they were satisfied that Danielle was safe. She became tearful and at that point the interviewer backed off.

The interviewing officer later checked Criminal Records to find that Lee Gaytor had a long record of convictions which included offences of violence against women and children and that there was a warrant outstanding for his arrest. He made a report to his senior officer before he went off duty. The case was lost in a pile of paperwork over the holiday period and nothing further happened for another four days. It was all too late for Danielle in any case.

It was 6 January when senior police officers realised that the case had drifted. Detective Inspector Steve Mackay was appointed senior investigating officer. Hugh McGrogan was formally interviewed and reiterated what he had said on Hogmanay. The next focus was the house at 66 Argyle Street. The detectives were keeping an open mind. Danielle might be there safe and well. No one responded to their knocking at the door. Later they discovered that someone, supposedly Gaytor, had climbed out of a window and made off when he saw them approach. As the day went on, inquiries revealed that Tracy Reid had left on a train for Edinburgh.

Police wanted to interview Christopher Gaytor about what he had told Hugh McGrogan and they found him in a favourite haunt, the Keg Bar. He denied having told McGrogan that Danielle was dead. The implications of giving false information were explained to him and he was released. McGrogan had been in his cups when he first talked to police about what Christopher Gaytor had told him but the officers were concerned that they had not been able to find Danielle.

They decided there was enough doubt about her welfare and accordingly Tracy Reid and Lee Gaytor had to be traced and questioned, under arrest if necessary. First they had to be found. Using, among other things, mobile phone transmissions, police discovered that Tracy Reid had got off the train going south at Aviemore and was heading back to Inverness on a train which was due to arrive late that evening. They were waiting for her when she disembarked.

In the car on the way to Burnett Road police station Tracy Reid admitted that Danielle was dead. She said that she had been so high on drugs at the time of Danielle's death and afterwards that she hadn't been aware of all that was happening. She told the police that her daughter's body was in the river. Even then she prevaricated. She gave them the wrong location.

Lee Gaytor was traced to a house in Nairn, where he was arrested. The following day, 7 January, Christopher Gaytor was detained again. En route to the police station, he told police of a phone call from his brother, Lee, in early November 2002, asking for his help. When he arrived at the house in Argyle Street, Lee told him that Danielle had fallen down the stairs after drinking half a bottle of vodka that had been left out. Lee told him that she was now dead, and her body was in a canvas suitcase. Christopher told the police how he helped Tracy wheel the suitcase through the centre of Inverness, past Crown Primary School, the school Danielle had briefly attended and down the High Street through the busy shopping centre, to the Caledonian Canal. Chillingly, Christopher told police that as they walked through the town Tracy had chatted asking him how his job was going. She hadn't shown any signs of distress or grief and hadn't even mentioned Danielle. When they thought no one was looking, he and Tracy had dumped the suitcase containing Danielle's body in the water beside the marina at Muirtown Basin, part of the Caledonian Canal.

Christopher Gaytor took detectives to the spot. Later that day, divers from Central Scotland police arrived and within an hour of starting their search they recovered the suitcase. It contained Danielle's body, together with stones, bricks and tiles to weigh it down. Detectives immediately gave credence to Christopher Gaytor's statement in relation to his own actions, but they didn't believe Danielle's death had been an accident.

On 8 January, Tracy Reid, Christopher Gaytor and his brother Lee appeared in private at Inverness Sheriff Court. They were remanded in custody, held on a holding charge of attempting to pervert the course of justice. Inverness, Scotland's newest city, woke to headlines that shocked its inhabitants. Many people visited Muirtown basin and placed flowers in memory of Danielle. Many stood a moment in silence, paying their respects.

The post-mortem report on Danielle's remains was awaited. It wasn't going to be easy with a body that had been immersed in water for two months. Scene-of-crime examiners got to work at Argyle Street. They soon found Danielle's blood spattered on her bedroom walls, the walls and flooring of the stairway, her mattress, pillow and duvet. On the stairs they found a tangle of hairs that had been pulled from her scalp. Following a media appeal witnesses from the Crown area came forward. They filled in details of Danielle's life while she lived in Argyle Street.

The post-mortem report, when it came, gave the lie to the explanation that Danielle had fallen down the stairs. Her injuries were consistent with her having been flung downstairs with such force that the veins under her skull had been sheared with the impact. Her injuries were too severe to have been caused by a fall and it would have been immediately apparent to anyone seeing her that she needed medical care. No responsible parent would have simply put a child to bed in that condition. Shockingly, in the opinion of pathologist, James Mackenzie, Danielle would have lived for anything between two and forty-eight hours after the attack that caused her death.

When Danielle's body was recovered and released for burial, Tracy's family made arrangements for the funeral. They were horrified that Tracy was allowed to change them. They were even more horrified at Tracy's choice of funeral music – the song 'Teenage Dirtbag' by the American rock band Wheatus. The lyrics include the words, 'She doesn't give a damn.' Tracy was on remand at Cornton Vale, Scotland's only women's prison, but she was allowed to attend the funeral. She wept over Danielle's grave in New Elgin cemetery, while other family members looked on disbelievingly. The family wanted to arrange for a gravestone to mark where Danielle was buried but Tracy's consent was needed and she wouldn't give it. All that marks the grave is the undertaker's small marker. For months before the case came to court for the trial, Tracy Reid was given bail. Her father supported her, and she moved in with him and his new family in Elgin till the trial began.

On 20 June 2003 the trial of Lee Gaytor, Tracy Reid and Christopher Gaytor began at the High Court in Perth. Lee Gaytor pled guilty to murdering Danielle by repeatedly striking her about the head and throwing her down the stairs at the house in Argyle Street. Tracy Reid admitted failing to seek medical help for her daughter and attempting to defeat the ends of justice by disposing of the body. Christopher Gaytor admitted his part in disposing of Danielle's body. The judge, Lord Hardie, deferred sentence, seeking psychiatric and other background reports on Tracy Reid.

After the reports were received, Lord Hardie fixed a date for a hearing of proof in mitigation. In the majority of criminal cases before the courts, the judge makes his decision based on the defence advocate or defending solicitor's speech to him. In this speech, the lawyer endeavours to tell the judge anything that should be taken into account and could influence the penalty to be imposed. (The Crown, in the shape of the Advocate Depute, or the Procurator Fiscal in less serious cases, will highlight anything that suggests greater culpability or blame should attach to the accused.) The judge will usually evaluate that information, along with any reports that have been requested. However, it is in the discretion of the judge – either at his own behest, or if requested by the defence – to fix a proof in mitigation. This involves witnesses being questioned about relevant mitigating factors, in the same way as they might be questioned at a trial, in the witness box and under oath.

In this case, Lord Hardie was concerned that the report from prosecution psychiatrist, Gary McPherson, was very different from that of the psychiatrist engaged by the defence, Mairead Tagg. He wanted to hear their reports tested in cross-examination.

Called to give evidence, Dr Tagg told Lord Hardie in court that Reid had been a victim too and that she suffered from post-traumatic stress disorder due to events in her life. She had been subjected to physical and mental abuse by Lee Gaytor, which had reduced her to behaving like an animal in order to survive. Having heard both experts, Lord Hardie said he believed Tagg lacked the objectivity necessary for an expert witness. He believed she had in effect been conned by Reid, taking her word for everything and not checking what she had been told.

At the end of the proof in mitigation, Tracy Reid's advocate, John Campbell QC, rose to make his speech. There is an important distinction in the way lawyers present such information to a court. It would always be improper for a lawyer to say anything to mislead a judge or jury – all lawyers are first and foremost officers of the court. For that reason, lawyers never ask their clients at a first consultation, 'Are you guilty?'. The question instead is, 'How do you wish to plead?'. If a client admits guilt but asks a lawyer to run a defence of innocence, then the lawyer must withdraw from acting and advise the accused to seek another lawyer. Campbell will have begun his address to Lord Hardie in Reid's case saying, 'My client instructs me that . . .'

Campbell recounted that a difficult family background had traumatised Tracy. He said that her father had a drink problem and her mother, Cathy Gordon, was neglectful of her children and spent much of her time in bed. Mrs Gordon had travelled to Edinburgh to be at the court and she was in the public benches, listening to what was being said. She began to seethe. While she and Tracy's father were married and living together, he was in the habit of having one night out every fortnight. He was not an alcoholic. Campbell continued, saying Tracy was the one who had got her two younger siblings up and ready for school. He went on to say that Danielle's father, Stanley Wells, the man Tracy had lived with for months, had raped her. Cathy Gordon believed this to be another lie and she could stay silent no longer. Tracy was trying to blame everyone else for her daughter's death, totally unjustifiably. Cathy shouted out that what was being said was rubbish. She is still amazed that the judge made no attempt to stop her outburst as what she did was in contempt of the court. The judge and the whole court waited till she said her piece and then Campbell resumed his plea in mitigation. He told Lord Hardie that Tracy Reid had been in the thrall of Gaytor, who was described as a psychopathic maniac, and that until her involvement with. him she had been a loving mother. Having weighed up all that he had heard and read in the reports, Lord Hardie sentenced Tracy Reid to eight years, Lee Gaytor to life and Christopher Gaytor to twelve months.

It is well known that even the criminal fraternity are disgusted by fellow prisoners who have ill-treated children. In Perth Prison, where Lee Gaytor was held prior to sentencing, he was kept in his cell twenty-four hours a day, seven days a week, under observation. Staff there described how prisoners were queuing up for the chance to get at him. After sentencing, he was sent to Wakefield maximum-security prison, which houses 600 of the most dangerous criminals in the UK. Wakefield has been dubbed 'Monster Mansion' by some of the popular press: inmates have included Ian Huntley, Harold Shipman and Robert Black. Most of Wakefield's inmates have committed serious crimes against women and children, and are unlikely ever to be released by the Parole Board because of the nature of their offences. Lee Gaytor will have fitted right in. At Cornton Vale, where many of the other inmates are drug addicts, Tracy will probably have told her own story, coloured by what she wanted fellow inmates to believe.

After sentencing, lawyers must consider whether to advise their client to lodge an appeal either against conviction or against sentence. In deciding whether to appeal in this case, Reid's lawyers will have referred to a recent case which, at least superficially, seemed similar. In May 2002, thirteen-month-old Carla-Nicole Bone was murdered by her mother's partner, Alexander McClure, while Andrea Bone, her mother, stood by and failed to intervene. In November 2002, at about the time Danielle died, Andrea Bone was convicted of culpable homicide and sentenced to three years in prison. She successfully appealed against her conviction. The appeal judges heard that she suffered from personality disorders which would have inhibited her from challenging McClure; she was tiny in comparison to him; at the time of the brutal assault which ended her child's life she was eight months pregnant; they lived in an isolated cottage in Aberdeenshire where help was not to hand. The argument that availed on her behalf was that the judge had not directed the jury to give consideration to the reasonableness of her being able to intervene, given all the factors enumerated above. Those factors did not apply to Tracy Reid's case. And of course, Andrea Bone did not try to hide her dead child's body, nor did she continue cashing Child Benefit for months after her child had died, as Tracy Reid had done.

How and when did the catalogue of events begin that led to Danielle's death? Problems with Tracy Reid began when she was just eleven. She grew up in Elgin, Moray. Her parents were divorced when she was young. She lived with her mother – who reverted to her maiden name, Cathy Gordon – and two younger sisters, Katrina and Violet, but still saw her father regularly. He didn't move from Elgin and still lives there. After what her mother describes as a normal childhood, Tracy went off the rails at about the age of eleven. She started going out with boys, and even older men, staying out all night and even at that early age she was drinking and possibly also inhaling solvents. Of the three children, she was the one who gave her mother the most heartache and worry.

No matter how Cathy tried she couldn't control Tracy's behaviour. If she tried to ground her, she simply waited till her mother's back was turned for a moment and sneaked out. If she told her off, the girl would disappear and stay out all night. Cathy found empty gas cylinders in the bin in Tracy's bedroom and suspected her of sniffing gas. The stress affected Cathy Gordon's own health.

Elgin police knew Tracy well. Many times, Cathy had to ask them to find her when she had stayed out all night. If Tracy was at home sparks would fly as she was jealous of her two younger sisters. If Tracy was out, the atmosphere at home was more peaceful but Cathy Gordon would then be worried what her oldest daughter was up to and whether she was safe. Cathy asked the social work department to help her with Tracy. A social worker was appointed and kept in touch until Tracy left her mother's home aged seventeen. That was when she was given her own council house in Elgin.

Tracy was nineteen when Danielle was born. She had been living with Stanley Wells, Danielle's father, for some months but the relationship had broken down before Danielle's birth and Wells had little to do with his child. He and his parents tried to form a relationship with Danielle, but their attempts were thwarted by Tracy.

Tracy's mother has an inherited genetic disorder that affects the eyesight and can cause mobility problems. Tracy, her sisters and other family members also have the condition, causing varying degrees of disability. Danielle was at risk of developing it too and as an infant she was monitored regularly. At first, Tracy gave every appearance to health professionals of being a concerned and caring parent and she kept all the appointments made for Danielle. But right from the start family members were concerned that Tracy was not really interested in Danielle. Even in hospital, when Danielle was a newborn, it was usually visiting family members who picked Danielle up, changed her and fed her.

Once Danielle was home, her granny and aunts played a significant role in looking after her. Tracy often asked her mother to take Danielle for a couple of days, which she did gladly, but soon she had her grandchild for five days most weeks. Even when Danielle was with her mother, she was being neglected. By the time she was one, her mother seldom provided food for her. She often had only yoghurts to eat. Tracy kept open house for large numbers of young folk around her own age and younger. They were smoking cannabis in the house and spending time with them seemed to be Tracy's priority.

When Tracy's uncle, Nick Gordon, married in 2000, he and his fiancée Susan asked if pretty little Danielle could be the flower girl at their wedding. On their big day, they discovered not only that Tracy had not bought a dress for Danielle to wear, but that the child didn't even have underwear. Tracy left it all to them to do but she managed to come along to the wedding.

In August 2000, without telling anyone in her family, Tracy suddenly left Elgin for Dundee. Her father went round to her house the evening she left. When he discovered the house empty he phoned his ex-wife. She had been kept in the dark too. Earlier that day, she had travelled from Inverness to Elgin to return Danielle, who had been staying with her. In retrospect, she knew that something had been up. Tracy had been anxious to know what time she was leaving and quizzed her about when the train back to Inverness was departing. Cathy suspected Tracy might have gone to Dundee but she didn't know for sure.

A few days later, Tracy phoned her mother and confirmed she was indeed in Dundee, living with Shehanna, her best friend from school days. Tracy's explanation for leaving so suddenly was that she was concerned that Danielle's father, Stanley, was going to try to get custody of the child and she had to get away. Cathy says this was nonsense.

Tracy's Uncle Nick and his wife Sue had always tried to help Tracy. When Danielle was little they had bought a pram and toys but they later discovered Tracy had sold them. When she took off for Dundee it fell to them to empty the house in Elgin. They were shocked to see the conditions in which Tracy and Danielle had been living. The carpets were sodden and the curtains shredded. Tracy and Danielle had been sleeping on mattresses on the floor. There were candle stubs lying about. Nick and Sue didn't know whether the candles had been used for taking drugs, or simply because the electricity had been cut off. Although there was clothing hanging out of drawers and most of Tracy's property had been left, there were neither toys nor children's clothing. Sue Gordon says you wouldn't have known a child had been living there. In spite of Tracy's past and Danielle's potential health problems there had been no continuing contact with social services in Elgin. Danielle was invisible to the authorities, who should have been involved in safeguarding her. This pattern was set to continue.

In Dundee, Danielle attended Cotton Road Nursery and teachers there didn't notice anything about Tracy that caused them concern although it is known that Tracy was getting more involved with drugs by this time. She was using ecstasy and speed and smoking cannabis every day. She moved to a house of her own in Dundee but before long she became unhappy living without the support of her family. She didn't want them to tell her what to do but she did need them to lean on. After about a year Tracy applied for a house tenancy in Inverness to be close to her mother. Once again, she just moved out, abandoning most of her property and leaving others to pick up the pieces. Nick Gordon, her uncle, hired a van and went to Dundee to collect her things.

Tracy and Danielle moved in with Cathy Gordon and after a short time she was allocated a council house near her mother's in South Kessock, the part of Inverness known as 'The Ferry'. It's an area where there are many problem families and vulnerable children. Over the next few months, she shuttled about, taking Danielle with her. She lived in her own house then at her mother's, then at her sister, Katrina's. She moved back to her own house and then to her mother's home and her sister's again. As soon as someone said something to her she didn't like she moved again. Katrina had begun a relationship with Lee Gaytor at about this time. Lee lived in lodgings in South Kessock a short distance away from his mother's home. He had fallen out with his mother. Mrs Gaytor and her other son, Christopher, had moved to Inverness from Hull in about 1998 and Lee had come north to join them after about six months. Christopher often worked as a kitchen porter in Inverness hotels – work that was seasonal. Lee chose not to work. He preferred to live with someone who worked and would give him money. Someone like Katrina.

Danielle was enrolled at Merkinch Nursery. The catchment area for the nursery is The Ferry district. Among so many vulnerable children, Danielle appeared well cared-for and staff had no concerns about her except some muscle deterioration in her legs. Tracy explained away Danielle's many absences from nursery saying that her daughter was receiving physiotherapy. This was a lie. Due to a breakdown in communication between a GP and the community paediatrician, no appointments were being made. When Tracy made her explanations she was given more leeway than she would otherwise have received because of the genetic condition that she suffered. She was registered blind, though family members say that she could read well enough.

Young friends of Tracy visited her home often and Danielle was sent to her bedroom when there were visitors. The youngster was spending much of her time in her room even then. On one occasion Cathy, saw a gang of boys going into Tracy's house. Worried for her grandchild's welfare, she collected Danielle from her mother and was only just back in her own home with the young girl when the drugs squad arrived. On another occasion, Danielle came to her granny's house on an errand for her mother. She was supposed to ask for 'baccie' (tobacco) but instead she asked her granny for hash. Cathy Gordon was very worried about what was happening to her wee granddaughter.

Sue Gordon tells of a family gathering to celebrate Katrina's birthday at around that time. Tracy and Katrina asked their mother to look after their children as they wanted to go out. By the time they returned at ten, the two little girls were having their supper and Danielle was messing about with her food. Her mother gave her a slap across the face. Danielle said, 'Mummy you've marked me,' to which Tracy replied, 'If anyone says anything I'll just say you fell.'

Cathy thought about reporting her daughter to social services but was fearful of Tracy's reaction. She had gone in the huff with the family so often and cut herself off. When that happened Cathy couldn't keep an eye on Danielle. By November 2001 she was so worried that she asked Tracy's uncle to make an anonymous phone call to the social work department, reporting that people were coming and going at Tracy's house, Tracy was drinking and using cannabis and Danielle's needs were taking second place.

Following that call, a social worker checked with Merkinch Nursery, to be told that Danielle was a pupil there and that there were no concerns about her. The medical practice where Danielle was registered was also contacted. The health visitor there did not know of Danielle but knew of the extended family, which she believed to be supportive. The social work department closed its file.

The first four years of Danielle's life had been pretty chaotic. Tracy was a far-from-devoted mother but she must have been sufficiently devious to present herself as a convincing, caring and supportive parent at the nurseries Danielle had attended and on the rare occasions Danielle had seen a doctor or health visitor. Danielle's life, already a long way from perfect, was about to take a turn for the worse. In April 2002, Tracy obtained the tenancy of the privately rented house at 66 Argyle Street, Inverness. Katrina, her boyfriend Lee Gaytor and her little girl, one-year-old Adele, moved into the two-bedroomed house with them. Gaytor immediately forced the two little girls to spend most of their time in a bedroom, particularly when he or his friends were in the living room doing drugs.

Crown Primary School was within 100 metres of their home and Danielle was enrolled to begin school there in August 2002. It wasn't long before Lee took a shine to Tracy and Katrina left the same month, after finding the pair in bed together. Having 'stolen' Katrina's partner and so brooked family disapproval, Tracy's reaction was predictable. She cut herself off from her family. When she had tried to do this in the past, her mother, then more mobile, had simply ignored her and had kept coming to the house to see her little granddaughter. But by now Cathy Gordon was in a wheelchair and Argyle Street was some distance from The Ferry.

Danielle was often seen in Crown out and about, sometimes late at night, sometimes in her nightie or scantily clad, going to fetch cigarette papers for her mother. She befriended a neighbour, who was surprised she was out alone and that her mother appeared unconcerned at having no idea where she was. Danielle asked neighbours for a loan of £5 to buy food. No one interfered beyond taking her home, probably deterred by the idea that it would be an intrusion; that it wasn't their responsibility; that someone else would look after the child's welfare. Tracy was taking drugs and drinking heavily. If Danielle dared to be in the living room at the wrong time Lee would drag her about by the hair and hit her repeatedly, with Tracy looking on. If Lee wasn't in the house, Danielle was left to her own devices to wander the streets.

Danielle started school and attended for about five weeks. She started a week late, due to her grandfather having had a stroke, according to Tracy. This was a complete fabrication. Danielle spent most of her time, when she wasn't at school, in her room. On 8 October, Tracy told Danielle's teacher that they were moving to Manchester and that the following day would be Danielle's last day at school. It is almost certain that Danielle was removed from school to hide the extent of the abuse she was suffering. By then it is reasonable to think that Danielle's life must have been intolerable. She had less than a month to live.

In late November 2002, Cathy Gordon contacted the social work department, expressing concern that Danielle was being neglected. No family members had seen Danielle for months though they did see Tracy in the city centre from time to time. The response to the phone call was for two social workers to visit 66 Argyle Street, but when there was no reply to their knocking a follow-up was delayed. The name on the door wasn't Tracy's and the social workers thought that Tracy might have moved or maybe they had the wrong address. It was weeks before a social worker contacted Cathy Gordon to check Tracy's current address and before a visit could be arranged the events of Hogmanay intervened.

In 2008, Tracy Reid was due for release after serving half her sentence with the usual fifty per cent remission for good behaviour. Often women are allowed to stay in houses close to the prison where they can come and go in preparation for release. Alternatively they are allowed out for home visits or day release. Early in 2008, Tracy Reid returned after day release and was found to be carrying drugs back into the prison with her.

A caring mother would surely have been shocked by her crime into getting clean and inside she would have had an opportunity to get support to help kick her habit. Obviously, even after four years inside, drugs still have a grip on Tracy Reid. She lost her remission and will likely have to serve close to the full eight-year sentence.

Nick and Sue Gordon found it hard to look back fondly on their wedding day. To them and other family members Danielle was a wee angel, fond of her Barbie dolls and music and very loving. Cathy Gordon misses her eldest grandchild, saying that a huge hole has been left in her life and the hurt will never go away. Violet doesn't even want to hear Tracy's name. Katrina can't understand why Tracy didn't intervene to protect Danielle. None of Tracy's immediate family wants anything to do with her when she is released from Cornton Vale. Even if she does serve the full term, they believe that eight years was too cheap a price for Danielle's life.

When Nick Gordon died in May 2008, his widow, Sue, arranged for his gravestone in New Elgin Cemetery to be engraved not only with his details but also those of Danielle, whose grave is a short distance away. Tracy is still adamant that no one will interfere and place a stone on the grave. As she said often while Danielle was alive, 'I'll do what I like, she's my bairn.'

Detective Inspector Steve Mackay, the senior investigating officer, spoke of the effect of the inquiry on his officers, many of whom had families, some with children the same age as Danielle. But it was not only those engaged in recovering Danielle's body or taking statements who were affected. Even those involved in a more peripheral way in the investigation found the case harrowing. In view of the long-term effects such a case may have on those involved, investigators were given a general debriefing. Confidential support was offered to anyone who felt they needed it through Northern Constabulary's welfare officer, who could call on more counselling expertise if and when it was needed.

As with the other shocking cases where a child has been murdered, an inquiry into the role of the authorities has been carried out. A full and thorough inquiry was led by Dr Jean Herbison, a consultant paediatrician who works at Yorkhill Hospital in Glasgow. Her report highlighted shortcomings of the various bodies – police, social workers, medical professionals, school and nursery staff – who could and should have been more proactive in protecting Danielle. Dr Herbison also pointed to failings in the system, particularly in communication. She posed the question,

'How, therefore, do we make agencies more approachable and easily accessible, if a member of the family or local community has any concerns for a child's welfare?'

Changes were made to all the systems that might matter. For example, it is now standard practice in Inverness that when a child leaves a school, that school must ensure that the child has been enrolled in a new school within ten days. If not, contact must be made with police and social services. Sadly, no matter how good the systems in place may be, there will always be cases like this. It is the nature of domestic violence that it is hidden – it happens behind closed doors and devious adults can hide it well. But usually, with the benefit of hindsight, there are clues that someone might have picked up.

A child like Danielle may be resilient and appear to be happy. She may be in the care of adults who are clever and manipulative and who can put on a caring public face while they are monsters behind closed doors. The fear of interfering unnecessarily should not weigh heavily in the scales when a child's life is under threat, so if we see anything that just doesn't seem right we shouldn't brush it under the carpet or leave it for someone else. The Scottish Government has set up a helpline for anyone concerned about a child's welfare. The number is freephone 0800 022 3222. We might be saving a child's life.

6

A LADIES' MAN

On the day he retired, John Cameron left two piles of files on his desk. The former chief of CID in Northern Constabulary, Cameron told his family that there were sixteen files relating to missing persons and seventeen relating to bodies that remained unidentified. They did not match up with each other. For a time it looked as if the case of Fiona Torbet would remain in the first of these piles.

In July 1993, retired consultant gynaecologist Edgar Torbet reported his sixty-two-year-old wife, Fiona, missing. She had not returned from a walking holiday in the West Highlands. The couple lived in Busby, Glasgow and had a second home in Tighnabruich. It was close to the many marinas and safe anchorages of the west coast, allowing Mr Torbet to indulge his passion for sailing. His wife had shared that interest in the past, but more recently ill-health had prohibited her from sailing. For some years she had pursued an interest in hill-walking, an interest her husband didn't share. The couple had amicably agreed to holiday separately, he on his boat and she in the hills. Not only was Fiona Torbet an able and experienced hill walker, she wrote for *The Great Outdoors* and other magazines for climbers and walkers. She was also a campaigner on environmental issues such as the fluoridation of the public water supply.

Police rightly take the view that an adult is entitled to disappear if they wish. Sometimes there are reasons, which have nothing to do with crime, why a person might want to walk away from their existing life and start again somewhere new. The last person known to have seen Fiona Torbet told a story that made it appear as if that was what had happened.

Mrs Torbet had booked to stay at Grianan House, a bed and breakfast establishment at Inverinate on the shore of Loch Duich, one of the most spectacular areas of the Highlands. Skirted by tiny villages such as Kintail, Inverinate and Dornie, the loch often features in photographs – particularly those showing picturesque Eilean Donan Castle – which appear on items such as tins of short-bread and cartons of fudge. It's an area very popular with hill-walkers. Many of Scotland's 284 Munros, (mountains over 3,000ft, named after Sir Hugh Munro, who first catalogued them), and smaller Corbetts and Grahams are within easy reach. For this reason, it was a favourite place for Fiona Torbet.

Every third house in Inverinate is a guesthouse. Mrs Torbet had been a guest of Jessie McMillan at Grianan House on several occasions and other local B & B proprietors say that Mrs McMillan looked after her guests very well. Her large modern bungalow lay in extensive gardens between the narrow strip of pebbled shore on the north side of the loch and the A87 road to Skye and the north-west. So it wasn't surprising Fiona Torbet took her repeat custom to Mrs McMillan. She will not have been the only loyal, regular visitor.

As was their regular arrangement, Mr Torbet knew his wife's plans. It was usual for them to remain in close and frequent contact when she was away on a walking trip. His first thought when she didn't return must have been the possibility of an accident in the hills.

On this particular stay, Mrs Torbet had been the only guest in residence at Grianan House. She was left in the care of Donald McMillan, former army tank driver and son of the house, who lived in a caravan in the grounds. His parents were away in Aberdeen, visiting a critically ill relative. As well as Donald, a cousin and his wife were also staying in another caravan in the garden. The McMillans' sick relative died, and they extended their visit to Aberdeen to attend the funeral.

Detective Inspector William McDonald was appointed senior investigating officer in charge of the missing person inquiry. He visited Grianan House and interviewed Donald McMillan, the last known person to have seen Mrs Torbet. McMillan said that Mrs Torbet had received a phone call in the evening before she left and had told him she was going to start a new life with another man. The following morning she had driven off with a man, leaving her own car behind. She said she would return for it later. McMillan showed the detectives that, for the first time in several visits to Grianan House, Mrs Torbet had signed the visitors' book. He also said that she had paid her accommodation bill in cash rather than by cheque. These two changes in the usual pattern of her dealings at Inverinate were noted, but police did not think them significant.

If Fiona Torbet had indeed disappeared intentionally, the police had to respect her wish. McDonald released photographs and posters and appealed via the press and TV, asking her to contact him in confidence, simply to confirm that nothing untoward had happened. Edgar Torbet travelled to Inverinate and inspected his wife's Volkswagen car, left parked at Grianan House.

When he looked in the car Mr Torbet found his wife's walking stick. Maps marked with houses for sale on Skye were also in the car, which was taken to a police compound in East Kilbride. The investigating team were relieved when Mr Torbet told them his wife would not have gone walking without her stick. If Mrs Torbet, experienced hill-walker though she was, had succumbed to some mishap in the hills then the chances of finding her in such a vast area were very remote. That scenario didn't fit the information from Donald McMillan either.

When someone disappears and the circumstances are at all suspicious, police attention first focuses on those closest to the missing person. In the case of an adult, that is usually their husband, wife or partner. Mr Torbet was sailing alone off the west coast when his wife disappeared, so he had no alibi. Police spoke to neighbours, relatives and friends of Mr and Mrs Torbet and no one said anything that dislodged the initial impression police had formed that the couple had had a long and happy marriage. There was no apparent cause for Mr Torbet to have done away with his wife. They simply each had separate hobbies, which each pursued with the full agreement and approval of the other. At the same time, police were learning from those who knew the couple that there was no reason to suppose Mrs Torbet had been discontented and likely to have gone off with another man.

If the missing woman had left her husband, though, one thing struck them as strange. Why would she have chosen to do so from Inverinate, with only the very basic items she had packed for a short hill-walking holiday? Her luggage was missing. The inquiry team set up a caravan in a lay-by close to Grianan House and the area was searched by a professional team using tracker dogs.

From an early stage, some of the police inquiry team thought Donald McMillan's story was improbable – including the senior investigating officer, William McDonald. McMillan was interviewed several times, but didn't deviate from his original story. He was asked the same questions so often that he complained to the tabloid press of police harassment, but he never made his complaints official. When police called to interview him his mother was very defensive.

On one occasion, McMillan was interviewed while his parents were away on holiday. He was easier to interview without his mother present and he told McDonald, 'It's lucky I have an alibi.' It was a strange thing to say as he obviously didn't. The detectives had nothing concrete to justify further interrogation, so they backed off and continued their investigation looking at other possibilities. Sightings of Fiona Torbet in Fort William and in Tighnabruich were reported but they proved to be false. These were enough to keep the case categorised as a missing person inquiry. With hindsight, police say it should have been upgraded to a murder case sooner than it was.

With no response to media appeals, the inquiry team talked to many folk who had known Fiona Torbet, including those in the climbing fraternity. They discovered that about a year before her disappearance she had written at length in *The Great Outdoors* magazine. She had compiled a list of hills then known as Lesser Corbetts (hills between 2,000 and 2,500 feet in height with a drop of at least 150 metres all round, of which there are 224 in Scotland). The article made it clear that she believed her list to be definitive. Alan Dawson, author of *The Relative Hills of Britain*, had produced his own list, which he believed to be more accurate and exhaustive. When he read Mrs Torbet's article, he contacted her to point this out. True to her character, she invited him to her house at Busby to chat. The pair got on well. They had a common interest, and agreed to collaborate to make one comprehensive list. They agreed too that his list should be the starting point as it was the more accurate. To avoid confusion, they decided it would be a good idea if the hills formerly called Lesser Corbetts were renamed Grahams. Graham was Fiona Torbet's maiden name.

This story is illustrative of Mrs Torbet's character. She was not the kind of person to be egotistical or even prickly and defensive of her opinion and was more interested in getting it right. It isn't unusual for hills to have more than one name. People living on opposite sides of a hill may call it by a different name. There was a hill between Fort William and Glencoe that had five possible names and when she discovered this while compiling her record, Fiona Torbet was scrupulous. After contacting the local police, who couldn't give her a definitive answer, she called a meeting of locals at Ardgower to try to arrive at a consensus as to the correct name to use.

As police flung their net out to gather in anyone who might have had a motive for killing Mrs Torbet they found out about this difference of opinion. About a week after Mrs Torbet was reported missing, Alan Dawson was astonished to find two burly cops arriving at this place of work to interview him as a potential suspect. His possible motive was professional jealousy, which of course did not exist. He got the impression the police thought then that Fiona Torbet was still alive but nonetheless they were

keeping an open mind. He very firmly felt he was being interviewed as a potential murder suspect.

As part of the ongoing inquiry, police were monitoring Mrs
Torbet's bank account. They also contacted her closest friends,
those she would have spoken to even if she had left her husband.
Over the months there was no contact whatsoever and there were
no withdrawals from her bank account. DI McDonald and his
team's fears for Fiona Torbet's safety grew as time went on.

The inquiry team were struggling to know where to devote
resources. There were no clues to indicate where Fiona Torbet's
body might be. By the time several months had elapsed, with no
contact or sightings, they were fairly sure it was a body they were
looking for. They could not completely discount the possibility of
an accident or even suicide.

There are vast areas of the Highlands where no one has walked
for many years. Forest ground can be undisturbed by human incur-
sion for forty years once trees have been planted. Inverinate is a
tiny place of little more than a dozen houses. Most were originally built for Forestry Commission workers, the majority nestling
right on the shore of the loch, the water lapping a tiny pebbled
beach at the bottom of their gardens. There are also a few houses
above the road. Peppered among them are modern private houses,
some with large gardens, such as Grianan House. Vast forests of
spruce and pine managed by the Forestry Commission fill the
lower slopes of the hills that surround Loch Duich. A body might
lie undiscovered in a shallow grave in a forested area like this for
a very long time. The best hope of it being found would be by a
casual dog walker. If Fiona Torbet had been murdered and the
killer had access to a vehicle, her body could be anywhere. Although
the case was very much open, police had no leads whatsoever
and were at a loss as to what to do next.

Then came a breakthrough. Muriel Mackenzie, a nurse tutor
living in Glasgow but originally from Inverinate, arrived in the
late spring of 1994 to spend a holiday with her grandmother. She
was out for a walk one day and as she strolled along the road

about 200 yards from Grianan House she spotted something in a ditch. That evening Ms Mackenzie and her grandmother were socialising with neighbours and she mentioned it. The neighbour thought it was worth a look; he believed it could have been a dead cat. When he investigated he discovered black bin bags, one of them containing a handbag. He immediately realised the potential implications and contacted the police.

The inquiry team raced to Inverinate; the incident caravan was long gone by then. The bag was identified as Fiona Torbet's from its contents, which included her chequebook, purse and diary. Other items discarded in the bin bags included some of Mrs Torbet's clothing. It seemed that when the area was searched originally a dog might have simply bypassed the bags; or perhaps the bags hadn't been there when the verge was originally searched. At that time, the ditch had been disguised by the summer flush of vegetation, but when Ms Mackenzie made her discovery it had died back so the bags were more obvious.

In the months that had passed since her disappearance, Mr Torbet hadn't believed for one moment that his wife had left him. He had known instinctively that something terrible must have happened to her and now this was confirmed. This very private man, who was suffering enough already, now had to suffer at the hands of the tabloid press. The discovery of Mrs Torbet's property put the case back in the media spotlight. A week or so later, nine months after his wife had gone missing, another issue came to light which further aroused the interest of the red-tops.

Edgar Torbet had resolved to sell one of the properties that he owned jointly with his wife. Because of her disappearance, he had been obliged to raise a legal action at Paisley Sheriff Court. This procedure is called an action for division and sale of property and is not unusual. But because Fiona's whereabouts were unknown, his solicitor had no alternative but to cite her to respond to the action, should she wish to oppose it, by advertising in the press. The tabloids pounced on this, creating lurid headlines from it. Worse was to come later.

The final entry in Mrs Torbet's diary recovered from her bag said, 'Strange letter awaited me from Donald McMillan. Embarrassing to cope with.' The letter was never found. DI MacDonald and his team decided that the case should no longer be treated as a missing person inquiry. It had become a suspected murder, with McMillan clearly considered the prime suspect. Detective Superintendent George Gough was appointed senior investigating officer, working with Detective Chief Inspector Norman McLeod, DI MacDonald and the team who had been on the case for ten months. The Procurator Fiscal in Dingwall at the time was David Hingston and he was notified when the case was reclassified.

In Scotland, the Procurator Fiscal is the person with legislative authority to be the investigator in all crimes and the police are his tool in carrying out inquiries. In practical terms, the Fiscal is not involved in most inquiries: police present a report after they have completed their investigation. However, when the case involves murder or suspected murder it can be a different matter and the Procurator Fiscal may be much more hands-on.

The Procurator Fiscal is also responsible for representing the Crown in the Sheriff Court, presenting the prosecution in all criminal cases there. When there is a murder on a one-man patch, such as the huge area covered from Dingwall, the normal procedures of the court can be seriously disrupted. The progress of a murder inquiry doesn't necessarily fit with the court timetable and when the presence of the Fiscal is needed at the scene in key moments of the investigation there can be major problems. On occasion, the work of the court has to be deferred till the following day, as prosecutions can't proceed without the Fiscal. In outlying areas of Scotland, where often solicitors have had to travel a considerable distance to represent an accused in court, this isn't ideal. Nonetheless, it is the system those charged with serving the ends of justice have to live with.

When Hingston and the police discussed the situation they agreed that the discovery of the handbag completely discredited the story told by Donald McMillan. What woman leaving her former life with a new man would open the car window as they drove away and lob out her property, including her handbag containing her purse, chequebook and diary? The idea was simply ridiculous. If attention had been focused on Donald McMillan before, it was even more so now. One question exercised the police and the Fiscal. Why had he told his story of Mrs Torbet going off with another man? If he had simply said that she had gone walking, which would have been entirely credible, then attention wouldn't have focused on him. If he was the killer – and that was looking most likely – why did he dispose of the handbag in such a way that it was almost certain to be found?

But two even more compelling questions were facing Gough and his colleagues. Where was Mrs Torbet's body? And how could they prove that McMillan was the killer? Thirty-three-year-old McMillan looked out of the ordinary – he had short-cropped hair in front and a long pony tail – but unusual looks do not necessarily make a killer; nor does telling strange and improbable stories. McMillan did have a criminal record, but there was nothing in it to suggest that he would commit a murder.

A missing body is a problem that police encounter in investigating many killings. Often the body can hold clues to the identity of the killer, particularly nowadays, when DNA can be extracted from the tiniest trace of anything the killer has left behind on his victim. This is now the tool that will often bring a killer to book. It has always been a difficult area of criminal law to prosecute a murderer where there is no body. Sometimes there is strong enough evidence without the body, sufficient to convince a jury of the guilt of the accused beyond reasonable doubt. This was true in the case of Elgin woman Arlene Fraser, who was murdered in 1998 by, or on the instructions of, her husband Nat. Sometimes the missing piece of the evidential jigsaw prevents justice being done – for example in the case of Renee and Andrew MacRae. (See Chapter 9, 'Where are They Now?')

In the Fraser case, the couple had separated and Arlene had

instructed a solicitor to sue for divorce. Nat Fraser had demonstrated jealousy and violence to his wife in the past and had told
friends he was angry about the financial implications of a divorce.
In the murder of his wife he had involved a friend, Hector Dick,
who turned Queen's evidence and gave a compelling account of
how Nat had told him that he had burned the body and ground
up anything that was left so that no trace of Arlene's body could
ever be found. Dick had been asked by Fraser to get a car urgently
and after it was used the car was burnt out deliberately. The timings
all fitted with the disappearance of Arlene. So there was strong
circumstantial evidence as well as that of Mr Dick to bring the
verdict home to Nat Fraser.

After the discovery of Fiona Torbet's bag, David Hingston and
the investigating cops considered where to focus the search for
the body. There were the extensive forests behind the house and
a sea loch in front. McMillan, by now prime suspect, had access
to a vehicle and if he had chosen to use it the area of search would
be beyond what was practicable. Forestry Commission forests, like
those adjacent to Inverinate, are fenced off and tracks leading into
them are usually protected by padlocked gates, but in the countryside many copies of the keys are kept by people without
authority to have them. This meant that McMillan might well have
been able to take the body into the nearby forest, or even a more
distant one, and bury it.

Against that, there are practical difficulties in disposing of a
body. It is literally a dead weight. It requires great strength to lift
even a slight person's weight if they are unco-operative and of
course there is no co-operation from a corpse. And then rigor
mortis starts to set in, adding another difficulty to moving a body.
Starting with the smaller muscle groups, over a period of eight
hours or so the body becomes progressively stiffer until it is just
like a board. It would be well-nigh impossible to put it in the boot
of any but the largest cars at that stage.

Rigor mortis loosens its grip after about eighteen hours, after
which the body will become flaccid again, but few killers know

this. Even if they do, they will not want to have a body on their hands for any longer than is absolutely necessary and risk being caught red-handed. Even a stocky, fit and healthy former soldier like McMillan would find it difficult to carry a body single-handedly, and forestry tracks are not easy to walk on, particularly with a heavy burden. So the most likely place for the body to have been dumped was close to a road or track. But police had to ask themselves: which track? If the culprit had carried the body to the nearest forest, he would have had to cross the main road, increasing the risk of being seen.

A team of police on the ground spent several days walking in a line through the forest nearest Grianan House. It is the smell of a body that is the giveaway and at one point the distinctive reek of rotting flesh stopped the search while the Procurator Fiscal was summoned from Dingwall, eighty miles away. The cops stood at some distance from the corpse, as procedure demands, to prevent corrupting forensic evidence. The Fiscal considered it part of his role as investigator to be responsible for the preservation of evidence and it was for him, along with a pathologist, to decide how the body should be removed.

On this occasion, however, when Hingston approached the 'corpse' he saw that it had horns. It was one of those moments when those engaged in the most gruesome of jobs could see humour in what was otherwise a desperately serious situation; the type of moment that has probably saved the sanity of a few cops. Even after the search was completed, the inquiry team could not discount the forest as Fiona Torbet's resting place. It would have been very easy to miss the grave and a fingertip search was out of the question given the size of the area.

Another possibility was that Fiona Torbet's grave was the bottom of Loch Duich. A body placed in water will sink, but then as putrefaction occurs it fills with gas and rises to the surface, where it will stay for a time. An undertaker in Ayr had not realised to what extent this made a body rise and was prosecuted when the bodies buried at sea, in conventional coffins – cheaper than the lead-lined variety – kept coming back. Had McMillan placed Fiona Torbet's body in the Loch, there was a great chance that it would have been seen during the period of buoyancy, unless he had taken steps to anchor it. If he had simply tipped it into the water, which lapped the shore right below Grianan House, anchored in some way with weights, then divers should be able to find it quite easily. He would have been taking a huge risk in carrying the body out from the shore in a boat to dump it in deeper water because of the probability of being seen. All the neighbouring houses over-looked the loch. Police divers searched the shore close to the house but found nothing.

Helicopters were deployed to over fly the area taking aerial photographs and looking for anything out of the way that might merit further investigation. Locals around Inverinate are used to the search and rescue craft that daily seem to pluck climbers and walkers in difficulties from the hills. This time, they were surprised to find the 'copters hovering only a few feet above their houses, scanning lower-lying land.

After these searches were completed, without success, the inves-tigating team came to the conclusion that their next focus had to be Grianan House and its extensive gardens. No one was looking forward to searching an obvious place – the septic tank. The problem was that there was just no evidence. It was only a gut feeling shared by the investigation team and Hingston, who had an uphill task to persuade his colleagues in the Crown Office in Edinburgh that a search warrant should be obtained. Mrs McMillan would never have allowed a search voluntarily. The initial view from the Crown Office was that the discovery of the bag was not enough to justify a search warrant. They would be aware of the allegations in the tabloid press that police were harassing McMillan. They wouldn't want to add fuel to the flames. Hingston argued the matter with his colleagues in Edinburgh strongly and successfully, with one proviso – there was to be no damage done to Grianan House during the search. The authorities didn't want to pick up the bill. Armed with the warrant, a large team began searching the house and garden.

Technology had produced underground radar by this time, though it was still relatively new. Technicians started to sweep the surface of the garden looking for anomalies. It was the same type of equipment as that used to search the basement and garden of Fred and Rosemary West's house in Gloucester. It had a footprint the size of an A4 sheet and was slow so the search of the large garden was going to take days. It was however efficient. Soon after the scan began, the equipment indicated something and a Rangers shirt was excavated with great care. Meanwhile other cops were searching McMillan's caravan and there they found a large number of pornographic magazines. They noted that McMillan had given the women featured points indicating their appeal to him. Younger women had been given scores of ten or twenty, while older women had been awarded up to 500. In retrospect Hingston regrets that the caravan was left unguarded overnight after the first day's search as there were also a lot of videos. He believes these would have contained similar material and which might have been useful evidence. When the search was resumed the following day the videos were gone. McMillan was asked to go to Dingwall voluntarily for questioning and agreed. His parents were asked to remain within their house to ensure that there was no interference with evidence. McMillan said nothing helpful during questioning and he was returned home.

Police had just brought McMillan back to the house when they made another breakthrough. Under the floorboards of the bathroom in Grianan House they found the rest of Fiona Torbet's luggage. They now had proof positive that they were on the right trail and Hingston was called from Dingwall to Inverinate again. Donald McMillan was arrested and taken back to Dingwall police station. He could be detained for six hours under section fourteen of the Criminal Procedure (Scotland) Act 1995, the equivalent of the Police and Criminal Evidence Act in England. At the end of the six-hour period, police had to either charge him with a crime or release him.

Until this point, McMillan's mother had been very protective of her son and vociferous in saying that he had done nothing wrong, but when Mrs Torbet's luggage was found in the house she was obviously shocked. Her husband had stood by virtually silent throughout. Hingston told Mrs McMillan that the police were going to search every inch of the house and garden and would be there for as long as it took to find the body. He also told her that he would need her and her husband to move out while the search continued. Hingston believes that Mrs McMillan influenced Donald McMillan's actions the following day.

Leaving a guard this time, the cops went home for the night. On the morning of 20 May 1994, ten months after Mrs Torbet had gone missing, in a police interview room at Dingwall, Donald McMillan silently, totally without comment, drew a sketch of the garden at Grianan House and placed a cross over the woodpile.

Police erected a tent over the part of the garden McMillan had indicated and carefully removed the logs to find a zinc sheet and then soil below. They removed the soil and sieved it through riddles to ensure nothing of significance was rejected. The area under the log pile was huge and the ground rough and rocky. The search started in the wrong place and those digging were working away from the body but luck was on the side of the police. A cop uncovered Mrs Torbet's fingers. It is just possible that they might have been missed and digging in that area could have been abandoned as a red herring. After all, McMillan had said nothing. When police later reviewed the evidence, in the aerial photos taken around Grianan House by the search helicopters, they found one in which Donald McMillan was standing right on top of the wood pile.

The body was lying in a shallow grave, with a carpet rolled around it. It was curled round a rock and there was some concern about how it could be removed without destroying evidence. Proof of the cause of death was going to be essential to a successful prosecution for murder – otherwise McMillan might say that Mrs Torbet had fallen and hit her head and he had panicked. In the event, McMillan's explanation for what happened was even more bizarre.

Dr Roslyn Rankin, the pathologist based in Raigmore Hospital, Inverness, arrived at the scene and following consultation between her and Hingston, police dug round the body as far as possible and lifted it out of the hole carefully. The following day, Dr Rankin carried out a post-mortem at Raigmore in difficult circumstances. The fans, which normally would help to ventilate away the smell of the decomposing body, were broken. The victim's head had been wrapped in bandages like a mummy and then trussed up with brown parcel tape. Dr Rankin's report gave the cause of death as mechanical asphyxia. McMillan was formally charged and appeared at Dingwall Sheriff Court for the first time on 24 May 1994. He was remanded to Porterfield Prison, Inverness to await his trial on charges of murdering Mrs Torbet and of perverting the course of justice.

He was tried at the High Court sitting in Inverness in September 1994 before a jury with Lord Cowie presiding. In the run-up to the trial, David Hingston recommended to Edgar Torbet that he didn't attend. The evidence of what happened to someone's nearest and dearest, particularly the medical evidence of how they met their death, can be very harrowing. It is advice given to most relatives and in the face of it a surprising number do sit through trials. Perhaps the need to see justice done is simply overwhelming. Perhaps there is a desire to see some remorse in the demeanour of the accused as he stands in the dock. Mr Torbet, however, took Hingston's advice and stayed at home. Yet again the tabloid press added to the misery he was experiencing.

Advocate Depute Iain Bonomy (now Lord Bonomy) was the prosecutor, with David Hingston sitting beside him. The evidence for the prosecution laid out every element of their case including the medical evidence of how Mrs Torbet had died. Initially, McMillan denied murdering Mrs Torbet. Suddenly, on 8 September, as the defence case started and the accused was in the witness box, he admitted that he had killed her and had made up a false story about her going off with a man. He then made a totally bizarre, and obviously false, allegation. He claimed Mrs Torbet had made advances to him and that when he rebuffed these she had tried to hit him. He said he had put a pillow over her face to try to calm her and had accidentally suffocated her. Hacks rushed to Mr Torbet's home where they doorstepped him and asked him to comment on these allegations. Their lack of sensitivity and apparent inability to assess the validity of what had been said is astounding. Meanwhile, in court, McMillan's legal team offered a plea of guilty to culpable homicide, which was rejected by the Crown.

In his summing-up at the end of the trial, Iain Bonomy said, 'I ask you to find that this attack was with intent to rape Mrs Torbet. It was a prolonged attack on a friendly and trusting lady who he bound and gagged for sexual gratification, an attack by a callous man who showed no remorse whatsoever. It was not the case that something went tragically wrong in an argument. This was murder.' The jury had to decide whether McMillan had murdered his victim or whether his crime was culpable homicide – that he had killed her without recklessness or intent. They took less than an hour to deliver their verdict. They found McMillan guilty of murder. Lord Cowie sentenced him to life for the murder and to five years for attempting to pervert the course of justice.

In 2003, two years after Scotland adopted the Human Rights Act, Lord Cullen, Lord Justice General considered the case, as he was required to do, and fixed a punishment tariff of fifteen years. That was the minimum sentence McMillan had to serve in prison before he could be considered for parole. Lord Cullen told McMillan at the High Court in Edinburgh, 'You had a fixation for older women and had sexual fantasies about them. It was a sexually motivated assault [on Mrs Torbet] and you must have subjected the victim to a terrifying ordeal . . .'

Donald McMillan died of natural causes in Saughton Prison, Edinburgh on 11 February 2007. He had not served his fifteen years. What had led him to commit murder? He had a brother and two sisters. They all enjoyed a normal childhood. After leaving school, he had taken a couple of jobs and then joined the army at eighteen. He served in the Royal Armoured Corps, but went absent without leave while his parents were living at Grianan House. After being arrested by Military Police, who searched the area and tracked him to his parent's home, he was handed down a punishment of six months' detention, which he served. He then left the army and moved in to the caravan in his parent's garden.

Locals at Inverinate had been familiar with the sight of McMillan and his brother, also in the army, in uniform waiting for the bus to Glasgow as they returned to their respective units after leave. When McMillan left the army and came to live permanently with his parents many locals became wary of him. He had a history of watching younger women, some just teenagers, in circumstances that made their parents nervous. They didn't say anything to his parents who were well regarded locally but took steps to keep their daughters safe by vigilance such as staying up till the young women were home.

McMillan didn't socialise with his neighbours but he did cycle regularly to Plockton, where he played football with local men. He was in the habit of writing letters to local girls, suggesting that their relationship was something other than it was. Understandably, they found this bizarre and frightening. He also gave them gifts of perfume, which was later found to belong to his mother. He had a problem with relationships with women his own age. It seems that given the opportunity of being alone with a woman who qualified for 'high marks' in his assessment was too great an opportunity to miss and he lost control. McMillan was not assessed as being mentally ill although he might have been diagnosed as suffering from erotomania or de Clérambault's syndrome. He appears to have had the erroneous and self-delusional conviction that Fiona Torbet was in love with him.

McMillan never explained where he had kept the body immediately after the killing. At the time of the killing, his cousin and his wife were staying in a caravan sited close to the log pile in the garden and they had access to the house. They were there for a couple of days after Mrs Torbet was murdered. Police are certain

McMillan wouldn't have buried Mrs Torbet during that time, as he would have risked being seen by his relatives. McDonald believes McMillan may have kept her body in his own caravan till his cousin and wife left and the coast was clear for his planned disposal. McMillan never explained why or when he had thrown Mrs Torbet's bag and property into the ditch close to Grianan House. He must have realised he was taking a huge risk. He could easily have put it with the rest of her property under the floorboards of the house, or even in the grave beside her. Had he done so, he might never have been brought to justice.

Police involved in the inquiry believe it is possible that while McMillan was stationed with the army in Germany he may have committed a similar offence.

It was only after McMillan was charged with Mrs Torbet's murder that locals spoke to police about him. However, even if his odd behaviour had come out earlier, detectives would have been able to do nothing about it due to the lack of evidence to point to him having killed Mrs Torbet.

It is David Hingston's proud boast that in twenty-six years as a Fiscal, no murderer operating in his area ever got away. He had a 100 per cent successful prosecution record. He is now a solicitor who defends those in court on criminal charges. His success rate in that role will inevitably be lower.

In researching this case I found that people in and around Inverinate were very reluctant to talk about it. Jessie McMillan and her husband moved away from Inverinate in the aftermath of the trial. They were thought of as good neighbours in the village. Their daughters married local men and settled in the area, where they remain. The family were all, except Donald, respectable, law-abiding people. The murder of Fiona Torbet made not only her family and friends victims but the killer's family too. They continue to live with the shame of association with Donald McMillan.

7

BEYOND REASONABLE DOUBT

There can have been few cases that disturbed the Highland community more than the brutal killing of thirty-six-year-old housewife and mother Elizabeth Sutherland. It happened in tiny Culbokie, a rural community twelve miles north of Inverness in an area known as the Black Isle. It was 24 September 1984 and the scene was the family home, Dunrobin, a three-year-old bungalow in Mounteagle Road. Mrs Sutherland was at home alone. Her husband, Kenneth, a self-employed builder, had gone to work and her two children, Jane (aged nine) and Steven (aged twelve) were at nearby Culbokie Primary and Fortrose Secondary schools respectively.

The village is within easy commuting distance of Inverness and has grown since 1984, with many new houses built to take advantage of the beautiful views of the Cromarty Firth and the hills beyond. But back then, it comprised just a main street with a village store, a pub and a clutch of houses. The village is only a couple of miles away from the busy A9 road, which links the north-east Highlands with the south of Scotland.

The Sutherland family home was located a short distance away from the nearest neighbour. In the Highlands, remoteness is not seen as a problem. Neighbourliness simply extends to people a bit further away. Just a short distance from the village is the Findon Burn. According to local legend, it was the home of a fairy who lured local men into the glen and kept them there. Culbokie was a close-knit community where everyone knew and trusted everyone else. Crime was virtually unknown.

What a horrific scene met young Jane when she returned from school. Her mother lay in a pool of blood. The girl summoned help but it was too late. Mrs Sutherland was only 4ft 9ins tall and known as 'Totsie'. A woman of her stature could not have put up much of a fight, but she might have been able to identify her assailant. Perhaps fearful of that, he had strangled and stabbed her and left her for dead in her bedroom, where he had closed the curtains.

Detective Superintendent Andrew Lister, then head of Northern CID, was the senior policeman in charge, with a team of twenty-four detectives dedicated to working on the inquiry full-time. They put up roadblocks and the scene of the crime was sealed off and forensically examined using the techniques available at the time. A police photographer took photographs of footprints in the garden and a tracker dog was sent through the dense woodland close to the bungalow. A caravan used as a major incident room by police was parked next to the house and computers were transferred from Inverness to the nearer police station at Dingwall to help analyse and collate all the information that was being gathered. The forensic laboratory of Grampian Police carried out scientific work.

Mrs Sutherland's husband Kenneth had an alibi, so he was not a suspect. Questions asked of locals soon made it clear that there was no local dispute that could have prompted the killing. It was obvious from the first that Totsie had disturbed an intruder in her home. Lister told the media at the first press conference that the likely motive for the murder had been robbery, although nothing had been taken and the house had not been forcibly entered. That last fact was not particularly helpful, because few people living in the area at the time locked their doors, the Sutherland family among them. The grieving and shocked widower, Kenneth, and his two children went to stay with relatives.

In the days after the killing, door-to-door inquiries were made in Culbokie and police issued several appeals. It was unlikely that the house would have been approached on foot by anyone other than the neighbours, so the appeals focused on vehicles and their users, but walkers were not ignored. Information about sightings were followed by appeals for more information. For example, police wanted to identify a man who walked into Conon Bridge Service Station, six miles from the murder scene, at about 9.45pm on the day of the murder. He was carrying a petrol can, which he filled and paid for using a £20 note.

A designated phone number for the inquiry was set up at Dingwall police station and publicised. Some callers rang up without speaking. To counter any fears a caller might have, public assurances were given that calls were being treated in the strictest confidence. Any callers who had hung up were urged to ring again as any information could be relevant. If they did then the information they imparted was not significant. There was to be no quick and easy answer to who killed Totsie.

Two weeks after the murder, police reiterated their request for information about the man who bought petrol at the Conon Bridge Service Station on 24 September. They were also asking about a man seen walking along the Tore to Mulbuie road that day at about 7.30pm, carrying a plastic container. Sightings of vehicles, even motorbikes, in the vicinity spawned other appeals.

Publicity was given to Totsie's last movements in an attempt to draw out information. The diminutive woman had visited her parents in the morning. Their house was just along the road and she had walked there. Totsie had been talking enthusiastically about bulbs she was going to plant in her garden. She left her parents' home at 12.30 to make the short walk home. She was brutally killed in the next few hours.

To the horror of people in the area, Lister said that the killer could be a local. He thought that aspects of the crime indicated local knowledge. The intruder had targeted a particular house where a successful local businessman lived so there would likely be good pickings. To Lister, awareness that doors would not be locked was another pointer to local knowledge. The inquiry team thought of arranging a mass fingerprinting of local men, but where

©MIRRORPIX.COM

Five times killer, Archibald Hall, after arrest and looking less suave than usual.

Career thief Michael Kitto was led by Hall into a killing spree.

©MIRRORPIX.COM

©MIRRORPIX.COM

Winter weather in Perthshire in January 1978 hampered the search for the body of Dorothy Scott-Elliott even after Hall had told police where to look.

©MIRRORPIX.COM

The national press reported on the trial of madman Iain Simpson, pictured left in his walking gear. Also featured on this front page are his victims, Swiss Hansreudi Gimmi (left top) and George Green (left bottom).

Daily Record

SAT. AUG. 25 1962

SCOTLAND'S NATIONAL NEWSPAPER No. 28,648

'The accused man escaped and he was not re-confined...I hope this case will never be forgotten'
—LORD KILBRANDON

● Lord KILBRANDON

'If our laws had been different my son would never have had the chance to kill. He would have been in a mental home'
—MRS. JANE SIMPSON

FREE TO KILL!

A9 mother attacks the law

By Jim Calder

PREACHER Iain Simpson escaped from a mental institution and stayed free for 28 days . . . and so became free to KILL.

Those 28 days of freedom meant that Simpson could not be returned to Hartwood Mental Institution, Lanarkshire.

● VICTIM Hans Gimmi . . . shot dead in a lonely wood.

The law says he could live a normal life. But the law is WRONG, Simpson's mother said yesterday.

"IF OUR LAWS HAD BEEN DIFFERENT MY SON WOULD NEVER HAVE HAD THE CHANCE TO KILL. HE WOULD HAVE BEEN WHERE HE BELONGED—IN A MENTAL HOME," MRS. JANE SIMPSON SAID.

Romancer

Iain Simpson was a romancer, a psyopath, a man who had hidden under the false facade of a minister's collar

"THOU SHALT NOT KILL" was the Commandment that 26-year-old Simpson preached.

But the "minister" did not practise what he preached. His white clerical collar was to become a dreadful symbol of death.

The High Court in Edinburgh yesterday was told of this man with "abnormal religious motivation."

Of Simpson's meetings with 30-year-old electrical engineer George Green, from Leeds, and Swiss student Hans Gimmi.

And of how the meetings ended in death for two young men who did not measure up to what Simpson regarded as "proper moral

● VICTIM George Green . . . shot dead on a lonely

Continued on Back Page

'THIS 'DEADLY PERIL'

LORD KILBRANDON, the High Court judge, yesterday attacked "the system that allowed Iain Simpson freedom . . ."

within hours of becoming an M.P. described it as "a deadly peril to society."

Mr. Kilbrandon, who committed Simpson to Carstairs Mental Institution, gave this warning as he said they will never be again by those responsible for the country's mental institutions."

'Public danger'

The M.P. who joined in the attack was Mr. James Dempsey (Lab. Coatbridge and Airdrie) in whose area Simpson's home lay.

At the end of the hearing Lord Kilbrandon attacked "the system" that allowed Simpson freedom.

He said: "The outstanding feature of this case is that the man arrested in 1960, had been certified as a public danger and sent back as such.

Escaped

"He escaped from this confinement. He was not discharged and cured and when he was found again he was not reconfined, but was subjected to the nonsense of a short prison sentence."

"I am not blaming anybody for this. It is the system."

He added: "If this gives

Continued on Back Page

'ORDAINE

IAIN SIMPSON felt almost a sense of triumph after he murdered twice.

He believed his victims died so . . . "

Robert Mone (left) was diagnosed insane and sent to Carstairs after he held a class of girls in a siege at his former Dundee school and shot their pregnant teacher. With Thomas McCulloch (right), another inmate at Carstairs with whom he established a close relationship, he broke out, killing Iain Simpson, Neil MacLellan, a nurse and PC George Taylor.

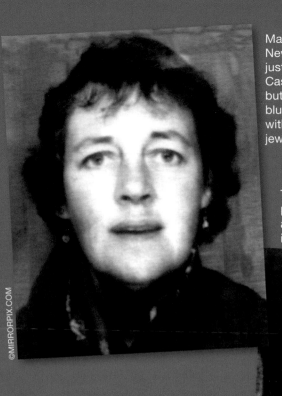

Margaret McOnie. One of Brian Newcombe's victims. Some just lost their hearts as the Casanova Killer wooed them, but she lost her life when he bludgeoned her over the head with a stone and stole her jewellery and chequebook.

The Casanova Killer, Brian Newcombe, in a photograph taken by a camera he stole. It's a picture that helped police discover the real identity of a con man with many aliases.

Jack Shuttleworth, a former prize fighter. At eighty-eight he was no match for Brian Newcombe who battered him to death before stealing the old man's wallet.

Likeable Bangladeshi restaurant manager Shamsuddin Mahmood was shot dead in an unprovoked racial attack that shocked Orkney.

Soldier Michael Ross as he made his way to his trial for the murder of Shamsuddin Mahmood in the High Court in Glasgow during May 2008. On the last day of his trial he had an arsenal of weapons waiting in a hired car nearby in case a guilty verdict was delivered. What would he have done if he had reached them?

The Mumutaz Restaurant, Bridge Street, Kirkwall – the site of the shooting of Shamsuddin Mahmood in June 1994.

Lee Gaytor, vicious killer of five-year-old Danielle Reid, now serving a life sentence in Wakefield Prison.

Tracy Reid, the mother who put her daughter to bed to die alone after a beating from her partner Lee Gaytor. She carried her daughter's body in a suitcase through Inverness city centre to dump it in the Caledonian Canal. She was sentenced to eight years.

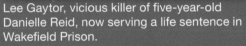

Helen Torbet, victim of Donald McMillan. She had the misfortune to choose his mother's guest house for her hillwalking holidays in the West Highlands.

Former soldier Donald McMillan who murdered sixty-two-year-old hillwalker Helen Torbet in his mother's guest house. He kept photos of women and gave them scores with younger women getting a 10 or a 20 and older women scoring up to 500.

Below: Detective Chief Inspector Peter MacPhee holds a replica of the Schmeisser pistol that was used to kill Alistair Wilson. Police were hopeful that the gun would afford clues leading them to the killer. Sadly, it did not.

Above: Respectable family man and banker Alistair Wilson spent the last day of his life walking with his family and friends through a forest near Nairn. Shot on his own doorstep, this apparently motiveless crime still baffles police.

Forensic team at work at the Wilson house in Crescent Street, Nairn in the aftermath of the killing.

Bill McDowell who was having an affair with Renee MacRae, his boss's wife. He has consistently denied having anything to do with the disappearance of Renee and her young son Andrew in 1976.

Renee MacRae's burnt-out car was recovered from the lay-by where it was seen ablaze on a Friday night in 1976. No trace of its occupants, Renee and her son, have ever been found. Renee's plans for that weekend were to spend it with McDowell and young Andrew at a hotel at Rannoch, Perthshire. They never arrived.

Renee MacRae whose disappearance remains a mystery.

The body of Kevin McLeod was recovered from Wick Harbour on Sunday, 9th February, 1997. Mr McLeod was last seen in the vicinity of the harbour about 3.30am on the morning of Saturday, 8th February, 1997 some time after leaving the Waterfront nightclub. The police investigation into Mr McLeod's death was incomplete and the circumstances of his death remain in contention. Anyone with information about Mr McLeod's death, however insignificant it may appear, is respectfully requested to contact the subscribers and in complete confidence.

John Macaulay & Company
Solicitors
46 London Road
Glasgow G1 5NB.
Tel. 0141 552 2831.

This poster appeal was launched by the MacLeod family who had it displayed in almost every shop in Wick.

Willie MacRae in full flight. He was a passionate and eloquent speaker particularly on politics and as a member of the anti-nuclear lobby.

Willie MacRae's Volvo where it came to rest on the banks of Loch Loyne. Some conspiracy theorists said that the car was removed before the police investigation began. This photograph was supplied by Northern Constabulary and is, along with other evidence in the case, available to view on the force's website.

would they draw the line to define local? There are lots of villages and small towns within fifteen miles of Culbokie and of course Inverness, now a city but then the Highlands' largest town, was not far off. In the event there were no fingerprints found at the scene to compare. Lister appealed to the public saying, 'Someone, somewhere must know something. No one can ignore the possibility that it might happen again. If someone is afraid, they can arrange to see me personally without becoming involved.'

Police had found the murder weapon at the scene. From what they knew of the scene itself and Mrs Sutherland's injuries, they said it was likely the killer would have been bloodstained. The public were asked to report anyone they had seen wearing bloodstained clothing. The comment about local knowledge fuelled fear that the killer was still in the Culbokie area. Locals lived in dread that he would strike again.

For weeks, no one came forward to identify the man who had bought petrol. Police were able to add to the description that he spoke with an English accent. If he was English, he might have returned to England and be beyond the scope of the media appeals. The Sutherland family offered a reward of £4,000 for information. No breakthrough was forthcoming. Locals were still coming forward with descriptions of unfamiliar people and vehicles. Successive appeals for information contained descriptions of vehicles as diverse as red and white Vauxhall Cavalier cars, a Land Rover towing a caravan, a motorcycle. Walkers seen in the area were also mentioned. Amazingly, when a suspect was caught it was discovered he had been driving an orange Transit van, but no one locally had noticed it.

The inquiry team threw their net wide. In the belief that an intruder bent on theft had been responsible, police identified and interviewed burglars known to operate in the area. This assumption later proved to be correct, and the killer was among those interviewed, but he appeared to have an alibi and slipped through the net. At the height of the inquiry, 100 policemen were involved and 5,000 people were interviewed. When the inquiry was stalling through lack of any useful leads, it featured on the BBC programme *Crimewatch*. Much was made of the peaceful nature of the area and the inexplicable brutality of the murder of this tiny and defenceless woman. No strong clues emerged after the programme.

As the manhunt continued, a local politician, James Munro, publicly made critical remarks about the ability of the police. These were reported in the press, but following a meeting of the Police Committee, at which the Chief Constable outlined in detail the extensive steps that were being taken, Munro said he had merely been expressing public concern and had no criticism to make. He also said that the police had the full confidence of the committee.

Criticism of police handling of major inquiries is a feature that recurs again and again in the Highlands. The tiny number of unsolved killings demonstrates that it is just as hard to commit the perfect murder and get away with it in the Highlands as anywhere else. There are so few murders that every one of them attracts a huge amount of attention. The killing of Totsie Sutherland was one of those that were hard to solve, but in the end, the cops got their man. Or did they?

Three months after the killing, Kenneth Sutherland took the difficult step of bringing his two children back to live in Dunrobin. The three spent their first Christmas without their beloved wife and mother in their own home, a house where happiness had been displaced by bad memories, particularly for young Jane. In the absence of any new leads the inquiry wound down.

Then, in August 1985, almost a year after the murder, there was a breakthrough. George McPhee, a known thief who had grown up at nearby Tore but was now living in the north of England, ill-advisedly drove a stolen car in Muir of Ord, just ten miles from Culbokie. He was spotted by the police, who fed his name into the system where information was stored about everyone suspected of committing crimes in the area at the time of Totsie's murder. The computer displayed the alibi given by McPhee. He had been with Colin Hawkins, an associate, on the day of the murder. McPhee and Hawkins had both claimed that on 24 September 1984 they were travelling south of Inverness in an orange van. The information on the computer bore an annotation that the pair had been eliminated as suspects in the murder. In all the reports of vehicles in the area on the day of the killing, no one had reported seeing their distinctive van. There was nothing to place them at Culbokie and no reason to disbelieve their story.

However, the sighting in Muir of Ord, and suspicion that he might have been thieving, prompted a search of McPhee's home in South Killingholm, South Humberside and there police found stolen property that had come from houses in the Easter Ross area near Culbokie. They noticed that some of it had come from a break-in that shared certain characteristics with the Sutherland home: the location of the Easter Ross house was also close to a wood and the bedroom curtains had been drawn. The similarity in the modus operandi was enough to focus attention on McPhee and Hawkins. They were interviewed first at Durham police station by Detective Angus McQuarrie and then brought north to Dingwall to be further questioned about the thefts. Hawkins immediately told police that McPhee was the killer. McPhee was arrested and charged.

In November 1985, George McPhee was tried before a jury of eight women and seven men at the High Court sitting in Inverness. There were fifteen charges in all on the indictment. One of them was the murder; there were also thirteen charges of theft and one of threatening a Dingwall barmaid with a knife. Lord Hunter presided, Mr Robert Henderson QC defended McPhee and Alistair Dunlop was the Advocate Depute prosecuting.

The charge of murder was in the following terms: 'On 24 September 1984 you did enter uninvited the house known as "Dunrobin", Culbokie, District of Ross and Cromarty and there assault Elizabeth Jessie MacKenzie or Sutherland, residing there, place your arm or hand around her neck, strangle her and did repeatedly cut and stab her on the neck and body with a knife and you did murder her.'

At the beginning of his trial, McPhee lodged a special defence of alibi to the murder charge, saying that at the time of Totsie's death he was in the Dundonnell–Braemore area with his associate, Colin Hawkins. He had no idea what Hawkins had told detectives and was in for a shock.

Jane Sutherland, by now ten years old, relived her nightmare as she told the court how she found her mother's body. On her return from school she had called out, 'I'm home,' and when she received no reply she had searched the house. She had found her mother's body on the floor of the bedroom, where the curtains had been drawn. She realised her mother was dead and ran the short distance to her grandparents' house to give them the heart-breaking news.

Detective Sergeant Gordon Ross gave evidence that there were no fingerprints at the scene that could belong to the accused. A cushion cover had been used to wipe the knife clean. The murder weapon was found in the kitchen drawer, with traces of blood on it. There was a lot of blood at the scene in the bedroom, but no sign of a struggle. We can only speculate that when Totsie came into her home, her killer had hidden and then pounced, grabbing her from behind and probably half-choking her. He may have dragged her to the kitchen, where he took the murder weapon from the cutlery drawer, and then pulled her into the bedroom, where he strangled and stabbed her.

Ross and Detective Constable Birnie of the Identification Branch told how they had photographed four footprints in the vegetable patch in the garden of Dunrobin and that they had made a cast of the most detailed of these. The footprint evidence proved to be very significant.

DS Ross was of the opinion that the prints had been made by someone who was running because of their position. He said there were also footprints made with soil on the carpet of the bedroom where the body was found, which had been made by the same person. He said it was hard because of movement to establish exactly the size of the print of which he and his colleague had taken a cast. He thought it was a size nine to ten. Birnie agreed that one person had made the footprints. His evidence as to the size was that they had been made by shoes larger than his own, which were seven-and-a-half or eight.

Detective Inspector Angus McQuarrie said he had taken a pair of shoes from McPhee when he was at Porterfield Prison on remand and that they were the same pair worn by McPhee when he was first interviewed at Durham police station on 9 August. They were size nine. When he interviewed Hawkins on 12 August at Durham he was wearing size seven shoes.

Colin Hawkins was the next witness for the prosecution. McPhee will have been expecting his former colleague to lie for him and back him up; instead his defence of alibi fell apart. Hawkins admitted that on the day of the murder he and McPhee were in Culbokie. They had travelled to the area in an orange Transit van with the intention of stealing snow poles from remote areas and selling them for scrap. They had stolen welding cable from a contractor's yard and stripped it in a quarry near Lairg, where they had slept in the van.

Alistair Dunlop, the prosecuting Advocate Depute, asked what had occurred at Culbokie. Hawkins told him that they had driven past the Sutherland home on the day of the murder with the intention of housebreaking and theft. McPhee, who was driving the van, had said to Hawkins it was 'a likely place to screw', as he had done on other occasions. McPhee had turned the van off the main road and parked on a track a short distance from the house, facing back towards the road for a 'quick getaway'. Hawkins had stayed in the van and watched McPhee as he climbed the fence into the garden. McPhee had entered the house by the back door after looking in a rear window. Hawkins said that he had expected McPhee to be no more than five or ten minutes in the house. When McPhee had returned to the van about forty minutes later he looked shocked and his behaviour suggested he was upset. His hands were clean which they hadn't been before he entered the house and his coat was zipped up. Hawkins related how McPhee had changed his clothes that night at a relative's house before the pair travelled back to England.

He claimed that he was approached by McPhee and another man a few weeks after the murder and told to say nothing about what happened in Scotland. He told the court he witnessed McPhee threatening the barmaid in the hotel in Dingwall.

When he was cross-examined by McPhee's advocate, Hawkins denied that he was the one who had entered the house and that McPhee was the getaway driver. He said he couldn't drive. He stuck to his story. He said he had lost his bottle years ago and wouldn't burgle a house. Hawkins admitted he had a cut finger on the day of the murder. He explained that he had cut it sawing down snow poles and he had kept his jacket zipped up to avoid getting blood on his shirt.

He admitted lying to English police, who questioned him shortly after the murder. At that point he had denied being in Culbokie, giving an alibi for 24 September. He explained this saying, 'It is habit, after years of criminal activity, to give false statements about anything.'

Just after Hawkins gave his evidence, there was a dramatic shift in the proceedings. Henderson, representing McPhee, withdrew the special defence of alibi on his client's behalf in respect of the murder charge. Instead he lodged a plea of incrimination, another special defence, naming Hawkins as the killer. He told the court his client was adhering to his defence of alibi so far as the charge of threatening the barmaid was concerned. His client was still claiming he was in Durham on the day of that offence – 19 September 1984.

A change of direction in the defence of a case is quite unusual. In the 1980s, the defence team would usually have taken a statement from all prosecution witnesses and have known what they were going to say in evidence. Hawkins was probably still living in England, which would have created practical problems, but the way round that would have been to ask the Procurator Fiscal for an indication of the evidence that Hawkins would be expected to give. In lodging the defence of alibi, it is apparent that McPhee's legal team weren't aware of what Hawkins was going to tell the court any more than their client and were wrong-footed. Nowadays, the Crown must make full disclosure of their case to the defence, showing them all statements, documents, reports etc. that they are going to rely on in the trial.

The next very significant evidence came from Trevor Proudfoot, who had been a prisoner in Porterfield Prison, Inverness. He had shared a cell for a few hours with McPhee in the summer of 1985 when McPhee was on remand. Proudfoot gave evidence of a confession that he said McPhee had made to him. McPhee had told him he had been getting a lot of hassle from police about the murder and that he had committed it but the police would never be able to prove it. After the confession, Proudfoot said, he had asked to be transferred to another cell away from McPhee.

He said police had approached him and offered to make a deal regarding drugs charges he was facing if he told them about McPhee, but he turned the offer down. After his own trial the cops visited him again, in prison. Detective Superintendent Andrew Lister, who was in charge of the investigation, told him that he could make things easier for him in prison and help him to get parole. Proudfoot said he had been reluctant to get involved but after discussing it with his solicitor, Robert Forrest, he eventually agreed to tell the Procurator Fiscal about McPhee's confession.

A pathologist gave evidence of the brutality of the injuries sustained by Totsie Sutherland. She had a horrendous neck wound and seven stab wounds in the chest. She had been held in a stranglehold from behind and stabbed in the chest and then her throat was cut. Her assailant would have had blood on his forearm.

Detective Superintendent Lister gave evidence that the footprints outside the house were at least size nine and possibly size ten. 'It was the same footprint in the garden as was in the house, and this was later confirmed to me, of course, by the lab,' he said. He also told the court that when he saw him in prison Hawkins was wearing size seven shoes and shoes taken from McPhee were size nine.

Lister was asked, 'Can you be sure that the imprint that can be made in soft soil by a heavy type of shoe or boot can, in actual fact, look much larger than the shoe or boot maybe when it is not on the ground?'

Lister replied, 'This is the point that was brought to us by the lab. They said that it could be a size smaller than the actual print, that there was some slippage in the soft soil.'

He was asked if he had considered Hawkins as a potential suspect and agreed vehemently that he had. He had examined Hawkins' feet for that reason but they were 'too fine' to have made the print of which the police had a plaster cast. He clarified that he meant they were too small and narrow.

When McPhee was apprehended, Lister had confirmed that his feet were the right size, although police had not managed to recover the actual footwear worn at the scene. Lister said he accepted that the size of the print would depend on the softness of the soil, the weight and size of the person and the type of shoe. He said that the shoe that made the print was a heavy-soled type. No finger-prints belonging to either McPhee or Hawkins had been found in Dunrobin. There were no unidentified fingerprints, except one set which experts thought were made either by a child or a woman.

McPhee and Hawkins were known criminals. McPhee's crim-inal career dated back to seven years earlier. Lister said that he placed reliance on Hawkins' allegations as, 'a lot of what he said tied in with what I already believed. He had to have been at the scene to tell me what he did. We went to see him several times and if we had doubted him we would have been on to him.' He said that all the while McPhee stuck to his story of being with Hawkins stealing snow poles.

Lister told the court that he had visited Proudfoot in prison when he heard he might have information. He said the man was afraid to talk as he risked being 'slashed up'. Lister said, 'He was terrified. I told him I would go to the prison authorities to make sure he was safeguarded. I also told him we would not oppose his parole.' He said that Proudfoot had refused to speak to him about the murder at first, even when a reward was mentioned.

At the beginning of the defence case, McPhee went into the witness box and gave his version of events. He said that when he and Hawkins were going along Mounteagle Road he saw Mrs Sutherland walking along the edge of the road towards Culbokie and away from the house. He said to Hawkins that she might be going to the shops and that there might be something worth stealing in the house. McPhee drove along the road and turned then parked the van close by. Hawkins got out and McPhee said, 'Make it quick. Get a television or video that's worth selling.' McPhee's account continued: Hawkins had gone into the house, and returned about fifteen to twenty minutes later, saying, 'Let's get out of here. I've been caught.' McPhee asked, 'Did they get a good look at you?' To which Hawkins replied, 'No, I don't think so.'

McPhee gave evidence that Hawkins had blood on his shirt, jacket and trousers but that Hawkins had said it was from a cut finger. According to McPhee, he then drove to a quarry near Lairg, where Hawkins asked him for a shirt and dumped the one covered in blood in a skip. There was no scrap in the quarry so they travelled to Dundonell to steal snow poles. He claimed that they then spent the night at North Kessock and travelled on to Edinburgh the following morning.

Asked by his defence advocate, Henderson, why he had changed his plea from alibi to incrimination, McPhee told the court that he had 'never grassed a man in my life'. He continued, 'When I heard Hawkins' evidence I decided to give the true version. I didn't think Hawkins would come to court and put the finger on me for a murder I did not commit.' He also denied ever admitting to Trevor Proudfoot, with whom he had shared a prison cell for three hours, that he had committed the murder.

Lord Hunter directed the jury, telling them that their job was to decide whether the accused was guilty or innocent and that they must weigh the evidence. He said that the footprints were the key piece of evidence: once McPhee had admitted that he was at the scene of the crime, it was a question of whether McPhee or Hawkins was the guilty party. On 3 December 1985, the jury failed to reach a verdict. The following day, they retired to continue their deliberations. After only forty-five minutes, they returned to the court to deliver a majority verdict of guilty.

Lord Hunter commented on the brutality of the killing:

'This was a murder of a peculiarly callous and brutal character and I must confess that having listened to the evidence I see no reason why the life sentence should mean anything different from what it says. But in order to mark the revulsion which the public must feel about the murder and because I think the circumstances merit it, I propose to make the recommendation to the Secretary of State on the minimum period which should elapse before you are released. The minimum period will be twenty-five years.'

McPhee showed no reaction when the verdict and sentence were given. There was however a response from the public gallery, where there was a spattering of applause. Totsie's husband said, 'I am sorry they have done away with hanging.' McPhee was also found guilty of the assault on the barmaid a few days earlier, which he had denied. By the end of the trial he had pled guilty to ten charges of theft.

George McPhee always claimed he was a victim of a miscarriage of justice and he applied to have his case examined by the Scottish Criminal Cases Review Commission (SCCRC). The commission was set up in April 1999 to look at possible miscarriages of justice. Cases referred to it are considered by a board made up of legal and laypersons appointed by the Crown, following a recommendation by the First Minister (Scotland's equivalent of a Prime Minister). Following consideration of the evidence presented in court and any new information submitted to them, they resolve whether to refer a case back to the High Court. To deal with the appeal, the High Court sits as an Appeal Court, normally of three judges but on rare occasions five, to reconsider the verdict. The Crown is asked to provide comments for consideration to the Appeal Court. SCCRC statistics show that in the eight years and eight months since it was established at time of writing, 965 applications were received. Only forty-two were referred back to the High Court and, of those, twenty-seven have resulted in a successful appeal. Not all are murder cases, but if ever proof was needed that the abolition of the death penalty was morally right and remains so, it lies in these figures. The criminal justice system is imperfect.

The SCCRC had serious concerns regarding certain aspects of McPhee's trial and in 2003 McPhee was released on bail pending reconsideration of his case. In December 2005 three judges, Lord Gill, Lord Nimmo Smith and Lord Osborne considered the appeal on the information they received from the SCCRC and the Crown.

The SCCRC was very concerned about Hawkins' part in convicting McPhee. The commission's inquiries discovered that Hawkins had given five statements to the police, providing various different accounts of the whereabouts and activities of himself and his accomplice. The Crown should have been aware of this when preparing for the trial and should have disclosed it to the defence so Hawkins could be challenged. It wasn't clear that this had been done. Not only had Hawkins' evidence changed over time; it was also either inconsistent with that of other witnesses, or uncorroborated. The jury should have been told to take account of Hawkins' position of self-interest. Hawkins' evidence therefore was discredited and in the opinion of the appeal judges it should not have been relied upon.

Then Trevor Proudfoot, the man who had shared a cell with McPhee, was interviewed by the SCCRC. He told them that at the time of the murder and during a period which extended beyond McPhee's 'confession', he had been abusing illegal drugs and as a result he remembered very little of what had been said or done. The report prepared by the Procurator Fiscal, which was sent to the Crown Office, was quite specific on this point, as the Fiscal had been concerned about Proudfoot's ability to recollect events accurately. Part of the Fiscal's job in preparing a case for trial is to assess the credibility of a witness when he precognoses him (takes a statement). He has to include his opinion of credibility in his report to the Crown Office.

When Proudfoot was given the opportunity to read a transcript of what he had said at the trial, he could not agree that it was a true reflection of what he remembered. The SCCRC was of the opinion that Proudfoot was induced by the police to give evidence to help them get a conviction. When asked by the SCCRC whether he had heard McPhee confess, Proudfoot was now unsure. The jury should have been told that Proudfoot was abusing drugs and that accordingly his recollections might not be reliable. The appeal court found that Proudfoot's evidence at the trial was thus discredited and should not have been relied upon.

The Crown had reviewed the evidence that had been given at the trial. It found that the police had taken photographs of the footprints and that these were probably all sent to the Grampian Police Laboratory, but that there was no record of a scientist there ever concluding what size shoe could have made the print. A number of pairs of shoes belonging to McPhee and Hawkins were examined after they were arrested but none were found to match the photographs.

Correspondence between the Fiscal and the Chief Constable of Grampian made it clear that the footprint in the plaster cast was incomplete, that only part of the heel was visible and that a double or triple application had occurred which made interpretation of the size impossible. The cast was so unclear that the laboratory found it impossible even to decide whether the print was of a left or of a right shoe. The two Grampian Police forensic scientists who had examined the cast print, Wilkie and Jensen, confirmed to the SCCRC what was said in the correspondence about it: that the photographs were inconclusive and they could not state the size from them. Jensen accepted he might at some stage have expressed an informal opinion that the cast came from a size nine shoe but he clearly had doubts and had expressed them. Part of the written forensic report was a sketch on which he had written 'size?'

Wilkie and Jensen were of the opinion that the footprints in the house were not 'distinctly different' from those in the cast and the photographs, but their report did not say that they were the same. The scientists had not been called as witnesses at the trial. If they had been, Detective Superintendent Lister's evidence would have been challenged.

The SCCRC report to the Appeal Court said it was inappropriate for an officer even of Lister's experience to have given the evidence he did regarding the footprints. It was virtually impossible that he would not have been aware of the lab report saying that the size could not be established from either the cast or the photographs. The original lab report regarding the cast was initialled by one of the two scientists who had examined it. Lister had countersigned the report, acknowledging receipt, less than three weeks before he gave evidence. It is hard to believe that he forgot what he read in the report. It looks very much as if, in his enthusiasm to get a conviction, he lied.

The Crown accepted that at the time of the trial there was information which, if given in evidence, would have called into question what was said in court about the footprints. Accordingly, the Crown could not support the conviction.

The SCCRC expressed concern at the lack of solid evidence to link McPhee with either the deceased, the murder weapon or the scene of the crime. The lack of forensic evidence to prove or rebut that the footprints had belonged to McPhee was unfair. Taken together with doubts over the veracity of evidence given by Hawkins and Proudfoot, this could have resulted in a different conclusion from the jury.

The three judges were critical of Detective Superintendent Lister. They said they thought he had acted in bad faith. Lister's evidence had effectively discounted Hawkins as the killer, so that at the end of the trial McPhee was found guilty. By the time the Appeal

Court considered the case and publicised their findings, Andrew Lister was beyond any disciplinary action or embarrassment. He had died in the interim.

In December 2005, Lord Gill told an impassive George McPhee that his conviction was quashed. He had served almost eighteen years behind bars. Speaking outside the court, his wife Pauline and his two sons with him, McPhee said he would like a public inquiry to find out why he had been in jail for so long. So far, there has been no sign of one.

Northern Constabulary said after the appeal that the file would not be reopened and that they were not looking for anyone else in connection with Mrs Sutherland's killing. So what is the truth? Was McPhee wrongly convicted? Or did he 'get off', having served eighteen years of a minimum sentence of twenty-five, because of a senior cop's determination to convict him whether the evidence supported it or not. Was he really the guilty party? Has Hawkins got off scot-free? I suspect we will never know the truth for sure.

PART THREE
UNSOLVED

8

RESORT TO MURDER

In the words of the old song, 'what a difference a day makes'. The Wilson family – Alistair, Veronica and their two little boys – could not have known on Sunday, 28 November 2004 that events that evening would change their lives forever.

The bright, winter afternoon had been spent out walking with friends in Forestry Commission-owned Culbin Forest, which extends eastwards from just beyond the outskirts of Nairn in Inverness-shire towards Findhorn Bay. Nairn is a popular seaside resort on the Moray Firth, with a links golf course. In years past, it was a favourite holiday destination for the film stars Charlie Chaplin and Burt Lancaster. It is easy to picture four-year-old Andrew and two-year-old Graham Wilson exploring the forest, most likely collecting fir cones and other childish treasures on the trails. When little Graham got tired, he was probably lifted onto his father's shoulders. No doubt the adults chatted while they watched their children play. It was a relaxed, family outing, like many that had preceded it and many that should have been yet to come.

At the end of a lovely day, the family returned to their home, a former bed and breakfast in Crescent Road that Alistair and Veronica had converted into a family home. They hadn't lived in Nairn long but were already fond of the area. They had built up a circle of friends and were finding their feet in the local community. Veronica had already taken part in a local sponsored cycle ride to fund a visit of children from Belarus in the summer.

Alistair was a thirty-year-old banker working out of the Bank of Scotland's business centre in Inverness, just sixteen miles away, and Veronica was a full-time mother, looking after their two young sons. After their day out in the fresh air, the boys would be tired and a warm bath before bed would help them to settle. At 7.10pm, the bedtime routine at their home was underway and Alistair was preparing to read a bedtime story to the boys when the doorbell rang. Veronica went to answer it. A short, stocky man wearing a baseball cap and a dark-coloured, blouson jacket stood on the step. He asked to speak to Alistair by name and held out an envelope. Veronica didn't know the man. She left the envelope with him and fetched Alistair.

Alistair went to the door and spoke briefly to the caller. He took the envelope from him and went back inside, where he had a short conversation with his wife, telling her that he didn't know the man. Then he went back to the doorstep. Police have never disclosed exactly what was said between Alistair and his wife except to comment that it was not certain that Alistair was going to return to the doorstep to speak again to the man. Police often keep back some information to weed out the strange and the mentally ill who sometimes come forward and claim responsibility for crimes. False confessions can be easily broken down when the interviewee is ignorant of details that are not in the public domain. If the substance of the conversation between Alistair and Veronica could have helped explain what happened next, it would have been disclosed.

Veronica was busy attending to her sons and she didn't hear what was said while Alistair spoke again to the visitor at the door. Only two people ever knew the details of who said what and why in that conversation. One of them is dead and the other . . .

The visitor shot Alistair Wilson in the head and body at point-blank range on his own doorstep and made off down Crescent Road. The sound of three shots brought Veronica rushing to the front door, where she found her husband in a pool of blood and his assailant making off, still clutching the blue or green envelope whose contents remain a mystery.

It was 7.13pm when Veronica's 999 call reached the police control room. She was hysterical, barely able to keep control enough to tell the operator what had happened. After making the call she frantically tried to administer first aid to her husband and then, distraught, ran to Havelock House Hotel across the road. Two nurses who happened to be in the bar raced out and did all they could to save Alistair's life. He was taken the sixteen miles by ambulance to Raigmore Hospital in Inverness, but it was too late. He was dead on arrival.

Detective Chief Inspector Peter MacPhee was appointed senior investigating officer on the case and all available police were diverted to Nairn to try to find the killer. Roadblocks were set up and searches for the killer began. The area around the Wilson home was sealed off to preserve evidence. Contrary to film and TV fiction, even the man in charge was kept behind the tapes till the scene-of-crime examiners had done their stuff. Veronica and her two little sons were taken into protective custody and stayed there for some weeks. They might have been the next planned victims and Veronica was, so far as detectives knew, the only person who could identify her husband's killer. That alone could make her a target.

The open ground of Nairn Links, a likely escape route for the killer, lies just a short distance from the Wilson home at the end of Crescent Road. It quickly became the focus of a search with sniffer dogs, but the speed of the response was in vain. The killer escaped, aided by darkness and the location.

Nairn is a small town with a population of about 11,000 people. Fortunately for the town's economy, tourists have not been deterred by the murder from bathing in the Moray Firth off Nairn's miles of safe sandy beaches, or from using the town as a base for exploring the area.

Locals were shocked when they woke the following day to find police, some of them armed, had taken over Nairn. They were even more alarmed to learn that one of the town's residents had been executed on his doorstep. Armed police are not a common sight in Highland towns. Underage drinking, vandalism and general youth disorder are not unusual, but in Nairn even those more minor offences happen on a scale smaller than in towns of a similar size. The only two previous murders in living memory in the town, in 1966 and 1986, had drink or disputes over a woman as their cause and were easily solved by the police. This case was of a very different complexion.

Alistair Wilson had moved into the area for his job with the bank. He had attended Garnock Academy and then Stirling University, where he graduated in accountancy and business law. He was a respectable business and family man, an upstanding member of the local community and well known in local banking circles. Veronica was a native of Fort William. There was nothing obvious in Alistair's family or business background to suggest a motive. Locals had to be asking, if the killing was random was the killer still in the vicinity? Who was safe?

Police began exploring every avenue, seeking a clue to the identity of the killer or a motive, which would usually provide pointers to his identity. Within a few hours of the shooting, police from Northern Constabulary's Financial Investigations Unit were at Mr Wilson's office, examining computers used by the dead man. He was head of a new business banking team but was shortly due to leave the bank to become commercial director of BRE Highlands, a new research and consultancy organisation set up to help Highland companies operate in an environmentally aware way.

Police appealed to the public, issuing a description of the gunman and asking for help to identify him. An incident room was set up in Nairn police station and later a custom-built Portacabin with communication facilities was sited at the rear of the police station to operate as an incident room and allow the normal business of the police station to continue unimpeded. A house-to-house inquiry began the day after the killing. The post-mortem on Alistair Wilson's body was carried out that day too. An extensive search of the beach and the shoreline was carried out.

Police began inputting information into HOLMES, the computerised system for collating statements and information. This investigation was to be the largest HOLMES inquiry ever run by Northern Constabulary, closely followed by that into the death of Shamsuddin Mahmood featured in Chapter 4.

The Havelock House Hotel, across the road from the Wilson family home, was very busy on Sunday nights with its popular Sunday dinners. The lounge windows overlooked the scene of the crime and there were people sitting in these windows at the time of the shooting. The killer had luck on his side, something he could not have relied on. It was down to pure chance that none of the potential witnesses in the hotel had been looking out in the several minutes he stood on the Wilsons' doorstep. The noise of the jukebox in the lounge masked the sound of the shots, which might have drawn the attention of clientele in the hotel. Did the killer know that was likely? He seems to have been undeterred by the possibility. The shooting could have been witnessed and he could have been pursued and captured.

Two CCTV cameras operate in the area near the Wilson home. One of them, belonging to the Highland Council, is attached to a church and should focus on a roundabout at the junction between Crescent Road and the main road through Nairn. A live lead connects it to the local police station, but no one sits and watches the screens constantly. The footage is recorded onto a hard drive for future examination and possible evidence. The camera's angle can be changed remotely, and MacPhee's team discovered that its view was directed down Crescent Road. Detectives were very hopeful the killer would be caught on film, but the hard drive was blank. Every possible way of recovering pictures was explored but nothing could be retrieved.

At the far end of Crescent Road there is a small hotel that has a private CCTV system. It is used to monitor an area used in summer, where customers sit at tables outside. It also looks along Crescent Road. Again, the detectives were hopeful, but they discovered that the machine hadn't been recording on the Sunday night;

the tape was full and had stopped running. The hotel owner had gone away that weekend and there had been a breakdown in communication between him and the person left in charge. Neither had changed the tape.

Northern Constabulary called in help from outside the area. The number of murders in the area does not justify the force having its own specialists in many areas of modern policing. Some specialisations are esoteric and provision is across the forces for the whole of Scotland. Grampian Police Laboratory and Strathclyde ballistics section assisted in identifying the bullets. The National Crime Faculty's Centrex Unit provided guidance. This unit was set up following the Yorkshire Ripper inquiry to provide an integrated approach to solving and reducing crime and, as well as top cops, it has a forensic clinical psychologist and behaviour specialists who will provide an offender profile.

Detective Chief Inspector Peter MacPhee began giving regular press conferences. He explained the strategies his team had adopted. 'We will continue to carry out background searches into the deceased to try and establish a motive. What we will do in these circumstances is take his life apart piece by piece and look at his business in depth.' At that same conference, Chief Inspector Andy Walker, Area Commander for Badenoch, Strathspey and Nairn, reassured residents of the area. They were fearful that the killer was still in their midst and could kill again. He highlighted the big police presence in the town, which had firearms capability. He reminded the folk of Nairn that this type of crime was very rare.

A week after the killing, police set up roadblocks and stopped every vehicle travelling through Nairn between 6pm and 8.30pm. The A96, the busy main road between Inverness and Aberdeen, passes though the centre of Nairn. Crescent Road runs off this main route. There were between 600 and 700 vehicles stopped in the hope that someone who had made the same journey a week before would recall something that could be of importance. Walkers were also stopped and asked if they had been there the week before. Police discounted a theory that the killer had escaped the area in a speedboat. The tide would have been low at the time of the shooting and no vessel could have left the harbour.

Crimestoppers put up the highest reward they had ever offered in Scotland – £10,000 for anyone with knowledge of the crime to come forward. The local community turned out in larger numbers than ever before to the switching on of the town's Christmas lights. That evening, Sandy Park, Nairn's provost, reflected on the feelings of folk in the town. 'I think it brought people together when they most needed that sense of reassurance,' he said. 'People were genuinely afraid last Sunday when there were fears that a gunman was on the loose and this evening, you get the feeling that the community is here because they need to feel that sense of togetherness.'

Then came an unexpected breakthrough. A complaint was made to Sandy Park by constituents about a blocked drain. Council workmen and a local contractor were sent to Seabank Road, another street off the A96 which, like Crescent Road, leads towards the links. As he was clearing the drain, one of the workmen found a small handgun. The following day, in a press conference, DCI MacPhee confirmed that it was of a type that could have been used in the killing. Subsequent examination established it was the murder weapon. Detectives were surprised that the killer had chosen to dump the gun in this location. Seabank Road is well lit and lined with houses whose residents might have seen something; particularly since the drain where the gun was placed was right under a lamp standard. Between Crescent Road and Seabank Road are many ill-lit places where the gunman was less likely to have been seen leaving his firearm. He had passed them by.

Incident tapes were used to block off part of Seabank Road and police carried out a close examination of the area, including the gardens of houses in the street. The area where the gun was found was outside the area of one square mile around the Wilson home, which had been thoroughly searched already. House-to-house inquiries were also instituted in the new area. Nothing of further interest was turned up. The amount of time that had elapsed since the shooting and the volume of traffic in Seabank Road since meant that there was little point in trying to find DNA traces on anything left in the street to help with finding the killer. The only useful thing was the gun, which was subjected to forensic examination to ascertain its provenance. Unfortunately there were no fingerprints on the weapon.

Peter MacPhee arranged for every householder in Nairn to receive a letter appealing for information and posters were displayed throughout the town bearing a photo of Mr Wilson and a telephone number to call. Witnesses came forward to tell of sighting a man on the Stagecoach bus between Inverness and Aberdeen. He was described as tall, but otherwise fitted the description of the wanted man. Cops were told that on the night of the murder he had left the bus at Nairn a short time before the shooting.

On 14 December, MacPhee appeared on the BBC's *Crimewatch* programme. He walked down the steps from the front door of the Wilson family home in Nairn, describing the suspect and the route along which he made his escape, assuming he had gone directly to Seabank Road. The detective asked the public to come forward if they had knowledge of a possible motive or of what could have been in the envelope. He asked if anyone knew anything about the gun or the identity of a person who fitted the description of the suspect. He also mentioned the Crimestoppers reward. Veronica appeared on the show, as did Alistair's sister Jillian and his parents Joan and Alan. They made heartrending personal appeals.

Jillian described her brother. 'Alistair was an ambitious, hardworking man. A lot of people knew him and respected him. He just adored his wife and doted on his two wee sons. When I heard the news I was at my home in Australia. I jumped on a plane the next day and was able to be with my family who are just so distraught at the moment. None of us know why this has happened. It is just a complete and utter mystery.'

His mother Joan said, 'Veronica has lost her husband. These boys will never have a Daddy that they will remember because they are so young. Not only that, but they have violated their home which they feel they are not happy to go back to. It means a complete upheaval in every way. And we have lost our only son.'

The following day, police said between thirty and forty calls had been received between the studio and Inverness HQ and that new leads had opened up as a result. In particular, a witness had come forward to say he had seen a person carrying a blue envelope close to the murder scene. Also police requested that someone who had phoned Crimestoppers anonymously make contact again. In the days that followed, police announced that the man on the Stagecoach bus had come forward and been eliminated from the inquiry, as had the person carrying the blue envelope.

A memorial service for Alistair was held in St Ninian's Church in Nairn. Veronica Wilson made an appeal to the media to respect the family's need for privacy. In deference to the inevitable interest of the press and public she agreed to speak to the press later that day and she read out the following statement:

Three weeks ago, my life was torn apart. All of us are still coming to terms with what happened on that night and we are still asking questions. Our lives since then have been an emotional rollercoaster. Every day we are asking who, we are asking why, and we are asking what for? These questions will haunt us for the rest of our lives.

'Al and the boys had a great Christmas last year and I wish I had known it was to be our last. I don't know what the next few days will hold in the run-up to Christmas, as it couldn't be further from all of our minds. We need to be together now as a family, without the bond that held us together and the boys will have to accept they are to spend their first Christmas without their Dad. I pray the police find the man who did this to my family. Only then will our questions be answered.

I thank the people of Nairn for their messages of support. I now ask that everyone allows me and the boys to begin to rebuild our lives and try to move on. My family and friends have been a huge support, although a lot of them have been as shell-shocked as me. The boys need a future and a Christmas and that's what is holding us together. At the moment we are only taking small steps forward. The who, why and what fors are the only things which will enable us to move forward.

The older child is more aware than the younger one that something's wrong. But we haven't discussed guns, killing and death so I am not sure how much he [the older child] fully understands. I would appeal to anyone who knows anything to come forward. It's unreal. I don't know why anyone would do this to us, but for our two young boys we need to know why.

MacPhee said the caller to Crimestoppers had rung again and the operator had obtained more information which was of interest. However, he appealed to the caller to speak to him directly. He believed there was still useful information he could get from that source and he assured the caller that their discussion would be in the utmost confidence. He also asked for members of the person's family to be in touch as he thought they too could have useful information.

Tests on the gun for trace elements were unsuccessful. Results came back from the lab on evidence collected at the scene of the shooting. DNA had been extracted and steps were taken to eliminate about 250 people who were at the scene legitimately, including those who had gone to the aid of the dying man and members of emergency services. In early February 2005 they were contacted and asked to attend at Nairn police station voluntarily to give mouth swabs for DNA comparison purposes.

Information was still trickling in. The occupants of a light-coloured Honda CRV 4x4 reported in the Lodgehill Park area of Nairn were asked to come forward. Police had been told a man had been behaving in an agitated manner on the evening of the murder.

On 13 April 2005 Peter MacPhee made a second appearance on *Crimewatch*. This time the focus was his appeal for help from the public to identify anyone who might have had the gun. After the programme, DCI MacPhee said around two dozen calls had been received.

Police contacted the makers of both the gun and the ammunition used in the shooting. Detective Inspector Gordon Greenlees followed up those contacts. He travelled to Germany and the Czech Republic to meet with the manufacturers. The gun is just four and a half inches long and weighs under 400g. It is a .25 semi-automatic Schmeisser pistol that had been manufactured by C. G. Haenal Waffen of Suhl, in what was then East Germany, between 1922 and 1925. The ammunition had been made in Vlasim, Czechoslovakia between 1983 and 1993. There were two possible sources of the gun. It could have been a Second World War trophy smuggled into the UK, or it could have been legally imported before the ban on handguns imposed in 1997, after the horrific Dunblane school massacre. It would not be the weapon of choice of a hit man. Normally a gun used by the criminal fraternity would have had its serial number removed. The gun used to shoot Alistair Wilson still had its serial number intact.

The manufacturer was able to say that about 40,000 examples of this type of gun were made and that there had been one legitimate importer in the UK. The importer had ceased trading many years ago and the owner of the business had since died. Diligent detective work traced the owner's grandson in the south of England. Surprisingly, after all these years, he still held the records dealing with his grandfather's business in his loft and he willingly made these available to the police. Once again, MacPhee's team were hopeful they had a starting point for a new thread of investigation that could lead them to the killer. There was a chance that the original buyer of the gun could be traced. If police followed changes of ownership by sale or inheritance, they might find the person who had used it to kill in Nairn.

The ledgers in the attic detailed the serial numbers of every gun the firm had imported and sold and the name and address of the buyer. In a wicked twist of fate, however, there was a ledger missing. One ledger contained serial numbers earlier than the one on the gun; the next one contained later serial numbers. The murder weapon may not have been listed in the missing ledger, but the cops had drawn a blank. Again. Every time they thought they were onto something it didn't materialise.

The response to the *Crimewatch* programme resulted in follow-ups over the whole the UK, as far distant as the Channel Islands, as police tried to find out who might have used the gun. Although DNA and trace evidence had not been found on the weapon, MacPhee disclosed that some DNA evidence collected at the scene did not match the DNA of anyone known to have been in Crescent Road on the weekend of the shooting who had been checked. It might belong to innocent parties, but equally it might provide a crucial link to the killer.

A year after the killing, MacPhee remained in buoyant mood, insisting that the killer would be caught. He said, 'I am confident that we will, in time, solve this murder. I remain convinced that the information we are looking for is in our system, because of the wide scope we set for the inquiry at the outset.' The motive has however remained elusive.

Theories abounded. Police interviewed about twenty men who shared the dead man's name, working on the possibility that the banker was killed as a result of mistaken identity. There was nothing in any of their backgrounds that pointed to a possible motive.

Alistair Wilson's working life was scrutinised. He had been a new business manager in the bank. Could the killer have been a failed businessman out for revenge? Someone he had refused a loan or whose business had failed? Had there been a colleague who might have borne a grudge? That theory was quickly dismissed as Alistair, in his last conversation with his wife, had said that he didn't know the caller at the door, the man who moments later took his life. There would be no reason for him to deny knowing someone who was a business contact. Could the crime have its roots in passion – could the killer have been obsessed with Alistair or jealous of him?

Bearing in mind that most killers come from within the family of the victim, Veronica had to be considered. Imagine, if you can, how it feels to be bereaved in these circumstances and then suffer the additional burden of the police and the media suggesting that you are the perpetrator. Veronica must have found this as hard to bear as Sally Clark, the English lawyer wrongly convicted of murdering her sons, or the parents of Madeleine McCann, the little girl who disappeared during a family holiday in Portugal. At least each of them had a spouse to support them. Fortunately for Veronica Wilson, it didn't take police long to discount her as a suspect.

Another theory put forward was that Alistair had declined to help the IRA launder money. Just three weeks after his killing, £26 million was stolen from the head office of the Northern Bank in Belfast in an audacious robbery that had obviously been carefully planned. The IRA is believed to have been generating around £30 million pounds a year from counterfeiting, robberies, extortion, racketeering and smuggling. That money would need to be laundered, but Alistair Wilson's job in the bank would not have given him opportunities to get involved in money laundering. Then of course there was the source of the gun and ammunition. Did that point to the involvement of organised crime from eastern European?

The dead man was a respectable person whose life was split between his family and his work. He had been ambitious, a genial host and helpful to others. His friends could not think of anything in Alistair's life or personality that could have resulted in his violent death.

A theory that seemed to gain credence for a time, as the inquiry was about to scale down, was that Alistair had borrowed £50,000 from loan sharks to fund a business venture for which he couldn't raise funds through legitimate means. The loan sharks then tried to blackmail him to help with money laundering and when he wouldn't or couldn't co-operate they killed him. But like the other theories, this one didn't hold water.

By midsummer 2007, other lines of inquiry were more or less exhausted. There were about 10,000 people entered in the records on HOLMES and of them about 6,000 were male. In November 2007, on the third anniversary of the killing, MacPhee disclosed that eighteen DNA profiles had been identified on material found at the scene of the shooting and that seventeen of these had been eliminated. The one that was still being investigated was found on a cigarette stub found close to the Wilson home in Crescent Road. The DNA on the cigarette stub was identified as belonging to a male.

MacPhee was keen to have further DNA testing done in an attempt to discover if the profile found at the scene could belong to the offender. DNA testing is expensive and police work has to be carried out within a budget so it was necessary to whittle down the numbers of men to be tested. The budget wouldn't stretch to testing 6,000. Criteria were used to create a matrix focusing on those who were more likely to be the offender. Points were given for men who lived in or within fifty miles of Nairn; men who had some contact with the dead man; men who had previous convictions for assault or firearms offences. About 1,300 men were scored highly enough in the system to warrant further investigation and the go-ahead was given to test their DNA.

The next six months were spent contacting these men and obtaining samples. Some of the men were not aware that they were on a database relating to the inquiry and were surprised to be contacted. When the letters were going out asking them to attend a 'surgery' to give a sample, debate was raging in the press about human rights versus a national DNA database. Scotland's legislation, unlike England's, allows people to provide their DNA for a particular inquiry only and to ask that it be destroyed thereafter. If the donor agrees, it can be left on the national database.

The advantage to an individual is that if their home is burgled their DNA can quickly be eliminated from the subsequent inquiry.

Some men objected to giving a sample on principle; others wanted to seek legal advice before giving it; others didn't read the letter properly and failed to understand what was wanted of them and why. Further approaches made by members of the investigation team resulted in a high rate of co-operation. About ninety-five per cent gave voluntary assistance. In other similar appeals in the south about twenty per cent have come forward. Nonetheless, at the end of the exercise, about seventy men had not been eliminated. Police had to keep in mind that these men were not suspects. If the DNA sample was matched it was always possible the owner would be someone who had been in Crescent Road quite innocently on or before the day of the shooting.

Police were faced with finding ways other than DNA of discounting these men as potential suspects. Family members, work colleagues and bosses would have to be interviewed. When this was explained to the men, some changed their minds about giving a sample and co-operated. At the end of the exercise there were only two or three men left who could not be eliminated from the inquiry by any means available. If this was crime fiction, police would be lurking in the local pub where these men drink, ready to snatch a bottle or glass with their DNA on it. Real life doesn't work that way. MacPhee prefers not to be too specific on exactly now many people are still in the frame but he says it is now a waiting game. If any of these men offend, their DNA will be taken and compared with the unidentified sample. Controversially, if any member of their family offends, familial DNA can also be used for comparison.

Sixty-three officers worked on the inquiry at its height and by the third anniversary seven were still dedicated to following up, working out of the police headquarters in Inverness. Later the team was cut to two. The Portacabin in Nairn is long gone.

Police cannot continue to investigate the case indefinitely when there are no leads to pursue, but until the killer is caught it will remain open. As the investigation wound down Mrs Wilson said:

'As time passes and both boys get older, the questions are more frequent and harder to answer. I have no answers to the questions, Who shot Daddy or Why did the bad person shoot Daddy? I would plead again that if anyone has any information that might help answer these questions, please contact the police, no matter how insignificant they feel the information may be. Someone knows something and I would say to them, please don't let another year pass without answers. I would like to thank everyone for their continued support and their co-operation with the inquiry.'

Inevitably, Northern Constabulary have come in for criticism for their failure to 'crack' this case. In their defence, they took the step of issuing a fact-sheet detailing the work that had been carried out in the investigation into Alistair Wilson's murder by May 2006. It read:

Statements taken during the inquiry so far:	3262
People interviewed:	4121
DNA Samples taken:	219
People checked whose name is Alistair Wilson:	19
Names fed into the system:	8242
Documents recovered during inquiry:	1680
Vehicles checked:	1730
Officers currently working on the inquiry:	19
Officers initially working on the inquiry:	63
Actions for officers during the inquiry to date:	7723
Computers forensically examined:	Over 30
Productions seized:	924

Two years after the killing, Northern Constabulary's Chief Constable Ian Latimer expressed his frustration at the lack of progress and said he was determined to bring the killer to book. He remains so. The puzzle is still unsolved and the officers involved in the investigation share Latimer's frustration. The police still have no clue as to why Alistair Wilson was shot.

The Wilson family live every day with the result of this mysterious violent death. When Veronica and her boys were taken into protective custody immediately following the shooting, police had to take a statement from the older boy who was potentially a crucial witness. By the Wednesday after the shooting, there hadn't been an opportunity with all that was happening. It was decided that the best way of drawing information from Andrew and of telling him his father was dead would be to have him interviewed by a child psychologist, with Veronica present. It was decided that the interview would be video-recorded.

In the run-up to the first anniversary of the murder, police sought opinion on whether they should use the recording in an attempt to reach someone who had information and was not coming forward. There must be someone – a wife, brother, or father – who knew what had happened and why. There were strong views both for and against using the video recording, but the consensus among psychologists was that it would be better in the long run for Andrew to think that he had helped the investigation. In the knowledge that release of the recording would provoke some disapproval, MacPhee's team went ahead. Sensitive to the feelings of the Wilson family, they didn't want the recording replayed on the news every time there was a mention of the killing – for example on an anniversary or if there were any developments in the case. They therefore took exceptional precautions. Two documentary programme producers were given the tape to use, only after signing a contract binding them to show the tape only once no matter how often their programme was repeated. Reporters who attended the morning briefing where the tape was shown had their cameras and mobile phones removed.

At the briefing, the tape-recording of Veronica's 999 call was played and the videotape of the interview with Andrew was shown. There were about twenty-five media hacks present. Usually the press vigorously seek answers to their questions throughout a press conference. For the first time ever, after the material was

played, there was total silence. What follows is a short extract of
the transcript of Andrew's interview.

Psychologist: And so where did Daddy go then?
Andrew: To the hospital.
Psychologist: And what do you think has happened now?
Andrew: Still in the hospital and I think he's OK.
Psychologist: Do you think we should ask Mummy if he's
                   OK? Mmm? Do you want to know if he's OK?

Andrew nods his head.

Psychologist: What do you think Mum?

Veronica acknowledges with a nod of the head.

Psychologist: Sweetheart, you need to come and sit and have
                   a cuddle with Mum. 'Cause Daddy isn't OK.
                   You know when you said you heard that big
                   bang? And that Daddy was shot?
Andrew: (*sitting on Veronica's knee*): Yes.
Psychologist: Well, Daddy's not going to come back.
Andrew: Why?
Psychologist: Because the shot made him dead.

Andrew begins to cry.

9

WHERE ARE THEY NOW?

On the cold, dark evening of 12 November 1976, a bus driver spotted a blazing car in a lay-by on the A9. This is the main road leading from central Scotland to the Highlands. The burning vehicle was on the southbound carriageway, about fourteen miles south of Inverness, at Dalmagarry. A disused quarry of the same name lies a few hundred yards away. Even in 1976, Inverness, capital of the Highlands was not immune to car crime.

Fire crews damped down the blaze as Constable Jimmy MacLean watched. His immediate concern was for the occupants of the vehicle, but there was no sign of anyone in or around the car, a blue BMW with the registration number JAS 219P. Constable MacLean was soon called away to deal with another matter in the town, an assault with a glass. Other officers at Northern Constabulary HQ in Inverness checked vehicle records and discovered that the car belonged to H. MacRae & Company Ltd, a well-established local building firm and a major employer in the town.

Although the car belonged to the company, it was always driven by thirty-six-year-old Christine Catherine MacRae, known as Renee, the estranged wife of well-known local businessman Gordon MacRae, who ran the business with his brother Charles. The couple had married in 1963 but the marriage had become unhappy. For a time they had lived separate lives under the same roof in a house in upmarket Drummond Crescent. Finally, in 1974, they had gone their separate ways. Renee now lived in a luxury bungalow in Cradlehall Park, a new Inverness housing development.

Petite, attractive Renee had told her husband she was driving south to Kilmarnock for the weekend to visit her sister, Morag Govans. She was taking three-year-old Andrew with her. The couple arranged that Gordon Junior, then nine years old, would stay with his father over the weekend. Renee would be back in plenty of time to collect him from school on Monday afternoon.

When Gordon MacRae Senior was told about the discovery of the burnt-out car he phoned Morag Govans and discovered that Renee and Andrew weren't in Kilmarnock. At first he was unconcerned. He had suspected Renee's story of going to visit her sister was a cover because he had known for years that Renee had a lover. He was about to be shocked when he discovered who the lover was. By this time, Gordon MacRae was already living with his secretary who subsequently became his wife. He was supporting Renee and the two boys financially, providing her with a top model car and her new home. MacRae told police he thought Renee had parked the car somewhere and gone on to her destination in another vehicle. It looked as if the BMW had been targeted by joyriders. The remains of the car were transported from the lay-by to a garage in Inverness's Longman Industrial Estate.

Morag Govans and Renee's best friend Valerie Steventon were not surprised either at the tale Renee had told her estranged husband. They too knew about Renee's lover. Valerie and Renee had been best friends since they were five or six years old. Their families had lived across the road from each other in Beauly. Their friendship had grown as they grew, with shared interests, firstly in dancing classes and cycling, through school, first jobs, marriage and starting a family. When Valerie heard about the car on the Saturday afternoon she was concerned but didn't think for a moment that anything dreadful had happened to her friend. She knew Renee loved her car and would be heartbroken that something had happened to it. She thought Renee was going to come back after her weekend away to find the car gone. Valerie drove through the Longman Industrial Estate to find out how badly the car had been damaged. She was horrified when she saw the burnt-out shell of the BMW up on a ramp in a garage.

On Sunday, 14 November, anticipating her friend's distress at the loss of the car, Valerie put a note through Renee's door at Cradlehall Park, telling her friend what had happened. She then drove south down the A9, hoping to catch Renee coming home. There was no sign of the lover's car.

Morag Govans and her sister Renee spoke to each other on the phone every Sunday and, when there was no call from Renee, Morag instinctively knew that something was very wrong. She called Valerie Steventon, who told her that Renee was safe. But Valerie knew more than she was letting on, and as the day went on, she began to wonder. She was in a quandary. Her friend had confided in her about where she was going and with whom. She felt it would be betraying Renee's trust to say more to anyone – even to Morag Govans. She expected Renee and Andrew to return to Inverness, safe and well, at some time over the next twenty-four hours. Renee would be home to collect young Gordon from school, of that she was certain. Valerie decided to keep her knowledge to herself for the moment.

Monday morning dawned and Valerie rang Renee's phone number. She received no answer. At intervals throughout the morning she tried the number over and over again. She had been anxious to tell Renee about her car but as time passed she became more worried about her friend. Where were Renee and Andrew? She went to the railway station in Inverness and met trains coming in from the south, expecting Renee and Andrew to come off one of them. Monday afternoon came and went with no sign of her friend and no message from her. Valerie Steventon became very concerned. During the day she had even phoned the home number for Renee's married lover and to her surprise the man himself had answered. Valerie hadn't spoken, but had simply put the phone down.

She didn't know what to make of it. She knew her friend to be reliable and considerate and she was sure that Renee would never have neglected to make contact if she had been unable for any reason to get back to Inverness to collect young Gordon. If anything had delayed her she would have been frantic. There was only one explanation – Renee and Andrew MacRae had disappeared. Valerie Steventon phoned Morag Govans and told her that she should report Renee and Andrew missing.

The following day, the police were gearing up to search for the missing young mother and her child. By now Gordon MacRae was also expressing grave concern for their safety. The unspoken thought of all those who knew Renee was that something terrible had happened to her and little son. She had left her older boy behind, something she would never had done had she been going to run away to a new life. Valerie Steventon says Renee just lived for her boys. No one regarded her as a suicide risk and she had no history of mental illness so it was highly improbable that she had taken her own and Andrew's lives.

Detective Superintendent John Cameron led the initial stages of the murder inquiry, although it wasn't labelled as such for a long time. The cops told the press that 'no crime had been committed', but in reality they were treating Renee and Andrew's disappearance as suspicious. From an early stage of the inquiry the police had information that only came into the public domain very much later.

The massive search for Renee and her son, alive or dead, started around the lay-by where the car had been found. Renee's description was widely circulated. She had been wearing a light-coloured sheepskin coat when she was last seen. Police appealed for any sightings. Experts from Grampian Police forensically examined the car and debris left in the lay-by using the scientific expertise available in 1976. Unfortunately the activities of the fire crews in the lay-by and the recovery vehicle would have destroyed or corrupted much of what might nowadays, with scientific advances, have been vital evidence. The trail was already around forty-eight hours old by the time the inquiry got under way.

Police leave and courses were cancelled and experts from other forces arrived in Inverness to help. Members of the Scottish Crime Squad (set up to assist all eight Scottish Police forces in defeating serious crime) were called in. A sub-aqua team from Stirling were engaged in searching the reservoirs, lochs and lochans.

Northern Constabulary officers were heavily involved. Many of them put in fourteen-hour days, searching, interviewing and collating information. The incident room was a large hall at Police HQ in Inverness usually used for courses or badminton.

Concrete foundations, cellars, attics and incinerators were examined. A BMW expert examined the car as well as the forensic scientists. Cops made a public appeal for information and disclosed that they were both puzzled and concerned. Their efforts were not limited to the extensive search and interviewing witnesses: they even consulted a Swiss clairvoyant.

Renee's last known movements on the day she vanished were pieced together. At first a ten-hour gap was unaccounted for between the last sighting of Renee and the discovery of her car. Then it was discovered that she had dropped into MacRae & Company's main office in the late afternoon and the gap narrowed. Gordon MacRae named his wife's lover publicly and said that when the police told him who it was it had been a bombshell to him. It was Bill McDowell, the company secretary and accountant at MacRae & Company, someone he had known for years. He felt betrayed. The connection between the two families extended beyond Bill McDowell; there were other McDowell family members who worked for the company. Immediately, Bill McDowell was fired.

About a week after Renee's disappearance, to the surprise of the police, McDowell walked into Police HQ. He said he wanted to speak to detectives voluntarily. Before he could do so his wife turned up, marched into the interview room and dragged him away, telling the cops to leave him alone. Had he been about to confess?

Meanwhile the search for Renee and her little boy went on. A sighting was reported of a man wearing a Mexican-style moustache in Renee's car, seven to ten days before she had vanished. This led to an appeal from the police for information about his identity and the release of a photofit image. A man had been seen on the night Renee's car was found, standing beside a parked car on the Shenachie side turning, just south of Dalmagarry. His identity was the subject of another appeal.

The Highlands is a vast area and even when a search can be focused fairly narrowly there are difficulties. The terrain is rough, uneven and often waterlogged. Some of the areas near the lay-by were heavily wooded and to compound the problems the weather was wintry, with lying snow potentially masking any area where the ground had been disturbed. The nearby army base at Fort George supplied about seventy soldiers from the King's Own Scottish Borderers, swelling the ranks of eighty local police. Two helicopters were used in the search.

Members of the public responded to an appeal from Donald Henderson, the Chief Constable, for help in the search and they turned out in large numbers. The Chief Constable thanked them, saying it was 'heart-warming' to get such a response. He instructed the searchers to apply the same diligence they would if they were searching for their own wife or small child. They were told to look for anything – a button, a buckle, a hankie – and to take it slowly and keep together as they combed the area.

Urged to do so by Provost Ian Fraser, civic head of Inverness, Gordon MacRae offered a reward of £1,000 for information regarding the whereabouts of Renee and Andrew. This was a considerable sum in 1976. Publicising the reward, MacRae stressed that he had been on very good terms with Renee. Although they had been apart for two years, he said, they had attempted a reconciliation during that time. He added that he was very concerned about her welfare and that of young Andrew, saying he was 'sick with worry'.

Bill McDowell was questioned about the weekend away he was purported to have planned with Renee and Andrew. He admitted that there had been such a plan, but said that it hadn't come off.

He said that he and Renee had a system of phone signals – silent calls with a certain number of rings – but that he had not received the necessary signal. He also revealed that he had received two such signals since Renee's car had been found ablaze and that one of them was when the police were in his house. This was significant evidence, as it suggested that Renee was still alive at that point. McDowell was questioned several times but remained adamant that he had no knowledge of the whereabouts of the missing pair.

The search went on. Renee's house at 4 Cradlehall Park and the MacRae & Company offices were subjected to a thorough examination. A total of 533 houses in Inverness, including over 100 at Cradlehall were searched, along with sheds and garages. More than 200 statements were taken. Many employees of MacRae & Company were questioned in the first two weeks of the inquiry.

A Canberra bomber from RAF Strike Command used 'Spy in the Sky' cameras to scan a fifteen-mile length of the A9. Searchers on foot completed the search close to the A9 and began combing side roads. Any search for a body in the Highlands, unless it is for a hill-walker or a climber, is generally focused on areas close to roads and tracks. The reasoning behind this strategy is that it would be difficult for a killer to carry a body across rough ground. It seemed unlikely that Renee and her small son would voluntarily have gone off-road for any distance.

Appeals to the public continued, both for volunteer searchers and for information. Cops said that a blue pushchair, which was normally in the boot of Renee's car, was missing. Two weeks to the day after Renee was believed to have set off to drive south, a checkpoint was set up to speak to drivers as they passed Police HQ. By this time, cops had a report of the last sighting of Renee by two witnesses, shortly before 5pm on 12 November. The missing hours before the burning car was seen had now shrunk to five.

By 24 November, the case had been designated a major crime inquiry and Detective Inspector Donald McArthur was given charge of a ten-strong team of detectives, boosted by two officers from the Scottish Crime Squad to continue the investigation. All crofters, and others living in the area, received a letter asking them to search all outbuildings. The searches by soldiers of the King's Own Scottish Borderers at Culloden and south of Dalmagarry Quarry continued. The quarry was also searched. Later events suggest not thoroughly enough.

The area already searched was revisited by a team comprising two geologists, shepherds and gamekeepers from the area and men experienced in tracking. They were looking in particular for any trace of freshly turned soil. It was hoped that they might spot what others had not. The inquiry team did not let up and soon had chalked up 5,000 interviews, but there was no breakthrough. The searchers were really looking for a needle in a haystack, but the haystack was enormous. Although it made sense to concentrate on the area close to where the car was found, there was a five-hour window from when Renee was last seen till her car was found. In that time a killer could have covered a lot of ground and potentially have disposed of bodies as far away as Caithness, Aberdeenshire, Wester Ross or Perthshire and still have had time to get back and set fire to the car.

Then two men contacted the police, saying they were heading for a nearby pub on the night Renee's car was found. They reported seeing a man dragging a heavy bundle towards Dalmagarry Quarry. They had though it was a dead sheep. Next, a couple that had been driving on the A9 reported seeing a man walking along the road in the dark, wheeling a pushchair.

Eventually the inquiry ran out of steam and officers were moved on to other cases, but there was always a willingness to reopen the inquiry if new evidence came to light. In 2000 there was speculation that remains found in a wood near Bonar Bridge could be Renee and Andrew but police quickly discounted the possibility. The remains were those of an adult male who had died two years before his body was found.

In 2001, the case was revisited when the residents of Greystone, a tiny village in Angus revealed that a man who matched the photofit picture issued in 1976 had lived there briefly. Locals described a man who kept his curtains permanently closed even though his house was remote from others and who dug up his garden under cover of darkness. They said that he left without warning the day after the photofit appeared in the press. The Greystone residents had taken a long time to pluck up the courage to speak. They were fearful that Renee and her son had been buried in the garden. The police took the information seriously but they found nothing to connect the strange resident of Greystone with Renee MacRae and her son.

In 2004, the case featured on a television programme, Scottish Television's *Unsolved – Getting Away with Murder*. Retired Sergeant John Cathcart, one of the cops involved in the initial inquiry, appeared on the show, and spoke openly about his suspicions. He told how on the Tuesday, just four days after Renee's car was found, he and a squad of eight men were searching Dalmagarry Quarry. The quarry, which was close to the lay-by where the car was found, was being infilled with waste from road works on the A9. The company engaged in the work offered to cease their operations but were told to carry on. The following day, the Wednesday, senior officers directed Cathcart and his men to search elsewhere.

Four months later, Cathcart was again searching at Dalmagarry Quarry, this time using a small tracked scraper – a tractor with a digging arm and bucket attached to it. In his work as a cop, Cathcart had come across bodies in various stages of decomposition and he said the smell is very distinctive. At Dalmagarry in April 1977 he noticed such a stench. The scraper driver, Hamish Borthwick, had noticed it too – he had been so affected by it that he jumped off the vehicle. Cathcart said that although he reported this to his senior officers, the search of the quarry was called off. He said that in 1976 or '77, a constable or sergeant would be aware of his place in the pecking order and would not dare contradict or face up to senior officers.

Incidentally, this view would be upheld by retired Detective Inspector Angus Chisholm, one of the senior investigating officers in the Mahmood murder case (see Chapter 4, 'A Position of Trust').

He confirms that the culture in the old days was not only that the lower ranks would not speak out boldly but that even if they did, they were unlikely to be heard.

Chisholm tells the story of an incident he attended when he was a young detective constable based in Inverness. A report came in of a stabbing at a pub in Baron Taylor's Street in the town centre. The victim was dead.

On his way to the scene, Chisholm passed a car that had collided with a fence. A bar from the fence had gone straight through the windscreen and out of the back of the car. He stopped, found the driver was drunk and called his uniformed colleagues to attend. When he arrived at the scene of the stabbing, he quickly realised that the description of the killer fitted the drunk driver. He tried to tell senior officers that he had the man in custody but they wouldn't listen. Their refusal to take an interest continued to the extent that he felt he had to dash back to the police station to ensure the drunk wasn't released. Later, the killer's knife was found, with his name on it, and Chisholm told his senior officer, Andrew Lister, that he had a man of that name in custody. Only then did his superiors pay any attention.

By 2004, all the senior officers involved in the MacRae inquiry had retired from the force. Cathcart said he remained convinced that Renee and Andrew had been buried in Dalmagarry Quarry.

Brian McGregor was among those who watched the *Unsolved* programme and he immediately took a keen interest in the case. He is a farmer at Bogbain, on the southern outskirts of Inverness, just a few miles from Dalmagarry. A veteran campaigner on issues such as planning and corruption, he is well known locally for his dedication to these causes. Later that year, when the news broke of Alistair Wilson's shooting (see Chapter 8, 'Resort to Murder') he was so absorbed by the case that he went off to work on the farm without his packed lunch. When his wife berated him for it, he responded that he had been thinking of other things. He now had two murders to solve.

McGregor was troubled by what he had heard John Cathcart

say on the *Unsolved* programme. He soon shared Cathcart's conviction that Renee and her son were buried in Dalmagarry Quarry.

McGregor visited the quarry accompanied by Cathcart and a diviner named Piercy Phillip. Using his divining rods, Phillip found what he believed could be a burial site close to the quarry's access track. McGregor offered to provide an excavator used in his peat business so that Cathcart could dig in the quarry – unless Northern Constabulary investigated themselves. The location identified by the diviner's rods was some 200 metres away from where Cathcart had reported noticing the smell during the search in April 1977. The men decided that publicising a second possible burial site might throw doubt on the quarry as Renee and Andrew's resting place, so they kept quiet for a time. They were also worried that there would be scepticism over the involvement of a diviner. They approached the owners of the quarry, but were not given permission to dig there.

Undaunted, McGregor began a campaign to pressure police into searching the quarry. He spoke to the media and launched a website. He also attached large, very visible signs to the side of a Land Rover, which he parked on his farm, immediately adjacent to the A9. Whether as a result of McGregor's campaign, the *Unsolved* programme, or quite independently, a cold case review started in December 2003. In August 2004, a massive ten-week project of digging in the quarry began. It was to cost £112,000.

About 1,800 trees grown since 1976 were felled to restore the quarry as nearly as possible to its 1976 state and then the excavators went in. Over a five-week period, parts of the quarry were excavated and victim recovery dogs were used. Professor Sue Black of Dundee University, an expert in forensic anthropology, was called in to advise. She had been a pupil at Inverness Royal Academy in 1976 and had known of the case since then. Professor Black had been involved in war-crime investigations in Kosovo and Iraq and, closer to home, had worked with Northern Constabulary to reconstruct the face of a man whose remains were found in Migdale Woods. It was her work that led to his identification, following a *Crimewatch* programme.

Professor John Hunter of Birmingham University was also on hand to advise. He had been involved in the search for the Moors Murderers' victims in 2001, and also had experience of assisting police homicide investigations in the UK, Iraq, Kosovo and the Balkans. His expertise was in guiding the digging operation so that it was carried out in a methodical and systematic way to make sure no area was missed.

At the end of the dig, Professor Black told the press that nothing had been found but a couple of crisp packets and some rabbit bones. She said that they had dug out the quarry to the original face, so that if there had been anything to find it would have been discovered. She mentioned that there was a competition advertised on the crisp packets with a closing date in 1976. She said they had found the trench where John Cathcart had noticed the smell of something akin to decomposing flesh but that no human remains had been uncovered. Professor Black admitted that everyone involved was disappointed, but that their disappointment would be nothing compared to that of the family and friends who longed for the opportunity to give Renee and Andrew a proper burial.

The quarry search had failed to turn up new evidence, but Northern Constabulary's Chief Constable, Ian Latimer, made a statement. He indicated that new information had come out of the review. He said that it had examined other lines of inquiry and that the police had new intelligence. He also said that he believed that the bodies had been in Dalmagarry Quarry at one time.

One of the lines of inquiry involved Gordon MacRae Junior being asked to give a DNA sample, another was a forensic re-examination of Renee's car. It had been kept at Dingwall Police station since 1976. What could DNA tests prove? Were there traces of blood in the car? Were police looking for confirmation that they belonged to someone related to Gordon MacRae Junior? In December 2004, excavators found a credit card with the name R. MacRae at a house at Island Bank Road, Inverness. Could this have been one of the clues police were putting together?

Latimer reported to the Police Board that there was a lot of information not in the public domain. It is easy to get the impression that one piece of the jigsaw is missing and if that was ever found Renee and Andrew's killer would be brought to justice. That piece is most likely the bodies of Renee and Andrew.

Probably prompted by fresh media interest in the case, an anonymous letter was sent to an Inverness newspaper. It claimed that five people, including a policeman who the letter said was the 'brains', had conspired to murder Renee. The letter said that Andrew was alive and living abroad. Police said they were sceptical and did not want to expend resources tracing the author. For reasons the police have never publicly acknowledged, they did not believe the letter was anything but a hoax.

John Cathcart and Brian McGregor responded to the absence of bodies in the quarry, saying that they believed that the wrong part of Dalmagarry Quarry had been searched. McGregor wrote regularly to the *Inverness Courier* on the topic of this case and he even advertised for information. In 2006, he was contacted by Eddie Tocher, a roadman who had worked on rebuilding the A9. Tocher now lived in Glenrothes, Fife, but had been told about McGregor's letters in the *Courier*. Sections of the A9 road were being replaced in 1976 under a contract that straddled the period of Renee's disappearance and the following year. It was the spoil from these works that was being used to level Dalmagarry Quarry in 1976 and 1977. Tocher told McGregor that one night he had knocked off work, leaving an area about a mile south of Dalmagarry Farm graded with a heavy roller. When he returned the next day the ground had been disturbed. He believed that it was the night of 12 November 1976. He had mentioned this strange discovery to his foreman at the time.

McGregor interviewed the man and adjudged him to be a credible witness and he followed it up by tracking down the foreman, William Traill, who was living in Milton Keynes. Traill remembered the incident too. Both men pinpointed the area where the disturbed ground had been – in the middle of the road. McGregor arranged to have the area scanned by a friend with a hobby-type metal detector. It must have been a bit like a farce as the A9 is busy with fast-moving traffic. McGregor and his companion would have been constantly rushing to the side of the road to allow vehicles to drive by. The metal detector picked up signals from the ground. There had to be something metal there. Could it be Andrew's missing blue pushchair?

McGregor went to the police with the information. They interviewed Eddie Tocher and showed him photographs of the area so he could indicate where he had seen the disturbed foundation works. The cops were reluctant to dig up the A9, so McGregor engaged his own team with more sophisticated scanning equipment. The scan found anomalies in the target area. There were three items buried about two metres down. Brian McGregor passed the scan report on to the police.

Then McGregor's A9 theory was disproved. Plans of the road replacement were discovered, showing exactly when work was carried out on each part of the road. The section of carriageway that had been disturbed, as observed by Tocher and Traill, had not been worked on till the year after Renee and Andrew disappeared. Unless the bodies were moved a year after their disappearance then the disturbance of the A9 was a red herring.

What was the information the police were keeping up their sleeves? Who did they think had killed Renee and Andrew? Statistics prove that most murders are committed by someone known to and usually in some relationship with the victim, and in the case of a woman, most likely her husband or partner. Gordon MacRae would have been the first and most obvious suspect. He insisted that he was on good terms with Renee. He was supporting her and the two boys financially, had set her up in a new house (although it remained in his own name) and had provided her with a car registered to his company. If she had been pressing to divorce him he would have had to come to a financial settlement with her. The accounts lodged with the Registrar of Companies for 1976 show that it was not a good year for his business. MacRae & Company returned a loss of just under half a million pounds. It would not have been a good time to be sued for divorce. Valerie Steventon says that Renee was quite happy with the financial arrangements with her estranged husband and had not taken legal advice to begin divorce proceedings.

If Gordon MacRae had just discovered the identity of Renee's lover, and other facts about their affair that could have been a possible motive. Could she have told him on the afternoon of 12 November, when she visited his offices? It was possible that he could have reacted violently to the news. Murders have been committed under much less provocation. But Gordon MacRae's shock seemed genuine when he discovered the identity of his wife's lover. He was himself in a new relationship and in any case he had an alibi for the evening when his wife and her little boy disappeared.

Could the killer be Renee's lover, Bill McDowell? He lived with his wife and family at Herdmuir House, Nairnside at the time. His relationship with Renee had been going on for four years. For part of that time, Renee had been living under the same roof as Gordon MacRae. Renee had confided to Valerie that Bill planned to leave his wife and make a life with Renee and her sons in Shetland. He said he had secured a job and a four-bedroomed home for them there. He had even described the house in detail to Renee.

When he was questioned after Renee and Andrew disappeared, McDowell admitted the affair. He also revealed a secret that fundamentally affected the facts of the case. He was the father of Renee's younger son Andrew. Having come clean about that, he denied that he had any intention of moving to Shetland with Renee. If she believed that, he said, it was a figment of her imagination. McDowell too had an alibi, for most of the five-hour time gap between the last sighting of Renee and the discovery of her blazing car. His wife, Rosemary, had decided to stand by him, and she provided it.

However, on the evening of Monday, 15 November 1976, Valerie

Steventon had spoken candidly to the police about Bill McDowell's relationship with Renee and had given them key information. Over a period of months, she was interviewed many times and reiterated what she had said in that first interview. She believed that Renee had been besotted with McDowell, but was not sure that McDowell was equally committed. Renee had told her about her plans for the weekend of 12 to 14 November. She said that McDowell had arranged a trip to a hotel at Rannoch, Perthshire, and had told Renee it was to enable him to start building a relationship with Andrew, in preparation for the move to Shetland.

On reflection, Valerie believes he wanted to have both Renee and Andrew as he planned to dispose of them both. It didn't make any sense otherwise. McDowell had been a regular evening visitor to the house at Cradlehall Park. He and Renee were discreet in their affair and were never seen together in public. Young Andrew already knew and recognised Bill McDowell. He was beginning to say 'Dada' when he saw McDowell. McDowell and Renee had been away for a weekend together once before. At that time, Andrew had been left with Valerie Steventon and her family, while Gordon Junior stayed with his father. Why not this time?

When police searched the house at 4 Cradlehall Park, they discovered that in one room things had been packed into boxes, apparently in readiness for departure. Renee had lived at the house for two years and she hadn't been living out of packing cases. Valerie Steventon's story fitted the known facts.

What motive could Bill McDowell have had for murdering Renee MacRae and his own three-year-old son? If Renee was planning an imminent move to Shetland – as the packing cases suggest – then she would have been disappointed to discover that it was not going ahead. McDowell would likely have anticipated this. He could expect that she would react badly to the news. It might well cost him his marriage and his job.

In October 2006, a report into the review of the case went to the Procurator Fiscal, who passed it on to the Crown Office. Cops thought there might now be enough evidence to start a prosecution. The Chief Constable had spoken of 'closing the evidential gap' shortly before the report was submitted. But it wasn't enough. In December 2006, the Crown Office said there was to be no prosecution. No one has yet been arrested. The cold case review cost almost £250,000.

Media and public interest in the case have not petered out. In 2007, the year that John Cathcart died, Dalmagarry Quarry was visited by two mediums, Jo Brocas and her husband Jock. Jo told a newspaper that they both felt there was nothing in the quarry linked to Renee and also that Renee had never been there. However, this is contrary to what police now believe. Jock believed there was nothing left at the quarry to help hunt down the killers. Jo said that a voice – Renee's, she believed – told her that she had never been to the lay-by where the car was found. People had been paid to kill her and had taken her then dumped the car where it was found later.

Gordon MacRae's has life moved on. He divorced Renee quietly in 1980, using the procedure available when a defendant's whereabouts are unknown, and married Vivienne the following year. They have a daughter. Gordon MacRae Junior was sent to boarding schools and then, after a short time at college in Edinburgh, worked in his father's offices. He now works as a storeman in another business in Inverness. Morag Govans lives in Inverness. Valerie Steventon lives near Inverness. They will all go to the end of their days bearing the scars of what happened to Renee MacRae, each in their own way.

Bill McDowell, now sixty-seven years old, lives in London. Inverness people remember the fires that seemed to follow him, destroying financial records at firms where he worked as an accountant. These included Ben Motors, Muir of Ord, Blue Circle and Logan Construction in Inverness. None of these fires resulted in a prosecution. One police officer commented, 'In the old days, that kind of thing would have got the person responsible the sack. The police wouldn't have been involved.'

After McDowell was fired from MacRae & Company he bought

a pub in Peebles called The Crook Inn. By the late 1980s, he was again working as an accountant, this time for Stancroft Securities, a company based in London. In 1990, he was charged with offences of dishonesty and forgery, the total sum he allegedly misappropriated just under £240,000. His former employer raised a case in the Scottish Court of Session, hoping to recover the money lost through McDowell's dishonesty, using a procedure which ultimately would have forced the sale of a substantial home McDowell still owned at Nairnside, near Inverness. It is believed that this was not the only time McDowell was brought to court. His mother, who continued to live in Inverness, died recently. McDowell did not return to Inverness for her funeral.

Where are Renee and Andrew now? As time goes on, it becomes less likely they will be found. Their killer is ageing and will inevitably be beyond the reach of the criminal justice system in due course. Morag Govans has set up a memorial to Renee and Andrew MacRae. It is a bench placed in Kirkhill Cemetery, on the outskirts of Inverness, the cemetery where Renee and Morag's parents are buried. Only one person knows where the bodies are and that person isn't talking.

10

DID HE FALL?

In February 1997, June and Hugh McLeod of Wick suffered every parent's worst nightmare. The reverberations shook the town and, indeed, the whole county of Caithness, and they are still echoing there today. June and Hugh's twenty-four-year-old son Kevin hadn't come home from a night out on Friday, 6 February and his Mum immediately knew something was seriously wrong. Kevin just didn't stop out overnight. If he was to be late home he always phoned. Occasionally he and his fiancée, Emma Sutherland, would babysit overnight, looking after her brother's children, but he always told his parents in advance. On this weekend, Emma was visiting Glasgow for a fitting on her wedding dress. She was to be married to Kevin in May.

Kevin was a steady, dependable lad. He was a qualified electrician but in 1997 he was working as a labourer at Wester, just outside Wick, at a pipeline fabricator's yard. Kevin had no history of involvement with drugs or violence. He wasn't a heavy drinker either. At Hogmanay he was always the designated driver, driving his cherished Cosworth car, while other family members enjoyed a dram to see in the New Year. His father was a welder, also working at the pipe fabrication yard, and in his spare time a singer with Remix, a well-known local band. Kevin's mum worked as a care assistant in a local nursing home. He had two younger brothers, Andrew and Martin, who were then eighteen and twenty-two years old respectively. Until February 1997, the McLeods were an ordinary family living in Nicolson Street, Wick, getting on with ordinary lives. But events in the early morning of 7 February changed that forever.

Wick is a small town of less than 10,000 inhabitants on the north-east coast of Scotland. Its older buildings are constructed using grey local stone. These are circled about with modern housing, much of it local authority. The town clings to the steep-banked mouth of Wick River, which ebbs and flows into the often dramatic, seething North Sea. In the nineteenth century, Wick was a premier port of the herring fishing industry, then at its height. In the 1860s, the lighthouse engineer Thomas Stevenson (father of the famous author Robert Louis Stevenson) was engaged to design and oversee construction of a breakwater. This was intended to extend the shel-tered haven for herring boats beyond the existing harbour. But the North Sea tides proved too strong and his project failed. The end of the abandoned breakwater is still visible and until recently an estate agent's 'for sale' sign, planted there by some local wag, marked it as a hazard to shipping. Nowadays, two bridges join the north and south parts of the town that lie on either side of the Wick River. The harbour lies to the south-east of one of the bridges, called 'The Service Bridge', and is within the town centre. Houses, shops and commercial premises line one side of the road, the quay is on the other.

The town has its share of crime, including assaults, some serious, but sudden death at the hands of another is very rare. Wick's older folk remember an incident back in the 1970s when a lover's tiff ended tragically. A young woman stabbed her boyfriend, was convicted of culpable homicide and went to jail for twelve years.

When June McLeod rose on the morning of Saturday, 7 February, having not heard Kevin come in the night before, she peeped into his bedroom. She was surprised to see the empty, unslept-in bed. She spent the morning expecting Kevin either to phone or to arrive back at the house for a shower and change of clothing. At noon, June had an appointment to have her hair done but she had a strong sense that something was wrong. She was reluctant to go out and cancelled the arrangement. She tried to justify to herself the lack of contact from Kevin, while replaying the events of the previous night in her mind.

Kevin and Emma had recently been given tenancy of a council house in a relatively new estate on the south side of Wick, in Thistle Park. Kevin had spent the early part of Friday evening fitting new lights in the house. June had been there with him, to clean the house and help prepare it for furnishings. Kevin hadn't planned to go out that night. He was in the shower when his best friend Mark Foubister phoned from Carter's Bar, a lively venue at weekends and one of the key locations for young people social-ising in Wick. He asked June was Kevin up for a game of pool. June commented to Mark that it sounded like a party in the back-ground. When she heard Kevin come out of the bathroom, she called him to the phone. She heard him agree to go out. Mark would collect him in his car. As Kevin stood chatting to his mum, waiting for Mark, he pulled a wad of notes from his pocket and counted out some money. This was the sum due to a neighbour who had painted and decorated the house in Thistle Park.

He asked June to pay it over the following day. It was such a foul night of wind and rain that he didn't want to go to the neigh-bour's house and get soaked and he didn't expect his mum to do so either. June recalls suggesting Kevin wear a jacket but he just shrugged. He obviously thought he would be ferried to and from the house in Mark's car at the start and end of the evening. Just before 10pm, Mark called in at the house and the pair left.

The following day, trying to find an explanation that would fit the situation, June McLeod thought it was just possible that Mark, a car buff like Kevin, had decided to change his car and the pair had taken off for Aberdeen or somewhere else for the purpose. Mobile phones were still rare in 1997. Kevin didn't have one and if the boys were on the move a stop to make a phone call might have been an unwelcome diversion from the purpose of the trip.

By afternoon, Kevin hadn't returned and there had still been no phone call. Kevin's brother Martin was a typical, almost nocturnal, teenager, who had been at home playing video games with a friend late into the night. When he got up, he told his parents that Mark Foubister had called at about 3am and had asked if Kevin was home. He had even asked Martin to check his bedroom. Hugh and June spent Saturday afternoon trying to track down Mark Foubister, thinking that if he wasn't with Kevin he would most likely know where he had gone when they parted company.

It was nearly 6pm before they found Mark Foubister at his brother's house. When they asked where Kevin was, Mark put his head in his hands and said, 'Oh, no,' then promptly ran back into his brother's house. Hugh and June guessed from this that Mark suspected something had happened to Kevin and they believe to this day that he has held back information.

Both Kevin's parents were very concerned by now and Hugh called at the local police station to check that his son was not in the cells, although such a thing would have been totally out of character. Kevin had never been involved in anything that could lead to trouble with the police. When Hugh received a negative response he reported Kevin missing. The police told him that Kevin had to be missing for twenty-four hours before they could take any action, so the McLeod family immediately started their own search. June's younger brother Allan McLeod travelled north to Wick from Alness, about seventy miles away, to help in the search. When June and Allan's mother had died, June had taken him in, until he married and had a home of his own. When Kevin had worked for an electrical firm in Alness, he had lived with his uncle. Allan was particularly close to Kevin, Martin and Andrew, like a big brother.

Over the course of Saturday evening Emma phoned several times from Glasgow, obviously wanting to speak to Kevin. Seeing her number on caller display, Kevin's parents decided not to answer. What could they tell her? June was privately thinking that maybe Kevin had spent the night with another lass. By this time the improbable was becoming a possibility and it was easier to explain her son's absence away with something like that rather than the unthinkable.

On Sunday, 8 February, police mobilised to search for Kevin and they quickly established that he had been seen in the harbour area in the early hours of Saturday morning. As word of the search got around, a local cop who was off duty phoned in to report a sighting. He and a colleague had passed Kevin as they drove round the area in a police vehicle in the early hours of Saturday morning. There was nothing about Kevin at the time to make them suspicious so they simply drove past. Next came a report from the harbour nightwatchman, Richard Ewart. On his security checks he had twice seen Kevin slumped in the foetal position on the quayside opposite the Harbour Café. When he next checked the harbour area Kevin was gone. The cops called in a local diver, Gary Connor, to search the bottom of the harbour, close to where Ewart had seen Kevin. At 11am a body was found.

A local uniformed constable broke the news to Hugh and June McLeod. He told them that a body had been found, that they thought it was Kevin's and that there were definitely no suspicious circumstances. On their scant examination of the body, police saw that the button flies on Kevin's jeans were undone. They surmised that he had taken too much to drink, had felt the need to urinate, had gone to the edge of the quay for that purpose and had fallen in. All of that was perfectly reasonable, perhaps. However, it seems more likely that if he had been caught short in that location, he would have gravitated towards the buildings rather than the water's edge. Several men asked about this have all answered that in that situation they would not have gone to the edge of the quay.

The local cops made no preliminary examination of the body looking for obvious injuries before sending it south to Raigmore Hospital in Inverness for post-mortem. This was in accordance with the normal practice in Northern Constabulary at the time. Today, the mysterious death would have been treated as murder until evidence established there had been no foul play. There was no examination of the quayside as a possible crime scene, no early attempt to find witnesses to Kevin's last minutes by carrying out house-to-house and other inquiries. No steps were taken to preserve forensic evidence. The clothing Kevin wore that evening was lost or destroyed, apparently inadvertently. It is well known that the first hours after a crime are the most important in detection. In this case, these hours were frittered away.

Not surprisingly, the McLeod family was in a state of shock. The death notice printed in the next edition of the local paper, the *John O'Groat Journal*, reported that Kevin had died 'Tragically, as a result of a drowning accident'. However, when Dr Roslyn Rankin, consultant pathologist at Raigmore Hospital, began the post-mortem on the morning of Tuesday, 10 February she soon discovered that although the primary cause of his death was drowning, Kevin had suffered very serious abdominal injuries, injuries of a severity that might have been the result of an assault. She ceased her examination immediately.

In suspicious deaths, bodies are subject to a post-mortem by two pathologists instead of one so they can give corroborating evidence in court as is required by Scots law. This is vital should the death lead to a prosecution. Dr Rankin reported her preliminary findings to police immediately. The Procurator Fiscal based at Wick at the time, Alasdair MacDonald, immediately upgraded the case to a full-blown murder inquiry, and told police it should be given the 'full works'. Detective Sergeant Richard Martin, based in Wick, was put in charge of the inquiry.

The McLeod family now received a fresh shock. It was bad enough that their son was dead, but murdered . . . When the news came out, the report of a murder in their midst rocked the people of Caithness – much as it had in other Highland communities mentioned in this book. Bodies fished from Wick harbour are more likely to be suicides; there have been two since the body of Kevin McLeod was found. Wick sees very few incidents arising from serious crime. The most remarkable examples in the past twenty years were probably when an armed robber from England was arrested by armed police in a local hotel, and when a yacht involved in drug smuggling was brought into the harbour after it was impounded by Customs and Excise.

It was only a matter of days before DS Martin concluded that Kevin had fallen over one of the decorative bollards around the harbour and that this had caused his injuries. He sent photographs of the bollards to Dr Rankin, presumably suggesting to her that this had caused Kevin's severe injuries. (She did not visit the harbour herself – that would not be normal practice.) Her post-mortem report shows that she and her colleague T. J. Palmer completed the examination of Kevin's body. Their joint report, dated 24 February, records severe internal abdominal injuries, including a ruptured spleen, injuries to the liver and arterial tears. Kevin's ribs were intact. The conclusion of the report is that Kevin died from drowning, having suffered a major abdominal injury consistent with falling onto an object such as the bollards found at Wick Harbour. A faint abrasion was noted but the report states that the most likely source would have been the rope used to help lift the body from the water. Kevin's blood alcohol was measured at 153 micrograms per 100 millilitres – almost twice the limit for driving. He hadn't been driving, of course, but he had had a great deal to drink that evening – and this was a young man who was not a habitual drinker.

The post-mortem report also contains information from police reports regarding Kevin's whereabouts during the hours imme-diately before his death. The report shows that at this time the cops were aware that on the night he died Kevin had been involved in a heated dispute in the Waterfront, a local nightclub to which the town's youngsters migrate when the pubs close.

When the Waterfront nightclub closes, many people use taxis to make their way home or to parties, and taxis would be buzzing round Wick's streets in the early hours, about the time of the last sightings of Kevin alive. Allan McLeod asked Sergeant Martin if he had spoken to taxi drivers who were working that night. He insisted that he had, but within an hour of that conversation, Allan discovered this was untrue. He happened to be talking to one of the taxi-firm proprietors, who was also a driver. The taxi driver had begun the conversation by expressing sympathy, and by sheer chance Allan mentioned that he would have been questioned. The driver assured Allan he had not been approached by the police. The McLeod family concluded that the case was closed as far as Sergeant Martin was concerned. Still shocked, the family began to doubt that a proper investigation was being carried out. They became upset and angry.

In May 1997, having been told very little about the investigation, June and Hugh McLeod sought an appointment with the local Procurator Fiscal. Family liaison officers were yet to be introduced and at that time there was no methodical system or channel for providing information to victims' families. The senior investigating officer usually assumed the role of keeping the family informed.

At that meeting with the Fiscal, June and Hugh discovered for the first time the severity of their son's injuries. Mark Foubister had told them about the altercation in the Waterfront and had also revealed that the other person involved was Craig, a colleague of Kevin's working at Wester. They had reported this to DS Martin but were dismayed to discover that there had been no attempt to track down Craig among the fairly small workforce at Wester. This drove another nail into the coffin of the McLeod family's confidence in the police.

Hugh McLeod was working for the same employer at Wester and in June he easily managed to find out that the Craig of the incident was Craig Stenhouse. Hugh approached him and asked why he hadn't come forward to speak to the police if he had done nothing wrong and had nothing to hide. Shortly after their conversation, Stenhouse did go to the police and made a statement voluntarily.

Then, in July 1997, an article was published in *Scotland on Sunday*, which expressed the McLeod family's dissatisfaction at the investigation into their son's death. Shortly after publication, and perhaps as a result, Detective Inspectors Peter Black and Angus Chisholm, both normally based in Inverness, were assigned to investigate what was by then a cold case. They were backed by a team of junior officers, including local CID. At last, door-to-door inquiries were made in the harbour area and witnesses from the original inquiry were questioned again.

Ronald Hutchison, a taxi driver, had told June and Hugh that he had seen Kevin in the town centre with blood on his face and they passed on the information to the detectives. Eventually Hutchison admitted he had made this up, but investigating this allegation had taken up about a quarter of the resources of the second investigation into Kevin's death. As a result of that second investigation, the officers believed that Kevin's injuries were a result of his having fallen onto the *Gunnhilda*, a fishing boat moored at the quay, close to where his body was found. The bollard theory was discredited. There was no evidence discovered to indicate that any other person had been involved in Kevin McLeod's death. Again the case file was closed. Police took the view that all known lines of inquiry had been pursued, thoroughly explored and exhausted.

In September 1998, a Fatal Accident Inquiry (FAI) was held into the circumstances surrounding Kevin McLeod's death. In cases of sudden death, the Procurator Fiscal may make a recommendation to the Lord Advocate that there be an FAI. There is always an FAI when death results from an accident at work or occurs in custody, but otherwise it is discretionary. It is Scotland's closest equivalent to an inquest held before a coroner in England and other jurisdictions. The purpose of an FAI in cases like Kevin McLeod's is to decide how and when death took place. Sometimes at the end of an FAI, if it is appropriate, the sheriff will make recommendations to prevent a similar incident in future. This inquiry took place in Wick Sheriff Court and was presided over by the resident sheriff, Ian Cameron. Sheriff Cameron heard of Kevin's movements on the fateful night.

The second investigation carried out by DI Black and DI Chisholm had discovered that Kevin was involved in not one but two incidents at the Waterfront. The first involved another work colleague of Kevin's from Wester, one William Woods, now himself deceased. The second was that involving Craig Stenhouse. It seemed that the latter argument had begun when Kevin insisted that he hold his pint and Stenhouse declined to do so. The conversation had become heated. Stenhouse had allegedly pushed McLeod and punched him in the face, but not heavily enough to cause an injury that would have been revealed at the post-mortem. Stenhouse and Woods both said that the incidents ended amicably and in neither case were the bouncers involved. This suggests that the disturbances were short and that none of the participants' behaviour merited their ejection from the nightclub.

Mark Foubister was probably drinking at the same pace as his friend and when he gave his evidence at the FAI his recollection of this part of the evening was confused. He said he remembered calming his friend and trying to defuse one situation but couldn't recall which. He described how he and Kevin had left the Waterfront at 1.30am. They had taken a taxi to Loch Street, where they had planned to go to a party, but on arriving in that part of the town they decided instead to make their way back to the town centre on foot. Witnesses, including police passing in a car, saw Kevin stumbling and vomiting en route.

At Market Square, in the centre of town, where taxis then gathered in an informal rank and a kebab van catered for late-night revellers, Mark Foubister chatted to a taxi driver while Kevin sat on the window ledge of one of the shops nearby. After a time, Kevin set off alone, walking back towards the Waterfront in a direction that would take him to the Service Bridge and his route home. A short time later, Mark passed over the Service Bridge in a taxi with a young woman, but neither of the two passengers nor the taxi driver saw Kevin along the route. The taxi driver returned to the town centre by the same route in reverse and didn't see Kevin then either.

However, several people had seen Kevin that night in the area of the Service Bridge and the harbour, including the cop who later reported having driven past him. Calum Donn, a local fisherman, had seen Kevin sitting near the edge of the quay where the harbour nightwatchman also saw him. Donn had called to Kevin but received no response.

The medical evidence given at the FAI described faint bruising on Kevin's abdomen. This had probably been caused by the rope used to help lift Kevin's body from the water. There were two areas of injury, one of which was over the lower ribs. Dr Rankin thought that both abdominal injuries resulted from one event. However, Dr McFarlane, a consultant pathologist who represented the McLeod family at the hearing, believed that they could have been caused by two separate incidents. However, neither pathologist could be sure how the injuries had been sustained.

There was no evidence at the FAI of anyone who had seen an assault upon Kevin or any people close to him as he made his way from Market Square to the quay where Ewart, the nightwatchman saw him. A group of people who remained unidentified were seen in the vicinity of the town's swimming pool, which lies close to the southern end of the Service Bridge.

The sheriff's determination following the FAI was issued in September 1998. Sheriff Cameron found that the injuries sustained by Kevin could be explained in one of three ways. Kevin may have fallen on one of the bollards; he may have fallen from the quay onto the *Gunnhilda*; or he may have been seriously assaulted. Sheriff Cameron said he was not satisfied from evidence led at the FAI that the source of Kevin's injuries had been established. In his consideration of the evidence he was of the view that the injuries Kevin suffered, along with his intoxication could have contributed to his having fallen off the quay. He might have gone to the edge of the quay to urinate, felt faint and fallen into the water as a result of the injuries – but this presupposes that the injuries were sustained before the fall. Therefore they could not have been caused by his falling onto the *Gunnhilda*.

Sheriff Cameron's findings were critical of the scope of the initial police investigation, the lack of door-to-door inquiries, the failure of the police to identify Craig Stenhouse at an early stage and interview him, the failure to involve senior officers and the rapid conclusion of the first investigation. He also said that even had the investigation been carried out thoroughly and timeously there was no certainty that the result would have been any different. He was highly critical of Ronald Hutchison, the taxi driver who had reported having seen Kevin in the town centre bleeding profusely and who later admitted fabricating his whole story. Sadly there are many tales of people who tell fabricated stories to the police for no sensible reason. This is one of the reasons why the cops need to be circumspect about disclosing full information about a crime, even to those nearest to a victim. It can help to winnow out fantasy from fact in witness statements or purported confessions.

The solicitor representing the McLeod family asked the sheriff to recommend that Wick Harbour Trust be required to have additional nightwatchmen or to carry out more frequent patrols, but Sheriff Cameron considered that the harbour area was adequately illuminated at night. He added that people who drank too much had to accept some responsibility for themselves.

At the beginning of the FAI, Hugh, June and Allan McLeod and other family members were seeking answers. They were looking for closure, but sadly that was not the outcome. All they were left with were unanswered questions. They had hoped that the sheriff's open verdict would prompt the police to reopen the investigation but more than ten years later that has not happened. So Hugh, June and Allan McLeod have felt compelled to take matters into their own hands and carry out their own investigations, even though they lack the resources of the police force.

Iain Grant is a local journalist who has followed the case from the start and reported on it at length in the local press. He has said that the police made up their minds what had happened and 'squared the circle' to make the facts fit. Many people in Wick share the view of the McLeod family that Kevin McLeod was the victim of a vicious assault.

In 2001, Northern Constabulary invited forensic pathologist Dr Nathaniel Cary to examine the forensic evidence. Cary, based in

London, was a recognized expert. Two years later, he would be a key witness in the murder trial of Ian Huntley, killer of the Soham schoolgirls Jessica Chapman and Holly Wells. Information and photographs were provided to Cary. He dismissed totally the theory that a fall onto one of the bollards could have caused Kevin's injuries. He also concluded that it was improbable there was a third party involved. He said that Kevin had most likely fallen into the water having struck part of a creel and possibly then the gunnel of a fishing boat, the *Aurora*, as he fell, sustaining severe injuries. The theory now was that bruises on Kevin's abdomen matched the pattern on creels that are used by local fishermen.

Cary does not seem to have seen a creel, nor even a photograph of one, though three pieces of creel net were forwarded to him by the police. However, his findings indicate he is familiar with its basic structure – a net stretched over an inflexible steel frame. His report still leaves some unanswered questions. If Kevin had fallen from some height onto a creel, striking parts of his upper abdomen, would he not have suffered broken ribs? Dr McFarlane had reported that one of the areas of bruising was over the lower left ribs, but they were intact. None of the medical professionals have commented on this point. One earlier theory was that Kevin might have struck the MV *Gunnhilda* on falling from the quay. Now it was the MV *Aurora* that he was believed to have struck. The *Gunnhilda* was not creel-fishing in 1997. The *Gunnhilda* and the *Aurora* were moored about 25ft apart along the harbour quay on the night Kevin died. His body was reportedly found midway between the two boats and boatmen have told the McLeod family that Kevin would have gone straight down to the bottom of the harbour when he fell in the water. If that is right he could not have had a glancing blow off either boat.

Retired Glasgow detective Les Brown carried out his own investigation into the case and discovered even more compelling evidence. The skipper of the *Aurora* – who had bought the boat shortly before the tragic events of February 1997 – told Brown that according to his log he didn't have any creels on the boat till 11

February. If that is right, there were no creels on either the *Gunnhilda* or the *Aurora* at the time of Kevin's death. In the documents sent to Cary, sketches of the *Aurora* are listed as having been made on 19 September 2001. This would not reflect the gear that would have been on board on 9 February 1997.

In a small place like Wick, there is much gossip and speculation. Kevin's family have been given bits and pieces of information from many sources that have suggested lines of inquiry. They have diligently reported these to the police but so far there has been no new inquiry. June and Hugh don't wear rose-tinted spectacles when speaking of their three sons. They have tried, as honestly as they can, to think of anything that Kevin might have been involved in that could have made him a target for a severe beating. The obvious possibility would have been drugs. They are absolutely convinced that Kevin didn't use drugs. Even though Wick is far from the big cities of Scotland's central belt, it has its drug dealers and its addicts, who are often involved in crimes to fund their habit. There is, as in many places, a climate of fear that protects dealers from detection and many people may claim to have short memories when asked directly about those involved in supply.

When Les Brown visited the town in 2003 he discovered that even by then, two years after Cary's report, the police had not interviewed the skipper of the *Aurora*. He also found two women who in his opinion were telling the truth and who held vital evidence. One of them said she had seen Kevin receive a kicking from three men at the harbour. She identified one of them in enough detail to enable Brown to trace him. According to Brown, she had retracted her statement when local police told her that if she persisted in it her children would be taken into care. The second woman said a man had confessed to her he had killed Kevin saying, 'I have done something tonight I will regret for the rest of my life. I killed Kevin.'

In 2007, June and Hugh McLeod took part in a television programme called *Psychic Detectives*, in which three well known psychics use various skills they claim to have to help discover what happened in cases like this one. While many people may be sceptical even the police have used psychics on occasion to help in an investigation. Hugh and June were astonished at the extent to which what they were told matched the known facts.

The programme's production team say that the psychics are given no information about the case in advance and there is no reason to disbelieve that. Psychic Tony Stockwell described Kevin being hurt and then put in water. He said that a man named Michael was involved and so was a bouncer, a bald, older man. He described a witness who had come forward and whose evidence had been largely ignored. Stockwell said that Kevin had got sucked into something because of a young woman. He said Kevin was not afraid of saying what he thought and his outspokenness may have led to a beating, but that there had been no intention to kill him.

Stockwell travelled to Wick. On touching Kevin's cherished car, his Cosworth, he said that there had been three bags in the boot and that Kevin had carried them somewhere. He also spoke of men smuggling from a boat. He described three men involved in the attack on Kevin, with another man sitting back watching.

The second psychic, T. J. Higgs, also said that there was a female involved in what happened and that Kevin had done what he did to protect her. She described pain in Kevin's stomach like feeling winded, and unusual markings like a tread. The police investigation was hurried, she said. It was a cold night and the cops were keen to get back into the warmth.

Colin Fry was probably the best known of the three TV mediums participating in the programme. He used psychometry to give a reading, a process that involved holding something that had belonged to Kevin. He said he saw Kevin walking home in a deserted area, head down and his being attacked and later put into the water.

Although there has been no further investigation into Kevin's death, there have been two independent investigations into the police involvement in the case. The first was into Northern Constabulary's handling of the initial investigation, and the second focused on their manner of dealing with the McLeod family. The first was carried out, as procedure demands, by a senior cop, independent of Northern Constabulary. Andrew Cameron, Chief Constable of Central Scotland Police, was appointed. At the start, to ensure the candour of low-ranking officers, they were given an undertaking that no disciplinary action would be taken against them. The report, which was finalised in 2003, criticised the initial inquiry and the way the family had been dealt with. Cameron made recommendations of disciplinary action against senior officers, including Deputy Chief Constable Keith Cullen, whose correspondence with the family in dealing with their complaints was effectively intended to fob them off. Cullen refused to take part in a Police Board hearing and retired days before it was due to take place.

He is not alone. A Scottish newspaper used the Freedom of Information Act to discover that over a five-year period, twenty-seven cops had avoided disciplinary action by retiring. The Scottish Police Commissioner has since recommended that the Scottish Parliament look at setting up a procedure to prevent officers dodging disciplinary proceedings by retiring and taking their full pension rights. This would apply particularly to cases when the disciplinary actions, had they proceeded, might have led to the officer been demoted, or even dismissed with loss of pension entitlement.

Naturally, the McLeod family wanted to read Cameron's report, but Northern Constabulary blocked access. It was only after an appeal to the Information Commissioner, Kevin Dunnion, and a wait of about four years, that it was released to them. When they finally saw it in 2007, large swathes had been blanked out to comply with the Data Protection Act.

As a result of Cameron's report, police procedure for dealing with a sudden death has been reviewed and all deaths in similar circumstances to Kevin's should now be dealt with in a different way. The revised police manual says, 'Upon receiving a report of a sudden death, the officer attending will approach the inquiry from the perspective that a crime has, or may have, been committed.' If there is the slightest suspicion of a crime having been committed, the investigation should escalate immediately. A senior officer is to be involved, while the body, the scene and any potential items of evidence are treated as if a trial could follow. Lessons have definitely been learned.

A further investigation into the handling of the case was carried out by the Scottish Police Complaints Commissioner, Jim Martin. He described the force's dealings with the McLeod family as 'institutional arrogance'. As a result, Hugh, June and Allan McLeod met with Ian Latimer, Chief Constable of Northern Constabulary, in December 2007. At this meeting, he made an apology on behalf of the force. The McLeods were hopeful after this meeting that a new inquiry into their son's death would be initiated. So far, however, no new investigation has started, despite pressure from the local MP John Thurso and MSPs contacted by the family.

Psychiatrists say, and experienced police officers know, that parents who lose a child may never accept that it was an accident. Even if a comprehensive and diligent investigation concludes that death was caused by accident or suicide, some parents simply will not or cannot accept the conclusion. There are still many unanswered questions in the McLeod case, however, and few parents would be content to leave things as they are. It is a great pity that this inquiry went off the rails at the start. A great deal of time, money and energy has since been spent analysing what went wrong with the inquiry. Those resources could and should have been devoted to discovering the truth of whether Kevin McLeod fell or was pushed into Wick harbour.

11

STRANGER THAN FICTION

Not everyone who lives in a decent flat in Glasgow would dream of also owning a house in the Highlands, but that was the dream lived by Willie MacRae. His house at Dornie, Kintail, near the Kyle of Lochalsh, could not have been more different from his flat at 6 Balvicar Drive, Queens Park. The flat was well within the enormous conurbation of Glasgow and only a couple of doors away from a hostel that frequently housed former prisoners and oddballs. At the end of his street is the public park that gives the name to the area. In May 2008, years after MacRae lived there, the park was the scene of the brutal murder of Moira Jones, a forty-year-old sales consultant. MacRae's second home in Dornie – with the river running by the bottom of his garden and the silence broken only by birdsong – was his escape from sirens screaming at all hours in the city.

Willie loved his house in the north and escaped there as often as his other commitments would permit. On Easter weekend 1985 he set out towards his usual destination. His luggage included a briefcase with business papers he planned to work on while away. The manager of an off-licence where he was a regular customer was one of the last to see him as he prepared for the 170-mile trip. Willie bought a couple of bottles of his favourite Scotch and was in ebullient form. Donald Morrison, a cop who knew Willie well, saw him coming out of the off-licence, spoke to him and watched him drive away.

Willie had made the journey so often that the car would seem to drive itself. He should have arrived well before midnight on the Friday. His route would take him up the A82 road to the junction with the A87, where he would have turned westwards towards Dornie on the road that also led in those days to the Kyleakin ferry to Skye. He would pass close to Rattigan, where Iain Simpson picked up his second victim (see Chapter 2, 'Not Mad Enough') and travel through Inverinate, the tiny village where Fiona Torbet died (see Chapter 6, 'The Ladies' Man').

It was mid-morning the following day when Australian holidaymakers spotted MacRae's Volvo halfway down the slope between the road and waters of Loch Loyne. The observant pair saw that there was someone in the car and they clambered down the difficult, tussocky, wet, sometimes steep slope to take a closer look. They found MacRae unconscious in the driver's seat. Had he been there all night? No one saw him in Dornie, though it is possible that he had arrived at his home there and turned back again for reasons we will never know. There are no streetlights adjacent to Loch Loyne and if it had been an overcast night then many cars may have passed by without noticing Willie MacRae's car. That part of the A87 runs through a bleak and isolated part of the Highlands and in the north, old cars taken off the road as bothies for shepherds were not an unusual sight.

In 1985, few folk had a mobile phone so the next car to come along was flagged down to summon help. The Australians must have been relieved when one of the people in the next car told them she was a doctor; Dr Dorothy Messer from Aberdeen. Accompanied by one of her fellow travellers, she slipped and slithered down the slope to give what assistance she could till an ambulance arrived. David Coutts, her companion, was a Scottish National Party (SNP) councillor from Dundee. He noticed an SNP sticker on the car as he approached and when he got a look at the man inside he was shocked to recognise Willie MacRae, a man who was something of a hero in SNP circles.

The state of the car was consistent with it having rolled. The rear windscreen had popped out and was between the road and the car.

The driver's side window was either shattered or fully rolled down. The car was tilted over towards the driver's side, making it impossible to open the driver's door more than about a foot. The only injury visible was on MacRae's right temple. His thick hair was matted with blood and dried stains showed where blood had coursed down the right side of his face. Dr Messer climbed into the front passenger seat to better reach the injured man. The focus of those on the scene was, naturally enough, to preserve the life of the injured man, but David Coutts observed what he described later as a small, neat pile of papers and other items about twenty feet from the car, between it and the road. He said it included a bill from a Kyle of Lochalsh garage and MacRae's watch.

The local policeman attended and quickly assessed the scene as a road traffic accident. He concluded the driver had either lost control of his vehicle coming off a bend or had fallen asleep at the wheel. He reported accordingly. A single-manned ambulance arrived and with the help of the passers-by the paramedic recovered MacRae from his car, via the front passenger door, and transported him to Raigmore Hospital, Inverness. There MacRae was assessed as having a head injury. In accordance with the usual arrangements he was transferred urgently to Aberdeen Royal Infirmary, where the neurology department would be able to give appropriate treatment.

Soon after his arrival in Aberdeen, doctors diagnosed the unexpected cause of MacRae's head injury. A bullet was lodged in his brain. Dr Fergus MacRae, Willie's brother, made a dash to Aberdeen but the injured man never regained consciousness and he died at 3am on the morning of Easter Sunday.

Police were advised immediately the bullet was discovered and Chief Inspector Colin MacDonald was appointed senior investigating officer in what had suddenly become a potential murder inquiry. His boss was Detective Superintendent Andrew Lister, the man in charge of CID in Northern Constabulary at the time, who is a key figure in Chapter 7 of this book. Lister would have had no direct involvement in the inquiry.

Scene-of-crime officers, a production officer, a photographer and others arrived with haste at the scene at Loch Loyne and gave the locus a careful examination, looking for and recording evidence. Among other things, they were looking for the gun. Should it not be found, an armed man might be on the loose, but it was discovered at the site, in a small burn running down the hillside.

The day after Willie MacRae died, the only mention in newspapers was that he had been one of a number of victims of road traffic accidents over the holiday weekend. The usually vigilant press had not picked up on the rather more detailed inquiry that was by then under way.

Dr Fergus MacRae told police that his brother had been depressed. He was on antidepressant drugs and had been seeing a psychiatrist. He told them he believed his brother had taken his own life. Years earlier, when Willie had been in a distressed state and talking about suicide, Fergus had seen a small Smith & Wesson gun in his house. Willie told his brother he had bought it from an American while he was serving in India.

On the Thursday night before he left for the north, Willie spent the evening with his friend Howard Singerman, who says that MacRae was depressed and that the main topic of their conversation was suicide. MacRae was very worried at charges he faced for his third drunk driving offence. Singerman says he tried to persuade him to think things through over the weekend. Later that night, after a few drinks, Willie fell asleep while smoking in bed and set fire to his quilt. He put the smouldering article in the bath. The bath started to melt, giving off noxious fumes. MacRae was rescued by the Fire Brigade. It wasn't the first fire the heavy smoker had started by accident.

Ronald Welsh, MacRae's business partner, had told police that MacRae had asked him to visit him at home on the Friday morning and told him he was heading north for the weekend. He was very worried about MacRae's state of mind and when he phoned Dornie later that evening and got no reply, he phoned all police stations between Glasgow and Kyle.

The gun found at Loch Loyne was identified as being the Smith & Wesson belonging to Willie MacRae. It was unlicensed. There were no fingerprints on it, but that was to be expected because it had been lying in running water for several hours. Strathclyde Police ballistic experts forensically examined the bullet in MacRae's brain. It had been fired by the same gun. It appeared that Willie MacRae had shot himself using his own gun. In the absence of any evidence to the contrary, McDonald and his team were satisfied he had taken his own life. They reported accordingly to the Procurator Fiscal and the Crown Office and closed their files. That should have been the end of the matter.

However, to some, mostly SNP politicians and friends of Willie MacRae, this was accomplished with indecent and inappropriate haste. They saw reasons to look into MacRae's sudden death more thoroughly. The MacRae family simply wanted to lay their much-loved brother and uncle to rest and forget about the tragic end he had met, but his political friends were not satisfied. They said Willie MacRae's life was such that he would potentially have made many enemies, some of them belonging to the Establishment, including the then government, some of them in big business and some of them local criminals in the area to which he was travelling. The early closure of the case was, to them, a cover-up and they were determined to push for an inquiry. Fergus MacRae was offered an inquiry and turned it down. He and the other family members were satisfied. He must have regretted that many times since. It would potentially have laid to rest the speculation that raged for almost twenty-five years.

Who were these potential enemies? To find that out we need to discover who Willie MacRae was. He was born in 1923 and grew up in the bosom of a loving family in Falkirk with Kintail connections on his father's side. He did well at school and in the Second World War he joined the Argyll and Sutherland Highlanders. signing up while he was still underage. He served in France, where he was wounded. When his age was then discovered he was discharged.

He joined the Royal Indian Navy and spent some time there in naval intelligence. After the war, he studied law at Glasgow University and achieved his lifelong ambition to become a lawyer. Joining Abraham Levy in legal practice, he developed a strong association with the new state of Israel and wrote that country's mercantile law. He was an Emeritus Professor of the University of Haifa and after his death they created a memorial to him, such was his impact on Israel.

MacRae was an intelligent, clever man. In appearance he was distinctive – small, but with a huge personality that overrode his lack of dress sense. He was a chain-smoker. He had become involved in politics as a schoolboy. He was a leading light in the SNP for several years. His abilities as an eloquent and passionate speaker equipped him well for the role. He represented his party in four general elections and in 1979 he was one of three runners in the election for party leader. He lectured in law at Glasgow University and is remembered by students as being charismatic and inspirational, his enthusiasm rubbing off on the next generation of lawyers while they listened to him.

He was a vociferous opponent of the nuclear industry. In the late 1970s, there was a proposal to set up a high-level nuclear waste depository in Mullwharchar, a remote part of Dumfries and Galloway in south-west Scotland. This proposal was taken forward by Margaret Thatcher's Conservative government, but was ultimately rejected thanks to a successful campaign mounted by Willie MacRae and others. After victory at the planning inquiry, MacRae told supporters 'not to trust the political establishment in Scotland or Britain'. He had earlier told the inquiry, 'I suggest you put your waste where Guy Fawkes put his gunpowder.'

He had some involvement with a radical arm of the SNP called Siol nan Gaidhead. He may also have been connected with the Scottish National Liberation Army (SNLA), who are believed to have sent letter bombs to, among others, Margaret Thatcher. The extent of his involvement is disputed. Some say he played an active part in funding operations; while others say he acted professionally, only giving legal advice. Whichever it was, he told his election agent and friend, Peter Findlay, that he suspected he was being followed. His business partner Ronald Welsh believed it. At rallies, Welsh said, Special Branch officers could be picked out by their big police boots. It shouldn't be surprising that he was followed, if it was believed that he could lead security services to members of the SNLA, even if he was only providing them with legal advice.

The causes he espoused in his political life will likely have made him enemies within the government of the day. Nowadays, his telephone would be tapped and his movements watched, and maybe they were, even then. A documentary made for Channel 4, broadcast in 1992, contained allegations that Special Branch was following MacRae.

By 1981, MacRae was a partner in a law firm, Levy and MacRae, in Glasgow. His practice was mainly in litigation, an area of his life where he may well have gathered a few more enemies. Nothing gave him better satisfaction that fighting on David's side against Goliath. Giving big business a bloody nose would not be a way to curry favour with the rich and powerful. Most lawyers manage to separate the professional from the personal and are objective about the losses and victories that come to all of them. Indeed, sometimes their clients find the courtesy and good relations that exist between opposing sides discomfiting. But not all lawyers manage this, so MacRae might have had one or two enemies in legal circles as well as in the world of business.

On the face of it, he was successful in both his professional and his political lives. But sadly he was not happy in his personal life and he was drinking heavily. It is questionable whether he drank because he was unhappy or was unhappy because he drank. It seems likely the latter applied as his career seemed to be going well.

In spite of his radical views, he was well liked and respected among the SNP and he rubbed along with other members of the Glasgow bar. (Bar in the legal sense, of course, and not the public bars, though he was known to socialise with some of them there too). He was blunt and honest in his dealings and did not suffer fools kindly, though he was very caring and generous. He was liked and admired by most of his fellow lawyers, indeed he helped many to get a start in the legal profession.

Fergus MacRae, with whom he had a close relationship, was realistic about Willie's faults and he says by 1981 Willie was an alcoholic. He had already notched up one conviction for drunk driving. Then in early 1981, following a drive home from a Burns Supper during which he collided with two cars, Willie MacRae was arrested. The following day his brother visited him at home and saw, for the first time, the decorative Smith & Wesson. Willie was talking about suicide, as he had done in the past to his partners. He was clearly depressed. Fergus was very concerned about him. He took the gun from Willie and kept it for about a year, after which he returned it as he adjudged his brother's mental state better by then.

He had been given a warning by the senior partner of his legal firm on the first occasion he lost his licence for drink driving. Now, predictably, he was told to leave the firm. Both he and his partners would already have known the prosecution to follow would bring the firm's reputation into disrepute. So Willie MacRae was a man of many parts, as Scotland's national poet Rabbie Burns might have said.

He set up his own plate as MacRae & Co. with offices in Buchanan Street in the centre of Glasgow and for a time he had his drinking under control. He took with him Ronald Welsh who had trained under him at Levy MacRae, and who became a partner in the new firm. Then, in 1985, he was once again caught drunk driving, his third offence. The usual tariff for drunk driving in those days was a one-year ban for the first offence, a five-year ban for the second and then the possibility of a lifetime ban and a prison sentence for any subsequent offence. So Willie was in deep trouble. It has been said that his relationship with his partner was also going through a troubled period. Nothing has come to light to suggest that this would be anything serious. Ronald Welsh was a protégé of MacRae and wouldn't have become his business partner if the older man had not been satisfied at his abilities.

Welsh was struck off by the Scottish Law Society in November 1987, for failing to renew his practising certificate, failing to respond to complaints from former clients through the Law Society and breach of the accounts rules (the nature of which suggests carelessness of the rules but not blatant dishonesty designed to line his own pockets). Welsh said that he was so devastated by the death of his partner that he found it very difficult to carry on the business – and the decision of the tribunal to end his career as a lawyer bears this out. Had the firm been in difficulties before Willie MacRae's death, it is likely that the facts set out in the tribunal's decision would have pre-dated April 1985. They don't.

So we have a man with a high profile who undeniably had problems and enemies too; a man whose friends felt there had been a conspiracy to cover up a murder, some of their theories having more than a passing resemblance to those that surrounded the death of Princess Diana.

One story was that Willie was working on something just before his death that was going to lift the lid and embarrass the Establishment. If this was the case, there was a motive for security services to have dispatched him. Donald Morrison, the cop who spoke to him as he left Glasgow, said in that last chat Willie had been cheery. He had patted his bulging briefcase and said, 'I've got them.' What 'them' meant and what he had 'got' has never been explained.

When his friend Mary Johnston saw him just a few days before his death, he was very excited about something he had discovered. Mary Johnston and another friend, Jean Buchanan, say that MacRae's two houses were broken into shortly before his death. That might not have been unusual in Glasgow, but it certainly wouldn't have been a common occurrence in Dornie. Of the break-in at Dornie, Willie told Mary Johnston, 'They didn't get what they were looking for.'

Huge variations in his mental state were not unusual and Len Murray, a fellow lawyer and close friend from MacRae's days in Levy MacRae spoke of his mood swinging between ebullient and suicidal within a few hours. This behaviour could be explained by a diagnosis of manic depression or bipolar disorder, in which the mood swings from elation to deep depression. This seems to accord with what his brother knew of his mental health.

Nothing has come to light since Willie MacRae's death to explain what he meant in his conversations with Mary Johnston and Donald Morrison, but Morrison's assumption was that Willie was about to reveal something that would be, at the very least, shocking. As MacRae drove away on that final trip, Morrison noticed two cars following at a cracking pace, even going through traffic lights on red. It looked to him as though they were pursuing MacRae.

Did the person or people he referred to in his enigmatic remarks know that MacRae was about to reveal something? Were they ready to take steps to prevent that revelation? It was known that he was working on a book about the nuclear industry. There was also an inquiry planned into proposals to process nuclear waste at Dounreay, in which he would have played a part. His firm was down on the list as one of the objectors who would have been heard at the inquiry, which began a year to the day after his death. There is evidence that in the past, in the nuclear industry, some things were brushed under the carpet.

He might have found out about the shaft at Dounreay in Caithness built in the 1950s to allow low-level radioactive material to be discharged into the sea. In 1959, with government authority from the Scottish Office, it was used for disposal of all levels of nuclear waste until, in 1977, there was an explosion in the shaft. For a long time after the explosion, employees at Dounreay, all signatories of the Official Secrets Act, were gagged from disclosing facts about the use of the shaft or the explosion.

It is probable that the outflow from the shaft has been responsible for the many particles of nuclear waste still being found close to the site on the sea bed and local beaches, and it is certainly responsible for government expenditure running into many millions as it is 'cleaned up'. One stage of the process will cost an estimated £6.8 million. Was this what Willie MacRae had discovered? It would have been political dynamite at the time. His friends asked: could this, or something like it, have cost him his life?

There were compelling similarities between his death and that of Hilda Murrell, another opponent of the nuclear industry. Those similarities fuelled theories that the security arm of government was involved in both deaths. Just over a year before MacRae's death, on 21 March 1984, Miss Murrell had been about to appear as an objector at a public inquiry into a new nuclear power plant at Sizewell. She was abducted from her home in her own car and her body was found three days later about half a mile away.

At the time and for some years after, her death spawned even more speculation than the death of Willie MacRae. Books and films detailed various possibilities. Miss Murrell's nephew, Robert Green, had been in naval intelligence and it is understood he prepared two reports on the sinking of the *Belgrano* during the Falklands war; one for the cabinet and an edited version for parliament.

However, in 2005, following a cold case review, during which detectives re-examined DNA evidence in the light of scientific developments, the truth was established to be much more mundane. Andrew George, who was only sixteen when he committed the crime, was convicted of her murder at Stafford Crown Court. He was sentenced to life imprisonment. The killing had followed his bungled attempt to steal from Miss Murrell's house in Shrewsbury.

Anti-nuclear campaigners were targeted in other incidents around this time. The Edinburgh office of the Scottish Campaign to Resist Atomic Menace (known as SCRAM) was broken into and set alight. Dora Russell, another anti-nuclear campaigner, was attacked by two intruders in her home. Something of a pattern seemed to emerge.

The nuclear industry and the political establishment would not have been MacRae's only enemies at the time of his death. Although Dornie was then and is still a peaceful and safe place to live, the pestilence of illegal drugs had reached it by 1984. Drug dealers had moved into the area and were peddling their wares, to the dismay of locals.

A couple of local men took matters into their own hands and gave the dealers a beating. As a result, they found themselves in Dingwall Sheriff Court charged with assault. Sympathetic to local revulsion at drugs coming into their community and anxious to help, Willie MacRae offered to defend the men in the court. One of them, Allan MacLean, remembers MacRae mentioning specific premises where drugs were being sold during the hearings. He thinks that Willie knew more about the suppliers and was itching to name them. MacRae may have conducted his own investigation and might have been planning to hand over his findings to the police.

This might have explained why Willie MacRae was carrying his gun. Perhaps he knew more, as the local men believed. Perhaps he didn't know anything more, but those involved in the drug trade thought he did. Either way, there was another group of people out there, whose audacity and viciousness would be unlimited, fuelled by the huge sums of money involved in the supply of illegal drugs. They would have had a motive for gagging Willie MacRae, permanently.

The rugged west coast of Highland Scotland is not easily policed or monitored and is a place where major shipments of drugs have been landed in the past. In the winter of 1989, drug smugglers successfully landed a shipment of cannabis at Gruinard Bay, a little further north than Dornie. Buoyed up with the success of that venture, they then brought £100 million in Colombian cocaine which had been transported via Spain to be landed at Clashnessie, a beautiful sandy bay on the north-west coast of the Highlands.

Fortunately, the smugglers were being watched by police and customs officers. The boat involved in the first landing had aroused suspicion when it arrived at Ullapool, simply because it would normally have needed a crew of about six to sail it safely from Spain and it had arrived with only two men on board. That was enough to set the hare running and the cocaine didn't reach the streets of Britain.

More than twenty years after Willie MacRae's death, in 2006, a private investigator and former cop came forward with some information. He had an office in the same Buchanan Street building as MacRae & Co. He said he had been contacted by phone and asked to follow MacRae in the afternoon and evening of a Saturday, about five weeks before his death. The client seeking information about MacRae's movements was very keen to have a report from the investigator as soon as possible afterwards. He has never been traced. The investigator cashed the cheque received in payment of his fee and remembers it came from Newcastle. However, he was abroad at the time of Willie's death and didn't know of the importance of the information he had. By the time he realised the implications his paperwork had been destroyed and he couldn't recall anything else about the identity of the person who employed him.

Some of the rumours that have circulated about the cause of Willie's death have been plain ridiculous. An erstwhile friend of his, one Ian Watt, with the appropriate nickname 'Mad Watt' said that six months before his death Willie told him he was on a death list and that a hit man could be bought for £3,000 or less. Ian Watt also claimed that MacRae knew about the IRA bombing of the Grand Hotel in Brighton before it happened and that he was married and had a wife and children somewhere in Scotland. It was even believed in some quarters that Willie MacRae might have been in the British secret service himself.

A great deal of speculation hinged on the exact location where the gun was found at Loch Loyne in relation to Willie's car. If it was some distance away then it seemed less likely that MacRae could have shot himself. He would not have been able to throw the gun after pulling the trigger. Constable Kenny Crawford, the first cop on the scene, was reported as saying the gun was found some distance from the car. David Coutts, the SNP politician and one of the first on the scene, said that during an interview with a depute Procurator Fiscal in Inverness he was told the gun was found some distance away. He was told the authorities believed the gun had fallen out as the car rolled down the slope. Coutts says he was shown a sketched reconstruction with both the gun and the pile with watch and papers twenty to thirty yards from the car.

Some conspiracy theorists alleged that the police had already removed the car by the time they knew they were looking for a gun – they therefore couldn't have known its position relative to the resting place of the car when it was recovered. That was rebutted when the Lord Advocate, Peter Fraser (now Lord Fraser of Carmyllie) said in a public statement that the gun was found immediately below the driver's door. It is not surprising that those first on the scene didn't see the small handgun as they tended the injured man, particularly when the best access to him was through the passenger side of the car.

Forensic tests on the gun fuelled the debate. Two bullets had been fired. A nurse at Aberdeen Royal Infirmary breached confidentiality and went to Hamish Watt, a former SNP MP, saying two bullets were found in MacRae's brain. Experts said a dying man, which Willie was as soon as one bullet entered his brain, would not have been able to fire the weapon a second time.

The story of two bullets in his brain was contradicted by another nurse. She said that the X-rays had, at first, made it appear that there had been two bullets, but that there had only been one, which had ricocheted in MacRae's skull. That still left the question: was it the first or second bullet fired that lodged in Willie MacRae's head?

Perhaps MacRae fired an anguished shot into the air before turning his gun on himself. Perhaps he was checking the gun would fire. A fingertip search for the second bullet would not have been practicable at Loch Loyne; it would have been a needle in a haystack and would prove nothing. Post-mortem findings showed the muzzle of the gun had been held against his skin when it was fired.

If a killer fired the shots, was he travelling in the car with MacRae at the wheel? MacRae was found in the driver's seat and it seems unlikely he was moved there after being shot. A passenger in the car would be on the wrong side to fire a gun into MacRae's right temple while they were on the move and to shoot the driver in a moving car would be to risk severe injury and discovery.

If the car had left the road and rolled down the slope before the shot was fired, the killer would have had to clamber out of the car and round to the driver's door, in the dark, on rough ground, to place the gun at MacRae's right temple. Why would he go to that trouble? To make it look like suicide? And what would MacRae have been doing in the meanwhile? The conspiracy theories rolled on.

After his death, the Willie MacRae Society was established by Michael Strathern, a close and politically like-minded friend of the dead man, who has since died himself. The society was formed to keep MacRae's memory alive and to sustain pressure for an inquiry. The society sent countless letters to the Lord Advocate lobbying for an inquiry, but in vain.

On the anniversary of MacRae's death, a wreath was sent annually to the Crown Office. Strathern's son has taken up his father's role, and the tiny organisation still meets each year, on the anniversary of Willie MacRae's death at Loch Loyne. A cairn constructed of large stones lifted from nearby slopes was erected soon after his death close to the spot where he was found in his car. Later, a more permanent structure was made with the addition of mortar. The cairn carries a plate bearing the words: 'Willie MacRae, A Scottish Patriot, died here on 6th April 1985. The Struggle goes on. Siol Nan Gaidhead.'

In keeping with the disputes surrounding this case, on the first anniversary there was even disagreement about the exact spot where MacRae's car lay. Two different garages claim to have recovered the Volvo from different places along Loch Loyne. So on the second anniversary of Willie MacRae's death there were two separate gatherings at Loch Loyne. One took place where David Coutts said he and his companions found the car. The other was held a mile away, where John Farquhar Munro, who says he was there the day after the incident, led a small crowd of about fifty in a memorial gathering.

It is mainly, but not exclusively, SNP friends of Willie MacRae who have kept the debate over the circumstances of his death in the public eye. In 1990, Sir Nicholas Fairbairn, a Conservative MP and a lawyer who had served as Scotland's Solicitor General, sought a public statement or inquiry into Willie MacRae's death.

One of MacRae's former party colleagues, Winnie Ewing, a skilled criminal lawyer and one of his former students at Glasgow University, was charged by the SNP with making her own inquiry into his death. She took statements from witnesses but these simply threw up a lot of unanswered questions, so she looked to the Crown Office to fill in the blanks. She asked for information on the basis that she would be able to report to the party that she was either satisfied or dissatisfied that Willie MacRae had died at his own hand. She would not divulge anything detailed of what she was told or shown. It would not have been unusual for information to be disclosed, with an assurance of confidentiality from Mrs Ewing. Her reputation, among other things, as a former president of the Glasgow Bar Association would vouch her integrity but she met with a stone wall. To her mind, and that of many others, this suggested either that the investigation was not as thorough as it should have been and would show the justice system in a very bad light, or that the Establishment was indeed hiding something.

At the end of her inquiry Mrs Ewing said, 'I regret that I cannot say to the National Executive that Willie MacRae committed suicide.' Neither the current Solicitor General, Elish Angiolini, nor any of her predecessors in office have agreed to discuss the matter.

John Conway, a former ballistics officer with the Forensic Science

Office in Belfast and a member of the legal rights organisation Justice, investigated the case. He was highly critical of the police role. He believed that the security services were responsible for the speed with which the investigation was shut down. He sent a copy of his report to the Lord Advocate and in it said, 'There can be no doubt that at some time between the car crash and the first people arriving at the scene, someone searched through Mr MacRae's pockets and also ransacked the car.' Two years after sending his report to the Lord Advocate, Conway was involved in an accident which he believes was a 'frightener'. In 1990, Conway said that Justice would take this matter through the International Commission of Jurists to the Court of Human Rights in Strasbourg. It can only be assumed that either this did not happen or the Commission or the Court decided there was no case.

John MacLeod, writing in *The Herald*, claimed to have seen the Crown Office file. In a later article printed in April 1995, he fuelled even more speculation by stating that if he ever hears that the Crown Office has destroyed the file, he will reveal what he has seen, who showed it to him, what position that person held in 1985 and the part they played in the inquiry into Willie MacRae's death. MacLeod was preparing to write a book about the case, one that doesn't seem to have reached print yet, and this, the final paragraph of his article, could have been simply an attempt to whet the appetite of his potential readership.

Even MacRae's great friend, Michael Strathern, who believed that he was murdered, has said that reporters had to make up their stories because of the lack of information given to them. Questions have been asked in the Scottish Parliament as recently as 2006, when Christine Grahame asked what consideration the Scottish Executive would give to a full public inquiry into the death of Mr Willie MacRae. This was prompted by the disclosure of the private investigator who had been charged with watching Mr MacRae. Colin Boyd QC, then Lord Advocate, replied that the circumstances had been fully considered on a number of occasions and there was no basis for a public inquiry.

Dr Fergus MacRae, Willie's brother, was offered an inquiry shortly after his brother's death and declined at the time. He now regrets that. He was given special access to the Crown Office records and spent hours examining their file on the case. He was satisfied that his brother had taken his own life. As things stand, the MacRae family have been denied peace. Conspiracy theorists have worked hard and unremittingly to keep the circumstances of Willie's death in the public eye as they have pressed for a full public inquiry.

It is ironic that MacRae was a man who supported an independent Scotland. Had he died in England there would have been an inquest at which a coroner would have examined all the evidence to establish, as far as it could be established, the truth about what happened to him. In Scotland, a Fatal Accident Inquiry is not automatic, it is at the discretion of the Crown Office where the decision is made on the recommendation of the Procurator Fiscal.

In 2008, Northern Constabulary made unprecedented disclosures about their investigation into this case, in the hope and expectation that this might answer those who continue to question the official version of events. On their website it is possible to see a drawing showing the location of the car and the spot where the gun was recovered under the driver's door. There are photographs of the car on the banks of Loch Loyne, ballistics reports and correspondence, as well as lists of the dead man's property recovered from the scene. Intriguingly, for a heavy smoker, cigarettes weren't on the list of property and neither was a £100 note that Michael Strathern said MacRae always carried with him. Willie's briefcase – allegedly missing from the car; allegedly stolen because of the sensitive nature of its contents – was on the list of his property found at the scene, though its contents were not detailed. Out of respect for his privacy, the details of the drugs he was carrying are blanked out, but it is fair to assume they were not aspirin.

Since Northern Constabulary have released this material, few questions now remain unanswered. These are the reluctance of the police and Crown Office to be more forthcoming sooner and the pile of papers David Coutts said he saw. Through an SNP MSP, I invited David Coutts to contact me for his comment on the information released by the police. He has not done so. Are Willie MacRae's friends satisfied now? They seem to have been quieter since the police disclosure. To see the documents and photographs released go to www.northern.police.uk and search for 'Willie MacRae'.

EPILOGUE

Perhaps the most significant thing I have learned in researching and writing this book is that a sudden death produces far more victims than just the body on the mortuary slab or hidden in an unknown grave. Of course, there are the family and friends of the person killed, particularly the ones who are left with questions and who are still seeking closure. But whole communities can lose their sense of safety, their belief that this kind of thing can never happen among them.

Relatives of the killer can be victims too. They may be respectable, law-abiding families with an errant son or daughter. How awful to have a family member who has committed the ultimate crime. For the parents of such a person there must be an oft-asked question – could I/we have done anything differently? It is not only the perpetrator who may live with guilt.

Those involved in protecting the public can also be victims. I found the murder of Danielle Reid a particularly harrowing case to research and write about. How much harder must it be for police, pathologists and other people whose jobs put them on the front line of investigation and the pursuit of justice in such situations? The deaths I have written about are real, not fictional. These cases are interesting, often a puzzle. In reading about them we should not forget the victims.

I hoped in writing this book to try to discover a thread, a common feature that might point to a way of reducing the number of murders in Scotland and in particular in the Highlands. It quickly became apparent that the cases featured in this book are not representative of most killings in Scotland, or indeed the Highlands. Figures produced by the Scottish Government show that the fifteen-to-thirty age group commits half of all homicides, with a peak at age eighteen. Most victims are male and most are killed with a sharp instrument. Recent statistics are represented by politicians as showing that since 2004/5 there has been a reduction in the number of killers under the influence of drugs or alcohol or both at the time of their offence. In fact, this can only be judged in about fifty per cent of cases. The problem is that information about the influence of drink and drugs can only be accurately obtained when an accused is apprehended shortly after the incident. There will always be a problem in gaining meaningful figures.

Sitting in court, it is obvious that abuse of alcohol and drugs is a major factor in all types of crime, including the most serious. It has been suggested that legalising those drugs that are currently illegal would reduce crime by making them easier and cheaper to obtain. However, alcohol is not illegal, and for most people, it is not prohibitively expensive, so ease of availability and cost are not the only issues. One major issue has to be the effect that using these substances has on self-control. Policing possession, trafficking in illegal drugs and abuse of alcohol is right but prevention would be better.

Inculcating awareness of the damage that addiction to alcohol or drugs can do among our children should be a positive step in the right direction. In 1993, national guidelines to introduce this as a part of health education were implemented in Scottish schools as part of the teaching of children from five to fourteen years old. The impact of the programme in turning youngsters away from illegal drugs and promoting responsible attitudes to alcohol does not seem to have been assessed, but there has been no significant reduction in serious crime. The number of murders in Scotland fluctuates annually but there is no discernable downward trend. Multiple deprivation in some urban areas, a major challenge to Scottish politicians and policy-makers, probably plays a role.

Generation after generation of Scots in the cities are being sucked into a lifestyle of alcohol and drug abuse, addiction and crime. There are no simple answers to that problem.

Of Scotland's killers, twelve per cent suffered mental illness in the period before their offence. Not every mental illness will lead to crime, of course. The Mental Health Acts allow for compulsory detention of a person who is considered to be a risk to himself or others, with rights of appeal against that detention. It will rarely, if ever, be possible to prove that a person detained would have killed had he been free, but it must be assumed to be likely in some cases. Occasionally, a person receiving support for mental health problems by care in the community kills. This commonly happens when they have disappeared off the radar of the health and social-work professionals who were charged with their care, and have ceased taking prescribed medication.

Personality disorders raise quite different issues. They differ from mental illness in that they are incurable and generally considered untreatable. The incarceration of people afflicted with them could accordingly continue indefinitely. Many consider that the rights of the potential victim have fallen into second place behind those of the perpetrator. Invariably, among those holding this view are people whose friends or family have fallen victim to such a 'sick' individual. A Green Paper was produced in the Westminster parliament, followed by a White Paper redefining mental illness to include some personality disorders. But the problems of reconciling protection of the public with the human rights of people suffering from personality disorders seem to have been insuperable. The proposed amendment to the Mental Health Act in England and Wales has been abandoned for the moment. There has been no such initiative in Scotland.

Two-thirds of killers have a record, having committed previous offences. Could effective intervention strategies on a first or subsequent offence prevent these criminals, predominantly young males, from maturing into killers? In Belgium, there have been recent experiments with the involvement of victims, designed to increase young criminals' awareness of the effects of their crimes. It would be interesting to assess their effect on recidivism. Although changes in attitude among prisoners are anecdotally reported, there has been no measurement of reduction, or otherwise, in re-offending rates.

Those involved in the prison system in the UK are critical of post-release support given to prisoners. Would expenditure on greater support reduce the rate of recidivism and pay for itself by reducing the prison population?

In 2009, the Multiple Agency Public Protection Agency (MAPPA) is due to introduce a scheme for violent offenders into Scotland, similar to that in operation for sex offenders on the Sex Offenders' Register. According to the agency's online guidance document, 'The fundamental purpose of MAPPA is public safety and the reduction of serious harm. The protection of children, vulnerable adults and other victims is paramount.'

All violent offenders, including those with mental disorders, will be categorised according to the perceived risk they represent to the public when not in prison. They will be managed accordingly by a co-ordinated approach through all bodies involved – these will include police, criminal justice, probation officers and social work. Part of the operation of MAPPA may result in a means whereby a woman can discover whether a new partner has any history of violent or sexual offences. As with the Sex Offenders' Register, it is not likely that the public will be given direct access to records.

Many people feel that the right thing to with a killer is to put them behind bars and throw away the key. From the point of view of deterrence that is about as effective as trying to knock an elephant over with a feather. As pointed out already, most murders are committed in a moment of passion, with an intention to kill, or with a recklessness as to the result of violent action. A killer is not usually weighing up his chances of being caught, designing the perfect crime to ensure as far as possible he won't be caught, or weighing in the balance the length of sentence he is likely to have handed down. Even when a killer has planned his crime, the motive for carrying it out is the strongest impulsion. But imprisonment does have other legitimate purposes – public safety, retribution (or punishment) and rehabilitation.

In Scotland there was a major change in the way murderers were sentenced when Scotland's political masters signed up to the Convention on Human Rights in 2001. Previously murderers were simply sentenced to life and in fewer than five per cent of cases a judge would give an indication of the minimum sentence to be served in prison. In some cases, the judge would recommend that the rest of the offender's life should be spent behind bars. Human Rights legislation recognises that it is inhumane to give a lifer no hope of release, no specific date to work towards, even if it is in the distant future.

Since 2001, lifers have been given sentences with a fixed punishment tariff that must be served in prison, generally of between ten and thirty years. Law reports are highly regarded sources of law, which emanate from judgments in which judges often interpret statute. Sir Gerald Gordon, CBE, QC, LLD, who edited the *Scottish Criminal Law Reports* in 2002 commented that, 'It appears that the view of the court is that thirty years is the maximum for a penalty ... [This] is equivalent to a sentence of sixty years and is a period which would offer little or no hope of release.' (His statement acknowledges the usual fifty per cent remission of sentence given for good behaviour.)

All those sentenced to life since 2001 have had a punishment tariff specified. Those in prison serving a mandatory life sentence before then had their sentences reviewed. The judge who presided over the initial trial was consulted when possible. In fixing the punishment tariff, judges are not permitted to take into account any period of confinement that may be necessary for the protection of the public. After the punishment tariff is served, a life prisoner will automatically have release on licence considered by the Parole Board who are charged with ensuring, as far as possible, that the prisoner is no longer a risk to the public. The Parole Board's annual report, issued in December 2008, showed that out of Scotland's prison population of 791 lifers, 325 were eligible to have their cases considered and, of those, seventy-five satisfied the board that they could safely be released.

Sometimes, even after a very long sentence, the public can be apprehensive at the possible release of a killer, particularly one who has shown a propensity to re-offend and kill again. In fact, this is very rare – 0.05 per cent of lifers fall into this category and MAPPA may reduce that number even further.

The modern police forces in Scotland constantly update resources at their command to detect crime. The trend is towards forensic centres of excellence, providing service to all Scottish police forces – such as the laboratory in Dundee, which is expert in DNA profiling. In 2000, the Scottish Crime and Drugs Enforcement Agency was set up to assist all Scottish forces as and when necessary in the fight to combat serious and organised crime. All initiatives to reduce the number of victims of crime are to be welcomed.

It is coincidental that two of the people whose stories feature in this book share the same surname, just as it is coincidental that two of the victims were middle-aged women holidaying alone in the north of Scotland. In 2006, another lone female walker was killed in the Highlands, fifty-seven-year-old American Marty Layman-Mendonca, but these three cases straddle twenty-two years. Middle-aged women are not at high risk of becoming victims of crime in the Highlands any more than people who happen to share the surname MacRae.

The annual number of murders in Scotland has not varied significantly in the last ten years. The Highlands of Scotland is a place where it is relatively safe to live. Long may it remain so.

GENERAL BIBLIOGRAPHY

Crime and Investigation Network

Roddie Fraser, *The Divine Killer* (Ross-shire: Glen Books, 1998)

Roy Archibald Hall, *To Kill And Kill Again* (London: Blake's True Crime Library, 2002)

Dr Jean Herbison, *Protecting Highland's Children* (www.protectinghighlandschildren.org)

Alexander McGregor, *The Law Killers* (Edinburgh: Black & White Publishing, 2005)

www.hildamurell.org

Walter C. Paterson, 'Environmental Troublemaking' (Paper given at a symposium at Oxford University, organised by the students of the Human Sciences Department, November 1990)

Lorna J. F. Smith, *Violence in Society and in the Family* (Oxford: Oxford University Press, 2003)

STV news online (http://news.stv.tv/)

M. Stenton and S. Lees, *Who's Who of British Members of Parliament* Vol IV (Brighton: Harvester Press, 1976)

The Times

The *Yorkshire Post*

Scotland on Sunday

The Independent

Scottish Daily Record

Press and Journal

The Herald

The *Sunday Express*

The Scotsman
The *Daily Telegraph*
John O'Groats Journal
West Highland Free Press
The *News of the World*

EPILOGUE BIBLIOGRAPHY

European Journal of Crime: *Victims, Knowledge and Prisons*, 2006
The Mental Health Bill, 2006/07
Prison Statistics Scotland, 2007/2008
Scottish Criminal Law Reports, 2002
The Scottish Government, *Statistical Bulletin: Homicide in Scotland 2004–05*
The Scottish Government, *Statistical Bulletin: Homicide in Scotland 2007–08*
The Scottish Office Department of Health, *Towards a Healthier Scotland: A White Paper on Health*, 1999
The Scottish Office Department of Environmental Studies, *5–14 National Guidelines*, 1993
The Scottish Parole Board, *Annual Report*, 2007/08
The University of Manchester, *National Confidential Inquiry into Suicide and Homicide by People with Mental Illness (NCI)*, 2008

INDEX